THE NEW ENGLAND REGIONAL PLAN
AN ECONOMIC DEVELOPMENT STRATEGY

THE NEW ENGLAND REGIONAL PLAN
AN ECONOMIC DEVELOPMENT STRATEGY

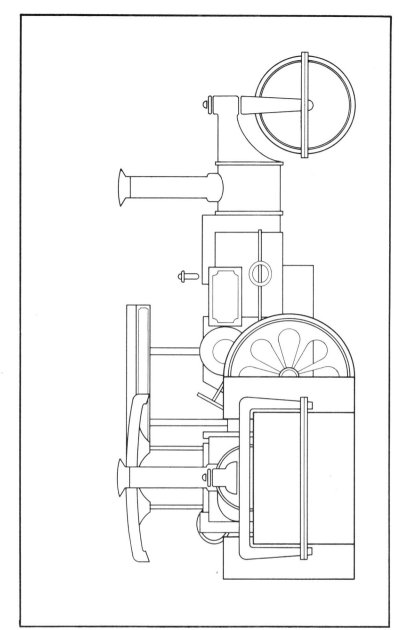

Published for New England Regional Commission *by* University Press of New England

Hanover and London, 1981

A Futures of New England Book

University Press of New England

Brandeis University
Brown University
Clark University
Dartmouth College
University of New Hampshire
University of Rhode Island
Tufts University
University of Vermont

Library of Congress Catalogue Card Number 81-50584
International Standard Book Number 087451-203-4 (Pa

Printed in the United States of America

Design/Graphic Ink
Photography/Diane Broadley, Fred Burnham
Typography/Altertext, Type Rite
Photograph, Chapter 1, courtesy of The Lowell Museum

Dedication

Because she cared about making government work so that all the people were served equally; because she understood that sound planning was necessary to accomplish this goal; because throughout the development of this Plan, both in public meetings and private working sessions, she went an extra measure in supporting, defending, and encouraging the individuals who devoted considerable time and energy to this effort; because she herself set the tone for this Plan when she urged in the Spring of 1980 that it be undertaken "in a hopeful and positive spirit"; and because she cared for and represented so well not only her native Connecticut but, in fact, all of New England and in doing so commanded our great respect and love, her colleagues and friends at the New England Regional Commission, with fond remembrance, dedicate this Plan to Ella Grasso.

Ella Grasso
Governor of Connecticut 1974–1980

New England Regional Commission

J. Joseph Grandmaison
Federal Cochairman

Joseph E. Brennan
Governor of Maine

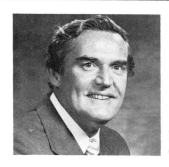

Edward J. King
Governor of Massachusetts

Hugh J. Gallen
Governor of
New Hampshire
State Cochairman

J. Joseph Garrahy
Governor of
Rhode Island

William A. O'Neill
Governor of Connecticut

Richard A. Snelling
Governor of Vermont

New England
Economic Advisory Committee

Richard J. Baker
Vice President,
Associate General Counsel and Secretary
State Mutual Life Assurance Company of
America
Worcester, Massachusetts

Nathaniel Bowditch
President
Maine Development Foundation
Augusta, Maine

Lynn Browne
Assistant Vice President and Economist
Federal Reserve Bank of Boston
Boston, Massachusetts

John J. Carson
Deputy Commissioner
Department of Economic Development
Hartford, Connecticut

Barbara Cottrell
Director
State Development Office
Augusta, Maine

Michael T. Daley
Director
Governor's Development Office
Commonwealth of Massachusetts
Boston, Massachusetts

Ralph Deslauriers
President
Bolton Valley Corporation
Bolton Valley, Vermont

Joel Eisenberg
Director
New England Economic Research Office
New England Congressional Caucus
Washington, D.C.

C. Stuart Forbes
American Realty Services Group
Boston, Massachusetts

Laurence Goss
Assistant Planning Director
Office of State Planning
Concord, New Hampshire

Professor William Henry
University of New Hampshire
Durham, New Hampshire

Douglas Johnson
Director of Economic Development and
Planning
Opportunities Industrialization Center of Rhode
Island
Providence, Rhode Island

Glen Kumekawa
Director of Intergovernmental Policy Analysis
Project
University of Rhode Island
Kingston, Rhode Island

Brad Peters
Vice President
Maine Central Railroad
Portland, Maine

Ronald Poltak
Director
Office of State Planning
Concord, New Hampshire

John Simson
Director
Office of State Planning
Montpelier, Vermont

Betty Tianti
Secretary/Treasurer
Connecticut State Labor Council
Hamden, Connecticut

Anne Wingate
Vice President for Planning and Research
Connecticut Business and Industry Association
Hartford, Connecticut

Contributing Authors

Written and prepared under the direction of:

Christine N. Knowles
Director, Economic Development
New England Regional Commission

*From the Economic Development Staff of the
New England Regional Commission:*

Suzanne Lorant
Special Assistant to the Federal Cochairman

Gail L. Kendall
Economist/Planner

Alan J. Miller
Economist/Planner

George Sahady
Regional Economist

Peter Schneider
Hazardous Waste Program Manager

Barbara L. Turoff
Environmental Planner

Christina G. Vouros
Production Coordinator

With assistance from:

Paul J. Tortolani
Director, NERCOM Transportation Program

Gordon Deane
Manager, NERCOM Alternative Energy
Program

Alan B. Sharaf
Federal Regional Council

Cornelia Potter
New England River Basins Commission

Acknowledgments

Robert A. Leone
Graduate School of Business Administration
Harvard University

Roger Schmenner
MIT-Harvard Joint Center for Urban Studies

Robert Bigelow
Director of Power Planning and Supply
The New England Electrical System

Belden Hull Daniels
Department of City and Regional Planning
Harvard University

Neal F. Finnegan
Senior Vice President
Shawmut Bank of Boston

Robert Patterson
Executive Director
Massachusetts Industrial Finance Agency

William E. Wetzel, Jr.
University of New Hampshire

John H. Kupjian
John H. Kupjian and Co.
Winchester, Massachusetts

William R. Osgood
Director
Massachusetts Business and Communication
Center Network

Judith Obermayer
Moleculon Research Corporation
Committee for Small Business Innovation

Robert Wallace
Framingham State College
Framingham, Massachusetts

B.J. Rudman
Massachusetts High Technology Council

Paul Osterman
Boston University

George Petersen
The Urban Institute
Washington, D.C.

Pierre Kisteneff
ABT Associates
Cambridge, Massachusetts

Lewis Bond
Corporation for Technical Assistance to
 Neighborhoods
Hartford, Connecticut

Rolf Goetze
Boston Redevelopment Authority

Joseph L. Rivers
J.L. Rivers Company
Boston, Massachusetts

Gail Leighton
New Hampshire Department of Forests and
Lands

William Serreta
Center for Human Ecology Studies
Freeport, Maine

David Kresge
Director
MIT-Harvard Joint Center for Urban Studies

Betsy Churchill
MIT-Harvard Joint Center for Urban Studies

John Hekman
Boston College
Currently on leave to the Federal Reserve Bank
of Boston

Charles B. Warden, Jr.
Strategic Information, Inc.
Waltham, Massachusetts

James Howell
Senior Vice President
First National Bank of Boston

David Birch
Massachusetts Institute of Technology

The New England Municipal Center
Durham, New Hampshire

Contents

Preface

As a development strategy, the New England Regional Plan is a policy guide acting at the intersection of public and private interests for the benefit of the greatest number of New Englanders.

The following *New England Regional Plan: An Economic Development Strategy* was formally accepted by unanimous resolution of the New England Regional Commission at the Winter 1980 Commission meeting, held at Woodstock, Vermont, on December 12th. The Commission is a Federal-State partnership, consisting of the Governors of the six New England States and a Federal Cochairman appointed by the President, and is charged with the responsibility of addressing the economic problems and promoting the economic growth of the New England Region. This strategy was developed at the request of the Commission members and is designed to assist them in fulfilling that mandate.

The growth strategy has been developed both to comply with the intent of Regional Commission enabling legislation (The Public Works and Economic Development Act of 1965 as amended), and to respond to the specific request of the New England Governors that better and more current information be developed on the economic problems and prospects of the Region since the post-1975 recovery. The Commission members intended that this Plan put into perspective some of the persistent myths about the problems of New England and that specific strategies be devised to combat those problems which continue to impact on the vitality of the Region. The strategy identifies shared, multi-state economic development issues and suggests Regional Commission programs and investments to respond to those issues. The Plan identifies common state problems and suggests areas of multi-state action working through the Commission and within state government directly. Recognizing that development planning involves both the public and private sectors, and that private sector investment is the essential ingredient to economic growth, the Plan identifies areas of common interest and joint action.

Perhaps most important, the Plan identifies regional priorities for Federal response. The information base about the Region has been developed to reflect how well New England fares as compared to the Nation as a whole. It seeks to identify regional differences, both strengths and weaknesses, so that Federal policies and problems can more clearly respond to the special character and needs of New England The Regional Plan will be presented to the Federal Regional Council, the Interagency Coordinating Council at the White House, and the U.S. Department of Commerce, identifying in so far as possible, areas of investment priorities, and legislative and regulatory changes. The strategy has been developed not as a long "wish list" of itemized investment needs, but as a policy guide for State and Federal decision making.

This document is the result of a concentrated fifteen-month planning process. In September of 1979, the Commission voted unanimously to staff and fund a concerted planning effort. At the same time the Commission created a seventeen member Economic Advisory Committee consisting of public and private sector leaders from the six states. The Advisory Committee met monthly to review and critique the work of Commission staff and to bring the expertise and concerns of individual members to bear on the process.

Prior to the initiation of Advisory Committee meetings, the staff surveyed state and sub-state planning agencies to identify prevalent concerns and problems facing all parts of the Region. These issues became the framework for staff work and Advisory Committee meetings and for the content of this document. The Advisors reviewed staff briefing papers, draft chapters and proposed strategies and recommendations, as well as taking individual responsibilities for their areas of expertise.

In addition to involvement by staff and economic advisors, many other New Englanders have been involved in developing information and issues in the planning process. Outside experts from the private sector, academia and government were invited to present their views at committee meetings. Members of the Federal Regional Council were given regular up-dates on the development of the strategy and FRC staff were invited to all regular meetings. Two specific outreach meetings were held in July to test the basic strategies in the Plan with representatives of target populations and communities in urban and rural parts of the Region. A draft strategy was presented to the full Commission on September 15 and this document was subsequently revised to reflect the suggestions and concerns of Commission members.

The planning process was initiated during a period when the national economic picture was dominated by concern for inflation. Much of

the work was accomplished during a recessionary period, and it was completed in a time of exceptional economic uncertainty. Serious efforts were made to look at the long-term prospects and problems of the regional economy and to pay less attention to near-term fluctuations of the business cycle. New England fared relatively well in the downturn of 1980, although unemployment exceeded the 1977-78 level. The focus of this document, however, is on the performance of the Region over the past 30 years and the policies and strategies necessary for the 1980's.

The result is a Regional Plan which addresses an agenda of multi-state issues with basic strategies and specific policy and program recommendations for each issue. The Plan does not cover all regional issues, rather it focuses on a limited list of priority concerns for Federal and Regional attention. It suggests areas where the public and private sectors should work together in the Region to promote economic growth. Finally, the document begins to identify a regional legislative agenda for FY81.

The *New England Regional Plan: An Economic Development Strategy* was presented to the New England Regional Commission on December 12, 1980, and was formally adopted by unanimous acceptance of the Commission resolution appearing below. The Regional Plan is being forwarded to the Secretary of Commerce. Individual state strategies reflecting both regional priorities and state-specific policies will be developed by each state and incorporated as part of the Regional Plan.

"The Regional Plan which we adopted here today is one important measure of our commitment to the economic future of New England. I, for one, am happy that it is upbeat. I think the statistics and data deserve recognition and that it is important that New England turn away from the poor-mouthing which has so often been at the center of our plans for the future. It indicates a dedica-

tion to work cooperatively with other private and public organizations."

Richard A. Snelling
Governor of Vermont
State Cochairman

"If New England is going to actually be in a position to determine its future, then we have never been in as good a position to do this as we are at the present time. The type of optimism that this sort of document as a strategy demonstrates should enable the six New England states as one region to have a significant effect upon the Region's economic development."

J. Joseph Grandmaison
Federal Cochairman

A Resolution of the New England Regional Commission to Adopt as an official statement of the Commission, the *"New England Regional Plan: An Economic Development Strategy"*
Whereas, the New England Regional Commission is charged in its enabling legislation with identifying economic problems and promoting economic development in the six-state region; and

Whereas, the Commission members at the September 1980 Commission Meeting accepted for review the Draft *"New England Regional Plan: An Economic Development Strategy;"* and

Whereas, an extensive outreach effort has been made by the Commission staff to make the Regional Plan available to appropriate persons and organizations, and to encourage feedback comments; and

Whereas, approximately 300 copies of the Regional Plan have been distributed in New England and elsewhere to persons and organizations including state and substate planning agencies, New England Congressional Caucus, Economic Advisory Committee members and other participants in the planning process, Academics, local development agencies, and others; and

Whereas, the revised Regional Plan has been updated with 1979 data and where possible with 1980 Census estimates; and

Whereas, the Commission has solicited and received numerous comments and suggestions for revision of the Draft Regional Plan; and

Whereas, specific state strategies will be developed at the state level to reflect state priorities and appended as chapters of the Regional Plan;

Now Therefore Be It Resolved by the New England Regional Commission that the revised regional strategy entitled, *"New England Regional Plan: An Economic Development Strategy,"* be adopted by the Commission to serve as a public statement on the status of the economy and a strategy for development in the New England Region, and as a framework for the development of state growth strategies which will be incorporated as components of the complete Regional Plan; and

— that the revised Regional Strategy will serve as an agenda for regional cooperation; and

— that the revised Regional Strategy identifies regional priorities for Federal response;

Now Therefore Be It Further Resolved that when the individual state growth strategies are incorporated into the Regional Plan they will be submitted to the Secretary of Commerce in the same manner as this Resolution approves and submits the Commission's *New England Regional Plan: An Economic Development Strategy* to the Secretary of Commerce;

Now Therefore Be It Finally Resolved that the Members of the New England Regional Commission extend their sincere appreciation to the New England Economic Advisory Committee and the many individuals in the Region who generously gave their time and effort in the lengthy process of developing this Regional Plan.

THE NEW ENGLAND REGIONAL PLAN
AN ECONOMIC DEVELOPMENT STRATEGY

Evolution of The New England Economy

In the nineteenth century, saws and axes made in New England cleared the forests of Ohio; New England ploughs broke the prairie sod; New England scales weighed wheat and meat in Texas; New England serge clothed businessmen in San Francisco . . . and New England dies, lathes, looms, forges, presses and screwdrivers outfitted factories far and wide. But by the twentieth century, New England plants were closing up and laying off workers. To most New Englanders the cause of the region's economic decline seemed obvious — loss of industry. They brooded upon reasons for this loss: cheaper labor in the South, obsolescence of the old brick factories along the rivers and beside the waterfalls, the decay of Boston's docks, imports from Switzerland and Japan.

Jane Jacobs, in *The Economy of Cities*

New England lags behind the nation and the pervasiveness of this lag is surprising . . . Although important bright spots exist, and offer promise for the future, the New England economy, in general has faltered since the end of World War II. The 1975 downturn in the nation's economy accentuated the 1975 basic problem: a slow but steady and pervasive deterioration of its economic base.

The New England Regional Commission, *Regional Development Plan*, 1976

New Englanders, as they say in the sandlot league, can't stand prosperity. It seems to embarrass them, a local condition attributable to an ethnic-philosophic mix of Celtic melancholia and Puritan miserableness. "The truth is things aren't all that bad . . ."

Ian Menzies, interpreting Robert A. Leone, in *The Boston Globe*, March 19, 1979

New England in 1980 has a strong economy with good prospects for future growth. The Region emerges from the 1970's with a new industrial mix, higher per capita income and lower unemployment than the rest of the nation. New England is the oldest contiguous economic region in the United States. It was the first region to experience the industrial revolution, and it has an infrastructure which reflects its history. The Region is comparatively densely populated with a few large cities, and many smaller cities, but with 40 rural counties with less than 200 persons per square mile. The perception of New England as a part of the declining urban Northeast has pervaded the thinking of government and private sector decision makers both within and outside the Region for over a decade. However, a careful reappraisal of the characteristics and performance of the regional economy over the past 30 years demonstrates that New England has grown significantly in terms of all major economic indicators and that the New England economy has evolved into a modern industrial mix which has excellent prospects for future economic growth.

The New England Region did suffer disproportionately in the early and mid 1970's under the multiple stresses of two national recessions, the accelerated decline in traditional manufacturing (apparel and textile, etc.) and abrupt increases in fuel costs. The impact of these problems was severe and masked the underlying strengths of

The underlying strength of the New England economy has always been skilled hard work that results in goods and services exportable to the rest of the country and the world. As the region emerges from the seventies with a new industrial mix, higher per capita income and lower unemployment than the rest of the nation, the prospects for future economic growth are excellent.

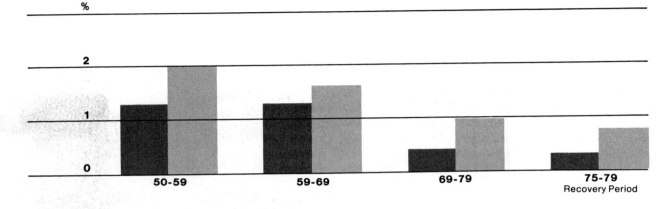

Figure I
Population Growth
(Average Annual Percent Change)

%

2

1

0

50-59   59-69   69-79   75-79
                            Recovery Period

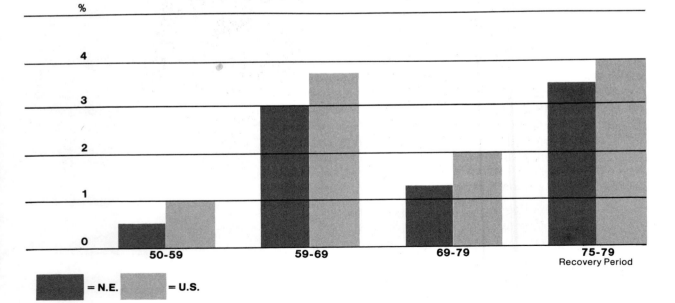

Figure II
Employment Growth
(Average Annual Percent Change)

%

4

3

2

1

0

50-59   59-69   69-79   75-79
                            Recovery Period

■ = N.E.   ▢ = U.S.

the evolving New England economy. In the years since 1975 New England has shown new vitality, even in the face of the current recession, and this vitality is not short-lived but reflects years of growth and some basic economic strengths.

Characteristics Of The New England Economy
Over the past thirty years, the New England economy has grown substantially in terms of employment, income and population. From 1950 to 1979 the Region experienced a net addition of over two million jobs, while real personal income climbed from $27 billion to over $66 billion. Population also increased over the interval - from 9.3 million persons in 1950 to 12.3 million in 1980.

In terms of every one of these aggregate measures the New England Region has exhibited positive trend growth over each of the time periods illustrated. It is only because the Nation has grown still more rapidly that New England has conventionally been seen as a declining region.

Figures I and II demonstrate that the Region and the Nation grew absolutely in terms of population and employment, but that New England lagged the country in rate of growth. However, in terms of the ability of the economy to provide employment and income for its citizens, New England has consistently outperformed the U.S. For every year measured, a greater percentage of New Englanders held jobs than the U.S. average, and real per capita income in the Region was consistently above the average. (See Figure III)

Contrary to the popular belief the New England Region has not been losing population. According to preliminary data from the 1980 Census more than twelve million people, 4 percent more than in 1970, live in New England in 1980. The proportion of this population that is of working age as well as the proportion that work, is higher than the national average.

But these ten-year figures tend to ignore the disruptions experienced in New England during the past ten years. Through most of the past decade, unemployment rates were unacceptably high in New England and, especially in recession years, substantially higher than the U.S. average.

As the figures illustrate, New England began the decade in prosperity with an unemployment rate of 4.9 percent, equal to the U.S. average. The impact of recessions caused unemployment to rise to 8.5 percent in 1975 in the U.S. and 10.4 percent in the Region. In 1976 the recovery began and since early 1978, New England's unemployment rate has been significantly below the national average. This trend continues through 1980 as the economy weathers the current recession.

The recent population and unemployment data are insufficient alone to give cause for general optimism, especially since New England has historically felt the impacts of national downturns somewhat later than the rest of the economy. Unemployment in 1980 is still significantly higher than it was at the beginning of the decade. But the Region's comparative strength in terms of unemployment, coupled with its persistent edge over the Nation in both per capita employment and real per capita income over the last 30 years, suggests grounds for optimism about the health and future of the Region.

The Region's Evolving Industrial Structure
The positive side of the Region's present situation becomes still more apparent from an ex-

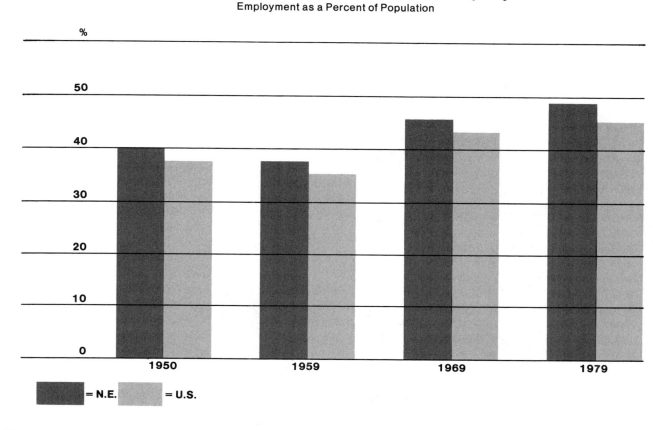

Figure III

New England's Changing Share of National Prosperity

Employment as a Percent of Population

■ = N.E. ▢ = U.S.

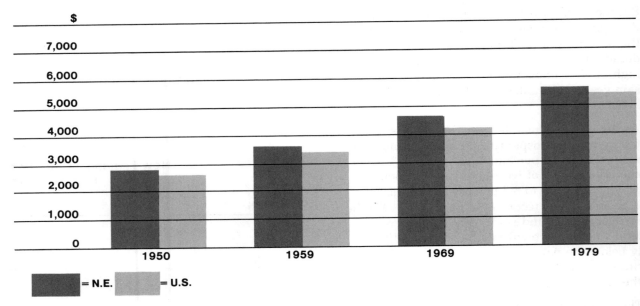

Figure IV
Real per Capita Income (1972 Dollars)

	1950	1959	1969	1979

■ = N.E.   ▨ = U.S.

Table I
**Population in New England
1970 and 1980**
(Number of Persons)

	1970	1980*	Average Annual Percent Change 1970-1980
Massachusetts	5,689,170	5,725,985	0.1%
Connecticut	3,032,217	3,096,951	0.2
Maine	993,722	1,123,560	1.3
Rhode Island	949,723	945,761	-.04
New Hampshire	737,681	918,959	2.5
Vermont	444,732	510,711	1.5
New England	11,847,245	12,321,927	0.4

Source: U.S. Department of Commerce, Department of the Census

*April 1, 1980 Preliminary Data

Figure V
Unemployment Rates: New England and the United States
1970-1979 Annual Averages (Percent)

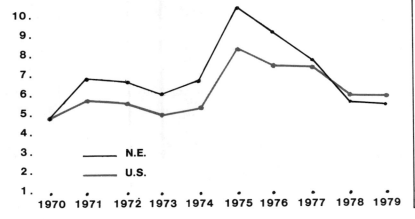

N.E.

U.S.

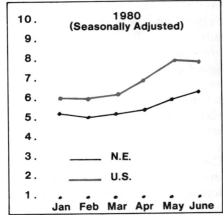

1980
(Seasonally Adjusted)

N.E.

U.S.

amination of the Region's changing industrial mix against the background of the Nation's evolving industrial structure.

Within New England's manufacturing sector there have also been changes — through attrition in industries which have been declining nationally as well as regionally, and by growth in such nationally up-and-coming industries as the high-technology computer industry. Non-durable goods have declined from 19.8 percent of the regional economic activity in 1950 to 8.6 in 1979.

Textiles, apparel, and leather have all declined significantly as shares of total, in both New England and the Nation. On the other hand, electrical and nonelectrical machinery, transportation equipment, instruments, and miscellaneous manufacturing have increased their shares of total manufacturing in New England and also nationally.

Through the process of differential growth over the years, New England's industrial structure has come to resemble the Nation's more closely than it did in 1950 — principally through a reduction in the importance to the Region of the manufacturing sector. At the same time, those industries which can be identified as rapid-growth industries nationally, both in manufacturing and non-manufacturing, have a strong presence in New England.

The manufacturing sector, as measured by employment in manufacturing industries, has been losing importance nationally as a share of the total, while the service-producing sector has grown. (Figure VI) Since this process is expected to continue, New England's economy — which was disproportionately weighted toward manufacturing in 1950 — benefits from the evolution of its own industrial mix in the same direction. Manufacturing employment comprised

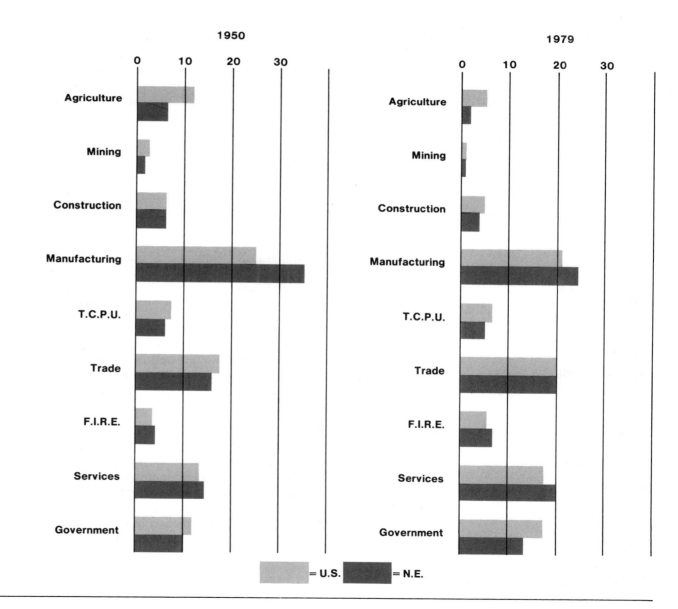

Figure VI

The Changing Industrial Structure of the N.E. Region and the Nation

Shares of Area Totals 1950 and 1979 (% of area totals)

= U.S.   = N.E.

Table II

The New England Region's Changing Industrial Structure 1950 - 1979

Industry Employment Shares of New England Totals
(Percent)

Industry	1950	1959	1969	1979
Manufacturing	**38.3**	**36.3**	**29.3**	**25.3**
Nondurables	19.8	16.3	11.6	8.6
Durables	18.5	19.9	17.7	16.7
Service-Producing	**51.4**	**55.7**	**58.9**	**63.8**
Transportation, Communication, Public Utilities	5.4	4.9	4.2	3.9
Trade	18.1	17.5	17.7	19.3
Finance, Insurance, Real Estate	3.9	4.7	4.6	5.2
Services	13.4	15.5	16.9	20.4
Government	10.5	13.2	15.6	15.0
Agriculture, Forestry, Fishery*	4.6	2.5	1.7E	1.4
Mining	0.2	0.1	0.1E	0.1
Construction	5.5	5.4	4.1	3.2
Total Excluding Non-farm				
Proprietors			94.1	93.8
Non-farm Proprietors			5.9	6.2
Total			100.0	100.0

E = Estimate
* Includes farm workers and proprietors

20.0 percent of total employment in the United States in 1979 down from 26.8 percent in 1950, in New England manufacturing employment represented 25.3 percent of total employment in 1979 down from 38.3 percent in 1950.

Naturally, it is the weakest among the Region's manufacturing industries that have declined. Thus, to some extent the Region's economy is healthier than it was thirty years ago simply because the moribund industries have nearly faded out of the picture. Meanwhile, the service-producing sector, in the wide sense including trade, finance, insurance and real estate, government, transportation, communication and public utilities as well as services in the traditional sense (professional services; trade, tourism, etc.) has grown rapidly in New England so that total employment has expanded. The service-producing sectors taken as a whole comprised 64.0 percent of total nationally in 1979, up dramatically from 54.1 percent in 1950, and New England's economy also followed this general trend, with the service-producing sector growing to 63.8 percent of total in 1979 from 51.4 percent in 1950.

Overall, New England's industrial mix at the end of the seventies, viewed in terms of regional aggregates, is a relatively healthy one compared with the situation thirty, twenty, or even ten years ago.

Within New England's manufacturing sector there have also been changes — through attrition in industries which have been declining nationally as well as regionally, and by growth in such nationally up-and-coming industries as the high-technology computer industry. Nondurable goods have declined from 19.8 percent of regional economic activity in 1950 to 8.6 percent in 1979.

For example: textiles, apparel and leather have all declined significantly as shares of total, in both New England and the Nation. On the other hand, electrical and nonelectrical machinery, transportation equipment, instruments and miscellaneous manufacturing have increased their shares of total manufacturing in New England and also nationally.

Some traditional New England industries are among those which have become uncompetitive nationally as well as in the Region, and it is futile for New England to try to compete for jobs within those industries without technological breakthroughs or new product development. Conversely, to the extent that the national economy continues to evolve toward a more service-oriented industrial mix; and within manufacturing toward a sophisticated, high technology mix, it is to New England's benefit to share in, and where possible lead, the expansion of the growing sector.

Distribution Of The Benefits Of Economic Growth

The preceding analysis suggests that the New England economy is relatively healthy with good prospects for economic growth in the near future. However unemployment remains high as compared to 1970, and employment and income data from selected areas and population groups indicate that not all New England residents enjoy equal access to the benefits of the Region's expanding and evolving economy. The number of individuals below the poverty level is 7.8 percent of the Region's population and that population tends to be centered in older urbanized communities in Southern New England plus rural counties throughout the three Northern States, Southeastern Massachusetts and Rhode Island.

Region-wide unemployment has averaged 5 percent for the past two years while Boston, the

Region's major city, has sustained an average unemployment rate of 7.6 percent. The smaller cities of the Region, identified most closely with the decline of traditional manufacturing, are most severely impacted: New Bedford's rate was 9.3 percent, Brockton's 8.0 percent, Bridgeport, Connecticut's 7.7 percent, Pawtucket, Rhode Island's 7.6 percent and Berlin, New Hampshire's 8.2 percent. Unemployment in rural communities in Northern Vermont and Northern Maine reached 8.6 percent and 12.2 percent, respectively, for the same period.

Access to employment and income opportunity is not solely a function of location in New England. The minority population of New England makes up 4.2 percent of the total population (as compared to 12.3 percent nationally) and tends to be disproportionately impacted by unemployment and low income. Over 44 percent of Blacks and 43 percent of Hispanics tend to seek employment in manufacturing which is declining in importance as a share of the Region's economy.

Women are disproportionately represented in the New England labor force compared to the Nation, yet women in New England earn less than one-half of male median income (1978 Census data) and full-time working women earned $9,602 in 1978 as compared to $15,745 for full-time working men. Finally, the problem of youth unemployment is a national, as well as a serious regional issue. In the age between 16 and 19, 15.6 percent of those in the labor force are unemployed, and this problem is more acute for minority youth and residents of distressed communities.

Insuring that the New England labor force will have the capabilities to take advantage of the growth and change in the Region's economy will be a major challenge to public policy mak-

ers. The location of expanding industries within the Region will affect the access of rural and urban residents to new job opportunities.

The Need For A Growth Strategy
The preceding overview of the New England economy rebuts the conventional perception of a region in decline, and suggests that the regional economy is healthy and will continue to grow in the future. The evolution of the regional economy offers new benefits in terms of increased employment and income which should be better distributed throughout the resident labor force. But this generally positive view should not give cause for complacency. Just as the economy was impacted by a series of severe problems in the early 1970's, other constraints may emerge to cause similar impacts in the future. The health of the Region is in large measure dependent on national economic policy and the changing nature of the regional economy requires continuous monitoring to insure that constraints do not occur to retard or alter that growth.

The *New England Regional Development Plan* identifies the characteristics of the evolving economy, isolates constraints to continued growth and proposes strategies and policy recommendations that promote the overall economic development of the Region and the specific needs of its target populations.

Framing a
Development Strategy
for New England

2

. . . traditional approaches to economic development . . . are no longer relevant to the real economic development problems of the country, its regions, states or communities. . . . economic policy must . . . be concerned with . . . the performance of major sectors within the aggregate economy; and the geographic consequences of national policy and technological change.

Ralph R. Widner, "Revising Our Development Strategies: A Challenge for the 80's" *CUED Commentary January 1980*

A new understanding of the strengths and weaknesses of the New England economy is important background to the development of a growth strategy for the Region. The preceding overview indicates that New England is in relatively good shape compared to the rest of the U.S. New England lags the Nation in terms of growth of both population and employment. But, at the same time, employment per capita and the percent of the population in the labor force are higher than they are in the Nation. Since 1978, unemployment in New England has remained consistently below the U.S. average. Thus, the numbers seem to indicate that the comparatively slower growth of an older, more densely populated region is not a disadvantage or a sign of decline as long as there is a balance between population and employment growth, and as long as per capita personal income remains high.

The prospects for future growth of the New England economy are good, as the structure of the regional economy shifts to a more modern industrial mix and grows more like that of the U.S. The Region is more dependent on manufacturing than the U.S. as a whole. But, over the last 30 years, the manufacturing base of the Region has diversified away from a concentration in older non-durables (apparel, textiles, etc.) into a broader mix of newer industries led "high technology" durables. At the same time, the Region's service producing sectors have

At the heart of a successful economic development strategy for New England is her people, for they represent the strength found in the great variety of goods and services offered in our region: everything from education, medicine, and finance to computers, leather, fish, forest products, jewelry, agricultural products, and, of course, tourism—all resting upon a significant pool of skilled labor.

grown rapidly to make up 64 percent of total regional employment. Currently, the goods producing sector is larger than that of the Nation. Thirty-eight percent of the Region's industries are experiencing growth or rapid growth. The principal distinguishing characteristic of the New England economy is its very small agricultural, mining and other primary goods producing industries, making the Region a major importer of food and other raw materials.

The changes in industrial structure indicate that New England's prospects for sustained growth and prosperity in the 1980's are promising, as long as the national economy continues to do well. But, the data on New England also demonstrate that not all geographic areas within the Region are likely to share equally in this growth and prosperity. The new industrial mix dominated by modern technologies and high grade services tends to be centered in Southern New England, including the southernmost counties of New Hampshire and Maine (and Chittendon County, Vermont). Employment and income data demonstrate that residents of the Region's older industrial cities and more remote rural counties do not share in the Region's general prosperity. Disinvestment in cities and the continued dependence on declining, less productive manufacturing industries have caused economic hardship for portions of New England's urban population. Underdeveloped, less diversified economies and the lack of a strong primary sector, have impacted the employment potential of rural residents from Eastern Connecticut to the Northern Tier.

The particular growth problems of these sub-areas and the industries which predominate there point to some of the underlying issues facing the Region as a whole. The labor requirements of emerging industries do not match the job skills of the traditional labor force. Infra-

structure age and the cost of upgrading or replacing physical capital is an issue for New England's cities in particular, and the Region generally. Transportation costs and distance from U.S. markets are traditionally identified as New England problems which are most manifest in the Northern Tier and in more distant communities. The lack of abundant natural resources, especially indigenous energy supplies, and the fact that the Region must import most of its fuel affect the growth potential of the Region as a whole.

In proposing a growth strategy for New England, it is important to recognize the basic strengths of the regional economy. It is also imperative to further identify those areas within the Region which are less likely to prosper, and the constraints to growth which affect those sub-areas and the Region as a whole.

Establishing Goals For A Regional Growth Policy

In a region like New England with limited natural resources, relatively dense concentrations of people and economic activity and a comparatively slow rate of population increase, growth in and of itself will not always be beneficial. In order to develop a growth policy which is directed at benefiting the residents of the Region, some overall goals have been developed. These broad goal statements should be used as a framework for subsequent discussion and analysis.

Simply stated, the growth and development of the New England economy should be promoted in such a manner that:

- *Employment opportunity for the Region's population is enhanced. Public policy should be directed at the continuation of high labor force participation and low unemployment.*

Table III
The Changing Industrial Structure of Manufacturing in New England

Industry Employment Shares of New England Manufacturing Total (percent)

| | Total Goods Manufactured | |
	1950	1979
Nondurables	51.8	33.9
Food & Tobacco	6.1	4.0
Textiles	17.2	4.2
Apparel	6.3	4.3
Paper	4.7	4.5
Printing & Publishing	4.1	5.7
Chemicals	1.7	2.7
Petroleum	0.2	0.2
Rubber & Plastics	3.8	4.6
Leather	7.8	3.9
Durables	48.2	66.1
Lumber	3.2	2.2
Furniture	1.5	1.3
Stone, Clay, & Glass	1.6	2.1
Primary Metals	5.3	3.3
Fabricated Metals		9.5
Nonelectrical Machinery	9.7	13.5
Electrical Machinery	7.2	13.5
Transportation Equipment	3.3	9.0
Instruments & Miscellaneous	8.1	11.6
Ordnance, Fabricated Metals & Transportation	11.5	18.5

Table IV

Selected Durable Goods Manufacturing Employment (1979)

As Percent of Total Employment

	N.E. Share	Average Annual Rate of Growth 1975-79	U.S. Share	Average Annual Rate of Growth 1975-79
All Durables	16.7%		12.1	
Electrical	3.4%	7.2%	2.0%	6.2%
Machinery	3.4	7.3	2.4	5.2
Fabricated Metals	2.4	3.3	1.6	4.3
Transportation Equip.	2.3	5.1	2.0	5.7
Instruments	1.6	7.7	.7	6.7
Miscellaneous Mfg.	1.3	3.6	.4	2.4
Lumber	.5	6.8	.7	6.2
Furniture	.3	1.0	.5	4.9

- *Income and standard of living for residents of the Region continue to improve. Both gross regional product and average personal income should benefit from economic growth.*

- *Quality of life in the Region is maintained or enhanced.*

- *The Distribution of the benefits of growth in employment and income is shared throughout the Region in terms of geographic location and specific population groups.*

It must be recognized from the beginning that these goals will contradict each other, that job creation can impact on environmental quality and that higher-income jobs are more difficult to direct toward more distressed geographic areas. However, these goals collectively should be utilized as a basic framework within which specific strategies for growth can be developed and tested, and target industries identified.

Growth Strategies For New England

The following three pronged approach represents the overall strategy which the New England Regional Development Plan will emphasize in furthering these broadly-stated goals. Public policy at the State, Regional and Federal level should be directed so as to:

- *foster industrial expansion in those industries which are good candidates for economic expansion and whose growth is likely to benefit the Region.*

- *maintain employment of those resources — especially labor — which currently are employed in less productive industries throughout the Region.*

- *target alternative approaches to those geographic areas of the Region which are economically distressed and are unlikely to share in natural growth without intervention.*

Specific substrategies to implement these broadly stated goals should be based on what is known about the Region's economic strengths. A sector by sector review of the New England economy surfaces some important information with which to develop strategies for a Regional Growth Policy and Regional Development Plan.

Manufacturing In New England

Manufacturing is important to the balanced growth of the Region's economy because it tends to generate higher-wage employment than traditional services, and because it can generate income for the region that is disproportionately high compared to its employment share. Manufacturing has been and is important to export generation. In the past, however, New England has been identified as vulnerable because of its dependence on manufacturing, because economic growth of the U.S. has been based largely on expansion and diversification of the service producing sectors, and because manufacturing dominated economies can be prone toward cyclical fluctuation and recession. A review of the current size and growth potential of New England manufacturing indicates that manufacturing is a major source of optimism about the Region's prospects.

Currently, 25.3 percent (1979) of all employment in New England is in manufacturing as compared to 20 percent for the U.S. The non-durable goods producing industries make up 8.6 percent of all activity, which is very similar to the rest of the Nation. It is in durable goods, most notably electrical and non-electrical machinery, where New England is strongest, with both a greater concentration of activity and, during the recent economic expansion, a higher rate of growth than the U.S. as a whole.

As Table III demonstrates, the non-durable goods producing sector has declined from

51.8% of all manufacturing employment in 1950 to 33.9% in 1979. In the same period, the durable goods manufacturing sector expanded to make up 66% of all manufacturing as measured by employment and a slightly smaller proportion when measured in terms of income.

New England's five largest manufacturing industries are durable goods producers directly or indirectly related to "high-technology." Instruments, electrical and non-electrical machinery, in particular, are larger and faster growing in New England than nationally, which points to both the critical importance of "high-technology" to the Region and the excellent prospects for the future as long as these industries remain in the forefront of national growth.

Fabricated metals and transportation equipment are two large-share manufacturing industries which are also more significant to the economy of the Region than to the U.S. These two related industries are growing more slowly, not keeping pace with the U.S. as a whole, which is a cause for concern. The transportation industry in New England is dominated by defense related aircraft and shipbuilding (as opposed to automobile production), and its health depends as much on national defense spending as on the health of the national economy. These two industries may require greater energy use and higher shipment costs and it is worth investigating the impact of energy cost on the competitive position of the Region where they are concerned. Transportation equipment and fabricated metals are of special concern in Connecticut where together they make up 9.7 percent of all employment.

Two other durable goods manufacturing industries deserve special attention. Miscellaneous manufacturing, which is dominated by the jewelry industry, was a strong growth industry in the Region and in Southeastern Massachusetts and Rhode Island in particular where it makes up 7.7 percent of all employment. However import competition, the world-wide rise in the cost of precious metals and the costs associated with compliance with new hazardous waste treatment regulations can affect the future of this important sub-regional industry. The lumber industry is the second fastest growing industry in New England, with particular importance to the Northern states. When combined with paper and furniture, the forest product group ranks as a very significant industry for the Region, but furniture products is not growing significantly. In Maine, where lumber is of the greatest significance, the furniture industry is of less significance than in every other New England state.

It is in non-durable goods production that New England has been viewed as an economy in decline. The out migration of textiles and apparel industries in the '60s and early '70s aggravated the unemployment impact of recessions. Between 1969 and 1978 the apparel industry in New England declined at a rate of 1.4 percent per year, and textiles declined at a rate of 2.8 percent per year. Now the apparel industry is actually smaller in New England than it is in the rest of the U.S., and textiles make up only 1.1 percent of regional activity. Lastly, a special mention should be made of the chemical industry which is not a major employer in the region, but does contribute significantly to regional product particularly in Connecticut and Rhode Island.

Non-durables remain an issue of regional concern in terms of the reuse of the resources they left behind (labor and older industrial structures) and because of their continued impor-

Table V

Selected Non-Durable Goods Employment (1979)

As Percent of Total Employment

	N.E. Share of Total Employment	Average Annual Rate of Growth 1975-9	U.S. Share of Total Employment	Average Annual Rate of Growth 1975-9
All Non-Durables	8.6%		7.9%	
Printing	1.4%	2.8%	1.2%	3.7%
Paper	1.1	2.2	.7	2.5
Food	1.0	0.6	1.6	1.1
Apparel	1.1	0.5	1.2	1.2
Textiles	1.0	1.3	.8	0.7
Leather	1.0	2.0	.2	0.2

tance in certain geographic locations. Rhode Island still has 2.8 percent of its labor force involved in textile manufacturing, for example.

Leather is another industry which generally contributed to the Region's problems in the recent past. Leather employment declined at the alarming rate of 3.5% per year between 1969 and 1978. Now leather has stabilized and in Maine and New Hampshire has begun to grow again.

The printing and paper industries together make up 2.5 percent of the economy, another strong component of the forest product-related industry, which is based on the Region's principal natural resource: wood. The paper industry employs 3.6 percent of Maine's labor force, while printing tends to be located in Southern New England. The New England paper industry deserves special attention because it generates income to the region disproportionate to its employment size, and because it is in the process of a major $70 million five-year reinvestment program.

A review of current data shows that New England's manufacturing sector is healthy, with strong growth potential first in high technology industries, and secondly in those four industries related to forest products. The Region's durable goods industries are very strong but there is a need to pay attention to transportation equipment and fabricated metals. The non-durable goods sector is weaker but presents less of a problem because it has already declined in importance over the last decade. Even in Maine, where non-durables play a far larger role, the prospects are good because of the strength of paper and leather, the largest industries of the non-durable group.

The Service Producing Industries In New England

The service producing sector of the regional economy, including finance, insurance, utilities and government, as well as trade and personal services, has expanded to make up 63.8 percent of all economic activity as measured by employment and 67.5 percent as measured in terms of income. Services are important to New England, not only because they make up so large a share of the economy, but because some high growth services can be identified as part of the economic base activity of the Region. To the extent that export services can be identified it is possible to analyze their problems and target public policy toward promoting their growth.

One simple method of identifying certain key service exports is to compare their role in the regional economy with that of the Nation.

New England has evolved as a center for financial activity in which investment companies emerge as industry leaders with a growth rate of 10.5 percent per year since 1975. The insurance industry is also centered in the Region; within that industry, insurance carriers is the major growth component. Finance, insurance and real estate together comprise 5.2 percent of the Region's employment.

Perhaps the single most important growth industry for the Region is professional services, which includes management consulting and architectural firms, computer software, medicine and private education. These industries make up 13.2 percent of the New England economy and are growing rapidly. Medicine and services makes up one-half of professional services and has been growing at a rate of 4.6 percent per year. Private education is more than twice as important an industry in New England as it is in the rest of the Nation. And these

Table VI
Export-Related Service Industries (1979)

	N.E. % Employment	U.S. % Employment
Finance, Insurance, Real Estate	5.2	4.8
Insurance Carriers	2.0	1.2
Professional Services	13.2	9.8
Medical	6.4	4.7
Education	2.6	1.2

high-grade service industries are essential to the vitality of the Region, not only for the high skilled jobs they create, but also because of the close relationship between these industries and the growth of high technology manufacturing.

The balance of the private sector service-producing economy in New England includes wholesale and retail trade, utilities, and various other service activities. These support activities grow with the economy and amount to 30.4 percent of all activity measured in terms of employment. These industries depend largely on the economic health of the Region and the personal income of its residents.

At the same time, standard industry classification overlooks the importance of tourism as an economic base activity. Using a methodology developed by the U.S. Travel Data Center to isolate the significance of tourism in the Region, it was estimated that 5.2 percent of the Region's labor force is employed in tourism related activity (as compared to 5.1 percent for the Nation). The importance of tourism is greater for Northern New England, particularly Vermont where it involves over 13 percent of the labor force.

The relatively modest growth of the hotel industry between 1975 and 1978, following a no-growth period since 1969, suggests more attention should be given to this regionally significant industry group which has the capacity to fill employment needs of the target populations of both urban and rural communities.

Government employment in New England represents 15.2 percent of total employment as compared to 17.7 percent in the U.S. Excluding government, then, New England actually has a larger service sector than the nation.

Over the last decade, New England has suffered a major loss in federal military employment (4.1 percent per year) which hit Rhode Island the

hardest with a job loss of 7.2 percent per year. Rhode Island's unemployment rate remained the highest in New England until 1979, reflecting the duration of impact of a major Federal Policy on the economy of a single state.

Services make up a considerable share of economic base activity for New England, and the nurturing of New England's emerging mix of services is an important part of an economic development strategy for the Region for several reasons. These industries tend to be less susceptible to recession and more consistent with quality of life goals of the regional plan than does manufacturing; the presence of educational, medical and investment industries is important to the incubation and growth of high technology manufacturing; tourism is a service that merits attention because of its size and income generation potential for more remote areas and target population groups.

Primary Goods Production In New England

It is in the primary industries that the difference between New England and the U.S. is strongest. The primary goods industries (agriculture, forestry, mining, etc.) account for 5.2 percent of all employment in the U.S. and only 1.5 percent of activity in the Region. This discrepancy reflects the lack of abundant natural resources, particularly in energy extraction. The Region's smaller and slower growing construction industry may reflect New England's slower rate of population growth.

Primary goods production, however, has an importance disproportionate to its share of regional employment and income. The Region's fisheries, agriculture and forestry industries provide important inputs to food processing and wood products manufacturing. Value added to natural resources has a potential for manufacturing growth which is not reflected in

Table VII

Service-Producing-Sector Employment (1979)

As A Percent Of Total Employment

	N.E.	U.S.
Transportation, Communications, Public Utilities	**3.9**	**4.9**
Trade	19.3	19.3
Wholesale	4.3	5.0
Retail	14.9	14.3
Finance, Insurance, Real Estate	**5.2**	**4.8**
Banking	1.5	1.4
Insurance Carriers	2.0	1.2
Other	1.7	2.2
Services	**20.4**	**17.9**
Professional, Social Services	13.2	9.8
Other	7.2	8.1
Government	**15.0**	**17.2**
Federal	3.6	5.0
State and Local	11.4	12.2
Total	**63.9**	**64.0**

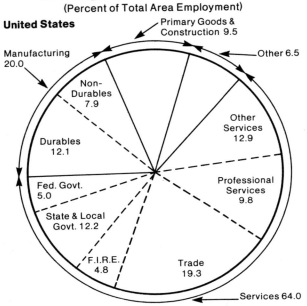

Figure VII
1979 Industrial Mix
New England and the United States
(Percent of Total Area Employment)

United States

Primary Goods & Construction 9.5
Manufacturing 20.0
Other 6.5
Non-Durables 7.9
Other Services 12.9
Durables 12.1
Fed. Govt. 5.0
Professional Services 9.8
State & Local Govt. 12.2
F.I.R.E. 4.8
Trade 19.3
Services 64.0

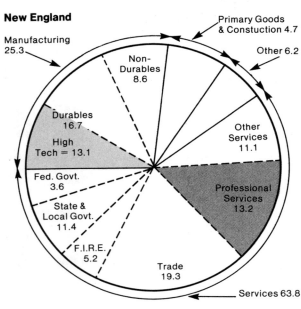

New England

Primary Goods & Constuction 4.7
Manufacturing 25.3
Other 6.2
Non-Durables 8.6
Durables 16.7
Other Services 11.1
High Tech = 13.1
Fed. Govt. 3.6
Professional Services 13.2
State & Local Govt. 11.4
F.I.R.E. 5.2
Trade 19.3
Services 63.8

historical statistics. Natural resource production is also important for import substitution. The increased costs of transportation make local food production more competitive, and the use of wood for fuel reduces need for energy imports. Finally, public policy toward the primary goods sector can have positive implications for improving the economies of distressed rural communities and for protecting the Region's quality of life through land use management.

Agriculture in New England declined steadily until the mid 1970's, but between 1974 and the latest Census on Agriculture in 1978, the industry has experienced new growth. The value of agricultural crops grew by 20 percent between 1974 and 1978. The amount of farm land under cultivation grew by 11 percent in the Region and by 17 percent in Rhode Island and 16 percent in New Hampshire.

Lumber output in New England has grown by 29 percent between 1970 and 1977. Currently 74 percent of the Region is in forest land, and the amount of wood available for harvesting (measured in cubic feet) has been increasing steadily since 1952. New England's forest differs from the Western forest because it is owned by many small landowners, and planning and management of the resource is very difficult. To insure the continued growth of the important forest product related manufacturing industries (lumber, paper, furniture, etc.), more attention should be given to the protection and development of the Region's most visible natural resource.

Since the enactment of the Fisheries Conservation and Management Act of 1976 protecting the Region's valuable fishing grounds, the fishing industry in New England has begun to expand. The catch from the New England fleet

declined from 852 million pounds in 1960 to 498 million pounds in 1975. After 1975 the catch increased annually to 709 million pounds in 1979. The expansion of the fishing industries involves additional employment opportunities in fish processing and in increased export income for the Region as a whole.

Primary goods production should be viewed as important to the Region's economic future, not so much as a provider of employment directly, but as an input to the production of other goods and services. As transportation and energy costs continue to rise, the importance of import substitution and value added to indigenous resources will also increase.

Constraints to the Growth of the New England Economy
The preceding overview demonstrates the renewed potential for sustained growth and prosperity of the New England economy. The Region's prospects have improved as the economic base has evolved to more closely resemble that of the Nation. In fact, in the areas of high technology and specialized services the Region currently outperforms the Nation. But this positive outlook should not give grounds for complacency. The very evolutionary nature of the Region's economic mix suggests a need for constant monitoring to insure that this trend continues and that constraints to future economic development do not emerge.

Serious problems which emerged during the 1970's must continue to be addressed if the health of the Region is to be preserved and enhanced. New England is a region with older infrastructure, limited natural resources and high energy costs. The current prospects will not be sustained without concerted government and private sector attention to these issues.

Energy

In spite of the Region's leadership in conservation, high energy prices and potential energy supply shortages disproportionately affect the cost of living and the ability to operate businesses in New England. These problems are especially significant because of the Region's high consumption of imported foreign oil and the fact that New England's winters are colder than winters in most other parts of the country.

In 1979, the Region paid approximately $17 billion for energy. This expenditure comprised more than 20 percent of New England's total personal income. Since the Region imports almost all of its energy supply, these expenditures result in a substantial outflow of capital from New England.

In addition to high energy costs and greater supply uncertainty, New England faces problems that result from energy use and supply in other parts of the Nation. Prevailing wind patterns carry air pollution generated outside of the Region into New England. Severance taxes on oil drilling and coal mining go directly into the general funds of oil and coal producing states so that they can offer lower taxes than states that are net energy consumers.

Skilled Labor

Traditionally, New England's most important economic resource has been its skilled, high quality labor force. The evolution of the New England economy and the particularly dramatic changes of the past decade have put a strain on the response mechanisms of the Region's labor market. The decline of traditional manufacturing jobs, accompanied by the growth of high technology manufacturing and services has created a demand for new skills and has resulted in a mismatch between industry requirements and existing labor supply.

Transportation

Located at one corner of the national transportation network, New England pays more to import raw materials and export finished products. Higher fuel costs, older transportation infrastructure, and short-haul intra-regional movements aggravate the transportation problems of New England. The recent deregulation of airlines has seriously impacted in-region air service, and deregulation of trucks and rail may have similar effects.

Industrial Waste

In water and air pollution, New England has been a leader in environmental management. However, the Region has no industrial waste treatment facilities to meet the needs of important industries such as electronics, metal-working, leather, and jewelry. The cost of transporting industrial waste out of the Region is high, and access to waste management sites may become limited. These problems are particularly acute for small firms. Industrial waste affects 4,600 of the Region's manufacturing firms and their 310,000 employees.

Implementation of a New England Growth Strategy

The preceding discussion of both opportunities and constraints leads to the following principal conclusions on which a growth strategy for New England should be based:

- New England is an export oriented economy, trading high grade manufacturing and services for fuel, raw materials and heavy goods with other parts of the U.S. and in International Markets.

- 38 percent of New England industries are in growth or rapid growth categories. This is of sufficient magnitude to justify a strategy based on developing

the strengths of the Region.

- New England's manufacturing base is proportionally larger than the national base. This is a benefit to the Region, because it is now led by high growth technology based industries and other durable goods.

- Traditional problem industries (apparel, textiles, and leather) are no longer major industries disproportionately located in New England. Recently, the leather industry reversed its decline and became a growth industry in Northern New England.

- Transportation equipment and fabricated metals need special attention because of their dependence on defense contracts.

- New England is an important exporter of high grade services — medicine, education, and finance.

- Tourism is an important industry to New England as an employer and a source of export income, especially to the Northern States.

- Because New England must import primary products, especially energy, and because income is directly related to the strength of the export base, export-related manufacturing and services are very important to growth.

- New England is an importer of primary goods, particularly energy, but the Region has potential in expanding fisheries, forestry and agriculture as inputs to manufacturing and for import substitution.

- Energy and transportation are interrelated issues which impact the cost of living and doing business in the Region and the economic balance between New England and the rest of the Nation.

- Skilled labor is critical to the continued strength of the Region's growth industries.

These conclusions suggest that implementation of the overall strategies of the Plan be based on the directing of public policies and resources at the key industries and issues which have been identified:

- Rapid growth industries, including high technology and high grade services.

- Maintenance of important industries, including transportation equipment and fabricated metals, as well as the resources which emerge from the decline of apparel and textiles.

- Industries which are significant to the special needs of sub-regions of New England and which have good growth prospects — natural resource related industries, especially forest products, leather, jewelry in Rhode Island, and tourism.

- Import substitution and value added to small share but potentially significant natural resource industries.

The goals identified earlier plus the basic growth strategy and the target industries implicit in the strategy should be tested against major issues, both assets and constraints, which affect the overall growth of the Region. In subsequent sections of this growth policy, the importance of major factors of production, e.g. capital, infrastructure, and energy will be evaluated and public policy options essential to implementation of the strategy will be introduced. Special attention should be given to the impact of these issues on the economic potential of the Region's poorer communities and population groups.

The Land and Natural Resources;
A Geographic
Framework for Development

However much New Englanders over the years may have talked of the harshness of their climate and the barrenness of the soil, the fact is that this region, in its own quiet and often understated way, is one of the most beautiful on the North American continent.

Neil Pierce in *The New England States*

Geographically, the New England Region includes the six states of Maine, New Hampshire, Vermont, Massachusetts, Connecticut, and Rhode Island, and encompasses about 67,000 square miles of the northeastern corner of the United States. The Region is characterized by three major physiographic regions: mountains, upland plateau, and lowland plains, ranging in elevation from sea level to Mount Washington, New Hampshire at 6,288 feet.

The shaping of New England's topographic features, the molding of the landscape, hills, valleys, and streams took place in the very recent past through the process of glaciation. During the glacial retreat of the Wisconsin Age which took place 12,000 years ago, all of New England was left covered by deposits of unconsolidated glacial till: clay, sand, gravel, and boulders. This factor is highly significant to the Region's soil quality and potential use for agriculture, the Region's groundwater resources, and settlement and land use patterns. For example, the most productive aquifers in New England are the glacial deposits of unconsolidated sand and gravel found along major waterways.

New England is known as a water-rich segment of the United States, with about 30,000 miles of streams, more than 5,000 lakes, and 6,000 miles of coastline. Some of the water supply is, however, contaminated, and the potable water supply is unevenly distributed throughout the Region. Therefore, some populated areas must

Long identified as a New England product, fish symbolize the characteristics of many of New England's natural resources: export item, highly prized, in limited supply.

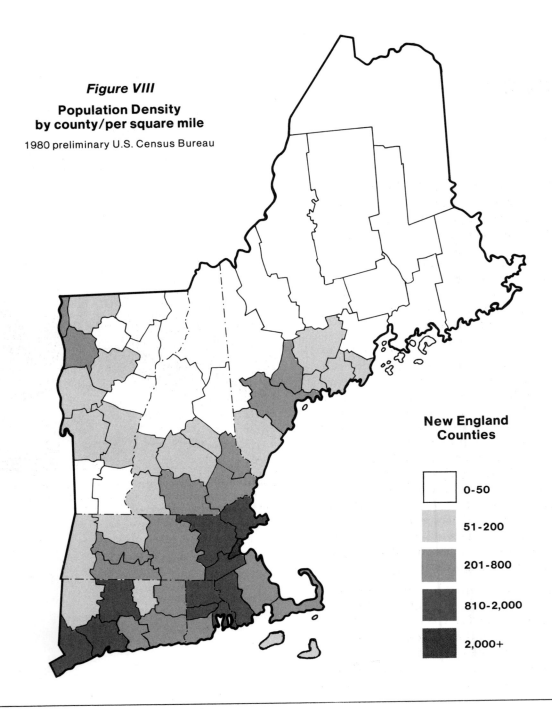

Figure VIII

Population Density by county/per square mile

1980 preliminary U.S. Census Bureau

New England Counties

	0-50
	51-200
	201-800
	810-2,000
	2,000+

rely on resources from the more rural areas of New England, in some cases involving inter-basin transfer of water.

With respect to use of water supply for energy generating purposes, New England has about 3,000 dams, half of which are used for recreational purposes, over 300 for flood control, and over 700 for water supply. Fewer than 300 now produce electric power, yet use of small dams for hydropower could benefit the Region's economy and help conserve fuel. Utilization of some of these dams for hydroelectric production could save New England millions of barrels of oil per year.

The Region's rocky coastline is located adjacent to the continental shelf, considered the actual edge of the continent and covered by only about 500 feet of water. These shallow waters provide one of the most productive fishing areas in the world. George's Bank represents a major factor in the Region's economic growth in terms of both the fishing industry and potential oil and gas reserves.

New England's climate, famous for being unpredictable, is the result of the interaction of several major air masses. The convergence of cold, dry sub-arctic air; warm, moist, Gulf of Mexico air; and cool, damp, North Atlantic air results in the sharply contrasting seasons. The Region's coastal climate is, however, somewhat modified by its proximity to the ocean. The area has abundant precipitation, with 42 inches for an annual average. The temperature averages 40°F–45°F and ranges from a low of 10°F to a high of 90°F. The Region's frostfree period, crucial in terms of potential agricultural yield, generally lasts from 100 to 150 days.

Population
According to the preliminary results of the 1980

Census, the population of New England is 12.3 million. Some of the most densely populated areas in the Nation are found in New England, a Region generally characterized as highly urbanized. The three northern New England states and sections of western Massachusetts and Connecticut, however, remain largely rural. Rhode Island, Massachusetts and Connecticut are between 80 percent and 90 percent urban, compared to a national average of 75 percent urban. Most of the people living in urban areas also live within Standard Metropolitan Statistical Areas (SMSAs). Nearly one tenth of the SMSAs in the United States are located in New England, an area with less than six percent of the total United States population.

Population distribution in New England reflects the growth of the Region's early centers, located near harbors and navigable waterways. In 1975, approximately one half of New England's inhabitants lived within 50 miles of the ports of Boston and Providence. The Connecticut, Housatonic, and Thames River Valleys supported another third of the total population.

In spite of recent national and regional trends of migration from urban centers toward rural, non-farm living and second home development, most sections of northern and western New England still maintain a strong rural flavor.

Population density in 1975 for the Region as a whole was 192 persons per square mile or more than twice the national average. However, there is a range from a low of 23 persons per square mile in northern Maine, to 1,012 persons per square mile in the Rhode Island and southern Massachusetts area. Although a greater percentage of the New England population lived in an SMSA in 1975 than the national average, urban densities were considerable lower. This may reflect the "urban sprawl" growth patterns

characteristic of the Region.

Land Use Patterns in New England
New England functions as a transition zone between Canada's Atlantic Provinces to the north and the New York City Metropolitan Area, lying at the northern end of the Atlantic Megalopolis. Land use in New England may be divided into six major categories, based on percent of land area covered in 1975, as follows: cropland, 6.3 percent; pasture and range, 2.2 percent; forest and woodland, 73.8 percent; urban, 6.1 percent; water, 5.6 percent; other, 6 percent.

Southern New England land use reflects the predominance of manufacturing, service, and financial activities with transportation routes and port facilities that tie in with a large consumer market to the south. Northern New England is heavily forested with population centers along the coast and river valleys.

Forestry
New England is heavily forested, with almost 74 percent of the total area forest and woodland. The pattern of forest cover is varied with over six major forest types and twenty-seven principal tree species. Forest types range from hardwoods in the north; hardwoods, hemlock, and pine in Vermont, New Hampshire, Southern Maine and Eastern Massachusetts; to mixed hardwoods and pine in southern regions; to pitch pine and oak on Cape Cod. The fauna which inhabit the Region are equally varied. Growth of new timber exceeds that which is cut by a slight margin, and the amount of wood harvested between 1950 and 1975 increased steadily. Maine is the leading state in that 70 percent of all timber harvest is utilized for pulp, paper and lumber, followed by New Hampshire and Vermont. Over 75 percent of New Eng-

Table VIII
Commercial Timberland Ownership
New England and the United States
1977
(1,000 Acres)

	Total	Federally Owned or Mngd	State, County, Municipal	Private
Mass.	2,798	10	356	2,432
Conn.	1,806	2	144	1,659
Maine	16,894	73	238	16,583
R.I.	395	—	32	363
N.H.	4,692	472	108	4,112
Vermont	4,430	213	209	4,008
N.E.	31,015	770	1,088	29,158
U.S.	487,726	105,744	30,858	351,124

Source: U.S. Forest Service

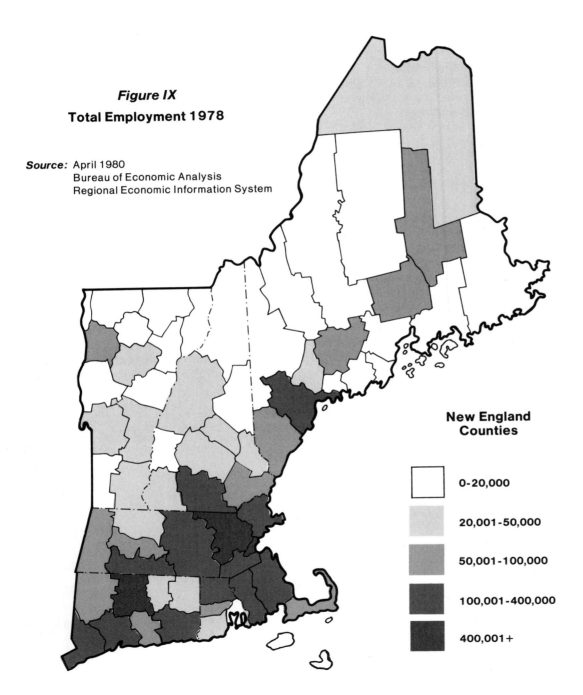

Figure IX

Total Employment 1978

Source: April 1980
Bureau of Economic Analysis
Regional Economic Information System

New England Counties

☐	0-20,000
☐	20,001-50,000
☐	50,001-100,000
☐	100,001-400,000
☐	400,001+

land's forest is privately owned, with average ownership less than fifty acres. Wood production, however, is not considered a major objective by the land owner, especially in Southern New England.

Individual forest stands reflect past agricultural practices, fire, hurricanes, and past timber harvesting methods. The United States Forest Service has designated much of the forest as "commercial" with the potential for commercial value for wood products. However, much of this so-called commercial forest is in poor condition, with over thirteen percent classified as rough or rotten. Forests serve not only as a source of raw materials for industry, but also for scenic and recreational purposes, as a source for the Region's water supply, as wildlife habitat, a fuel source, and a natural mechanism for flood control.

Agriculture
Between 1950 and 1974 there was a decline in farm populations and the number of farms in New England. However, between 1974 and 1978, sources indicate that the industry has experienced new growth. Output per farm remains as high as the national average and Connecticut, Massachusetts, and Rhode Island produce nearly twice as much value per farm as compared to the entire United States. High productivity is due in large part to specialty crops: tobacco in the Connecticut River Valley; a variety of truck garden vegetables in Massachusetts and Rhode Island; potatoes in the Aroostook River Valley in Maine; and sweet corn in Northern Maine. Cape Cod and the South Shore of Massachusetts produce two-thirds of the Nation's cranberries.

The most important agricultural product in New England is dairy products followed by poultry. Large urban populations in Northeastern New England and the New York City Metropolitan area constitute an enormous market for fluid milk produced in New England. Nonetheless, nearly one-third of all farms in New England have annual incomes of less than $2,500 per farm. About 60 percent of the Region's cropland is harvested and is expected to increase to 74 percent by the year 2000.

The Region has experienced a steady loss of prime agricultural land to residential and commercial development. The number of farm operators dropped by 42.4 percent between 1950 and 1960 and by 44.7 percent between 1960 and 1970 (as compared to national declines of 32.2 percent and 37.9 percent, respectively). However, farm size has increased, with average size of 200 acres for all of New England. Prime agricultural lands are often located near or on flood plains and aquifer recharge areas. Thus, agriculture is important to natural flood protection and ground water replenishment activity.

Fishing

New England's commercial fishing industry experienced a decline in the past several decades due to obsolete equipment, overfishing, financing and labor costs, closing of shellfish beds due to pollution and more stringent health standards, and competition from foreign vessels.

George's Bank is one of the world's most productive fishing grounds, as a result of a combination of physical factors. It consists of a shallow, oval-shaped platform between Cape Cod, Massachusetts and Cape Sable, Nova Scotia. The high productivity levels of the Bank are well established but the complexity of the ecosystem and its response to stress are not clear and therefore difficult to either predict or measure.

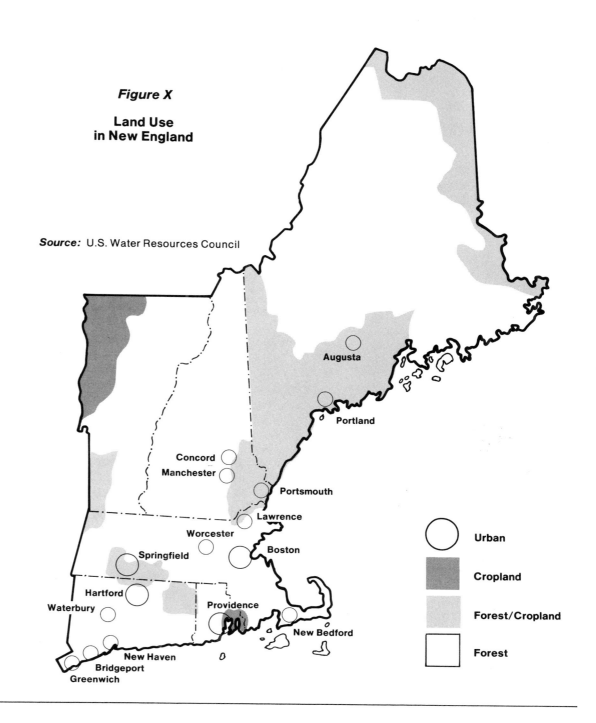

Figure X

Land Use in New England

Source: U.S. Water Resources Council

Augusta

Portland

Concord
Manchester
Portsmouth

Lawrence

Worcester

Boston

Springfield

Hartford

Waterbury

Providence

New Bedford

New Haven
Bridgeport
Greenwich

○ Urban

Cropland

Forest/Cropland

Forest

21

In March, 1976, the Fisheries Conservation and Management Act established United States jurisdiction over the management of fishery resources within 200 miles of the Nation's shore. Since the establishment of the 200 mile fishing limit, and with more effective management of these resources, New England's fishing industry has begun to expand. In 1974, the United States accounted for only 13.3 percent of the available catch from George's Bank. A 25 percent rise in recent New England catches on George's Bank, as compared to catches prior to the time the 200 mile limit went into effect, illustrates that the problems of competition and overfishing may indeed be easing. New England's commercial landings increased every year from 1976 to 1979.

Mining, Mineral Exploration and Development

Mineral and rock production in New England is less than one percent of the national total and there has been no substantial change since 1950. Valuable mineral resources such as sand, gravel, granite, marble, limestone, clay, some gemstones, and zinc are mined in New England. Coal deposits in the Narragansett Basin and copper deposits in Northern Maine are being evaluated. Total mineral production, primarily from sand and gravel mining, amounted to $173.5 million in 1970.

Sand and gravel deposits are localized and transportation costs are high. Past mining mismanagement in terms of lack of consideration of social and environmental impacts, have affected present mining operations, and extraction operations are limited, resulting in underutilization of these resources.

In addition to being a productive fishing ground, George's Bank is also scheduled for oil and natural gas exploration. Exploration and development of these reserves can pose potential environmental hazards, not only in terms of the placement of platforms and pipelines on spawning grounds but also the impacts of oil pollution. The three principal areas for conflict between fishermen's and the petroleum related activities involve traffic, debris on the sea floor, and pre-empted ground.

However, it has been estimated that the Region's share of petroleum jobs off shore could amount to 2,100 by the late 1980's. There will also be an increased demand for port related services such as vessel repair and maintenance capability in shore based activities.

Recreational Land

Abundant water resources, diversified land features, and seasonal variations provide much of New England with opportunities for a high quality recreational and living environment. Recreational facilities cater to skiing, hiking, swimming and fishing and have extended the use of many areas through four seasons.

The United States Forest Service and the Fish and Wildlife Service have identified 39,000 acres in five wilderness areas in New England. An additional 5,000 acres are designated as potential wilderness areas. There are twenty national wildlife refuges in the Region. The National Park Service administers sixteen parks, sites, and monuments (map).

New England contains a significant portion of the Nation's historical heritage with over 600 sites listed in the National Register of Historical Places, and 182 of these sites classified as National Historical Landmarks. The recognition of the Region's heritage is helping preserve what remains of the past centuries in New England. There is a sizable recreation effort included in some preservation strategies such as the de-

Table IX
Market Value of Agricultural Products Sold in New England 1974 - 1978
(Thousands of Dollars)

	1974	1978	% Change
Massachusetts	$179,653	$215,943	+ 20.2%
Connecticut	186,921	228,749	+ 22.4%
Maine	359,612	399,723	+ 11.2%
Rhode Island	22,219	26,402	+ 18.8%
New Hampshire	72,192	89,209	+ 23.6%
Vermont	207,889	274,745	+ 32.2%
New England	$1,028,486	$1,234,771	+ 20.1%

velopment of Old Sturbridge Village in Massachusetts and the Shelburne Museum in Vermont. There is also a developing trend toward reclamation and re-use of abandoned mill buildings and warehouses for commercial and retail use, including the redevelopment of waterfront areas in Boston and New Bedford, Massachusetts and Portland, Maine.

New England's population density and modification of natural resources near urban areas limit the amount of high quality recreational activity near urban centers, and the demand for recreational space is expected to increase.

Land Use Implications for a Regional Growth Strategy

Proximity to Markets
Geographically, New England is located close to major markets, an advantage that reinforces service industries and high value manufacturing. Of concern, however, is maximizing the efficiency of transportation systems to take full advantage of this locational proximity.

Water Supply
Water supply is not a problem in New England, however the quality of that supply is of great concern. In a number of cases, water quality is not appropriate for municipal or for industrial use. The existence of plentiful water supply in New England, if properly and wisely protected, will serve as an incentive for development in New England. By the year 2000, it is expected that 53 percent of the total freshwater consumption in the Region will be used in manufacturing.

Natural Resources
Natural resources are indeed limited in New England; however, existing resources are under-utilized. These resources are important to

Table X

Use of Farmland in New England in Acres 1974 and 1978

	Total Farmland			Harvested Farmland		
	1974	1978	% Change	1974	1978	% Change
Mass.	601,734	680,513	+ 13.1	188,015	214,220	+ 13.9
Conn.	440,056	501,419	+ 13.9	159,157	178,476	+ 12.1
Maine	1,523,696	1,614,180	+ 5.9	449,601	488,043	+ 8.5
R.I.	61,068	75,791	+ 24.1	21,422	25,141	+ 17.4
N.H.	506,464	543,347	+ 7.3	118,186	136,925	+15.9
Vermont	1,667,561	1,756,062	+ 5.3	514,801	581,583	+ 13.0
New England	4,800,561	5,171,312	+ 7.7	1,451,182	1,624,388	+ 11.2

Source: 1974, 1978 Census of Agriculture

Table XI
Value of Agricultural Products Sold in New England in 1974
Farms With Sales of $2,500 or More (Thousands of Dollars)

	MA	CT	ME	RI	NH	VT	NE	% Of Total NE Value
Crops	85,347	74,863	131,103	11,986	16,549	15,106	334,954	32.9
Grains	281	343	3,143	24	78	394	4,263	0.4
Tobacco	9,925	28,952	-	-	-	-	38,877	3.8
Cotton & Cottonseed	-	-	-	-	-	-	-	0.0
Field Seeds, Hay, Forage & Silage	4,136	5,096	4,714	331	2,410	7,544	24,231	2.4
Other Field Crops**	3,330	2,067	103,952	2,835	474	806	113,464	11.2
Vegetables, Sweet Corn & Melons	10,200	4,214	4,582	1,067	1,999	548	22,610	2.2
Fruits, Nuts & Berries	20,452	6,157	10,553	776	5,697	4,298	48,023	4.7
Nursery & Greenhouse Products	36,933	28,033	4,158	6,955	5,891	1,515	83,485	8.2
Forest Products	679	405	2,739	28	1,158	2,592	7,601	0.7
Livestock & Poultry Products	91,086	109,766	223,149	9,972	52,561	188,272	674,806	66.3
Poultry & Poultry Products	23,977	49,274	158,226	3,275	17,722	8,753	261,227	25.7
Dairy Products	50,396	50,551	54,662	5,278	29,337	160,265	350,489	34.5
Cattle & Calves	7,405	8,034	9,428	911	4,494	18,589	48,861	4.8
Sheep, Lambs & Wool	74	43	164	8	68	130	487	0.0
Hogs & Pigs	3,346	484	257	391	434	172	5,084	5.0
Other Livestock & Livestock Prod.	5,888	1,379	412	110	506	364	8,659	0.9
Total Agricultural Products	177,112	185,034	356,991	21,986	70,268	205,970	1,017,361	100.0

*The sum of the figures may not equal total due to rounding.
**Includes, Potatoes, Sweet Potatoes, Sugar Beets, Etc.

Source: 1974 Census of Agriculture; Bureau of the Census.

the Region in terms of import substitution and the potential for value-added industries. Protecting natural resources and utilizing best management practices benefit the economy of the Region not only in terms of recreation and tourism but also in attracting and maintaining a quality labor force.

Forestry
Forestry is an expanding industry (based on recent rapid growth trends in some New England states) even though it accounts for a relatively small percentage of total New England employment. Forestry is a critical input to the expanding, related manufacturing; paper, printing and publishing, lumber and furniture, which collectively account for 14.2 percent of total manufacturing employment in New England.

Processing of forestry products near their source could serve to foster new industry and expand employment. Although certain value-added industries such as paper and lumber are expanding, other forest product industries are constrained due to lack of information on supply of raw materials.

There is a need for an overall natural resource planning and management effort, including data gathering and timber inventories, development of marketing strategies and increased awareness about available resources. The potential of the forests for use as a source of raw materials for industries importing wood from outside the Region should be evaluated. Given a sufficient supply of raw material, new wood related businesses could be attracted to the area.

As the price of fossil fuels continues to rise, a great deal of attention is being paid to the use of wood as a fuel source. With proper management of this resource, including the education of small wood lot owners, wood can

Agriculture

Agriculture is another expanding industry, based on recent growth trends, and is even more important than employment data would indicate. The overall market value of agricultural products sold in New England rose 32.2 percent between 1974 and 1978. This expansion will provide an opportunity to reduce the Region's trade deficit and increase the amount of import substitution. Expansion of value-added industries such as food processing could serve to foster new industrial growth and higher employment.

Fisheries

There is enormous growth potential for the already expanding fishing industry with the extended United States jurisdiction and wise use of fishing grounds. Given the highly perishable quality of fish, it would be more efficient to process as close to the source as possible, thereby supporting a value-added industry. There is a need for better organization within the industry, provision of better port and related facilities, and improved marketing strategies for the finished fish product.

Recreation and Tourism

Open space and recreation facilities are New England assets. New England has an image of being picturesque: of white churches and village greens, colonial style architecture, autumn foliage, covered wooden bridges, lobster pots, ski slopes, and beaches. This blend of image and reality helps to provide a major economic benefit to the Region. Tourism is a rapid growth industry, a $6.9 billion industry in 1978. Employment in the travel industry in New England in 1978 was 269,000

not only grow as an alternative fuel source but also as lumber source.

Table XII

Ten Largest Agricultural Counties in New England By Value of Products Sold 1978
(Includes Farms with Sales of $2,500 or More)

	Value of Agric. Products Sold ($1,000)	Avg. Val. Per Farm	Acreage in Farms	Percent of Land In Farms
Androscoggin, ME	76,636	304,111	71,693	23.6
Aroostook, ME	71,004	59,071	420,247	9.6
Hartford, CT	53,989	93,730	79,490	16.8
Addison, VT	52,790	85,560	238,745	47.6
Kennebec, ME	48,706	111,967	120,217	21.5
Franklin, VT	48,172	71,366	226,205	53.6
Waldo, ME	47,174	130,676	94,514	20.0
New London, CT	46,470	121,332	80,378	18.8
Windham, CT	42,426	119,173	70,478	21.4
Middlesex, MA	40,657	93,038	41,866	7.9

Source: 1978 Census of Agriculture

Table XIII

New England Commercial Fish Landings

	Volume (thousand pounds)	Values ($000)
1976	544,119	175,436
1977	581,247	202,786
1978	660,717	256,510
1979	708,606	302,037

Source: National Marine Fisheries Service

persons. In Northern New England, in 1978, the travel industry accounted for 16.7 percent of the gross state product in New Hampshire, 14.6 in Vermont, and 13.8 percent in Maine.

Land Use Policy

New England's high population density and special environmental assets require particular attention to land use policy and growth management. Land use policy should ensure both continued availability of agricultural and forest lands, and the preservation of the overall attractiveness of the Region to residents and visitors while promoting growth and development. By encouraging appropriate development strategies in or near population centers, limited development capital will be preserved, existing transportation patterns reinforced, and natural resources and environmental quality protected.

Table XIV

Value and Output in New England's Fishing Industry (1979)

	Millions of Dollars	Millions of Pounds
New England	302	709
Massachusetts	176	375
Maine	80	232
Rhode Island	26	22
Connecticut	7	7
New Hampshire	3	8

Source: National Marine Fisheries Bureau

The Changing Labor Market: Priorities for Education & Training

If a man has no chance of obtaining work he is in a desperate position, not simply because he lacks an income but because he lacks this nourishing and enlivening factor of disciplined work which nothing can replace.

E. F. Schumacher, in *Small Is Beautiful*

The structure of the New England economy in 1980 reflects the significance of its most important 'natural' resource, the labor force. The Region has always been a center for machine tooling in manufacturing and specialized professional services. The new strength in high technologies is due in large part to the capabilities of the workforce. New England is not a center for mass production of high-bulk, low-value goods because of energy and transportation costs and lack of access to raw materials. Rather, the Region is healthy and growing because of its precision skills, its innovation of new products and provision of specialized services, all of which require a labor force characterized by productivity, flexibility and specialization.

A skilled labor force is important to New England not only because of its ability to attract business, but also because of its role in enhancing quality of life in the Region. The responsiveness of the labor market to the rapid changes in the structure of the economy is critical in terms of both the health of the economy and the ability of the population to share in the benefits of economic prosperity.

The evolution of the New England economy and the particularly dramatic changes of the past decade have put a strain on the response mechanisms in the Region's labor market. The decline of traditional manufacturing jobs, accompanied by the growth of high-tech manu-

While New England may justifiably boast of a large and highly skilled labor force, the exigencies of a rapidly changing economy require an increased emphasis on training by both the public and private sectors.

Table XV

New England's Changing Share Of National Prosperity
Employment In The Region As A Percent Of Population

	N.E.	U.S.
1950	41.6%	38.7%
1959	38.8	36.2
1962	38.8	35.6
1967	43.9	42.0
1969	44.7	43.2
1970	43.6	42.7
1973	44.6	44.0
1974	45.0	44.4
1975	43.4	43.3
1976	44.3	44.1
1977	45.7	45.4
1978	47.5	46.9
1979	49.0	47.9

Table XVI

New England and the United States Labor Force Participation 1979 As a Percent Of Civilian Non-Institutional Population 16 & Over

	U.S.	N.E.
All	63.7	65.9
Men	77.9	78.9
Women	51.0	54.3

Source: *Employment & Unemployment During 1979: An Analysis.* Bureau of Labor Statistics (not yet published).

facturing and services has created a demand for new skills and has resulted in unemployment of blue collar workers at approximately twice the level of office workers.

A regional strategy to address the issue of supply and demand for labor should be aimed at the maintenance and expansion of an educated and highly productive labor force on the supply side and, on the demand side, at the development of a diversified economic base, providing jobs at multiple skill levels.

The New England work force must have both the specific skills to match current industrial needs and, more importantly, the flexibility to adjust to the continuing changes in economic structure. The ability of the Region's education and training institutions to respond to this need should be a major concern of public policy makers. The Region has a competitive labor force, but the mismatch between the skills of some individuals and emerging job opportunities must be addressed by all levels of government and by the private sector.

In order to achieve full employment even of a highly-skilled, well-educated workforce, other components of economic development must also be in place. There must be industry and access to markets to provide jobs. The focus in this chapter is on developing the quality and flexibility of the Region's labor force. The other aspect of the labor strategy — development of industry to supply the jobs and networks linking industry to markets — is equally important and is covered in the other functional chapters of the Plan. Spreading economic development, in particular, desirable jobs, to disadvantaged groups and areas in the Region is the subject of the chapter on Targeting.

Characteristics of the New England Labor Force

The tradition of hard work in New England is demonstrated by the fact that employment as a percent of population has been higher than the national average for the past 30 years. Labor force participation, particularly by women, exceeds the rest of the U.S. Even in the worst years of the mid-1970s recession, a higher proportion of New Englanders was employed than the national average. (Tables XV and XVI)

The myth that firms move out of New England because of high labor costs and associated labor problems has had wide currency in recent years. Data on various measures of the desirability of the labor force from the point of view of the employer show this assumption to be false. In all of the measures examined (wage rates, degree of unionization and work stoppages) New England has lower rates (i.e., is more desirable to employers) than the Nation as a whole.

Wages In New England Industries
In 1979, average hourly earnings in manufacturing in New England ranged in statewide averages from $5.10 to $6.43, as compared with a national average of $6.69. With some small exceptions, this gap has generally prevailed since 1950. (Table XVII)

The differential wage rates can be partially attributed to the industrial mix of the Region. For example, the industrial category with the highest wage rates is petroleum refining, of which there is very little in New England. The lowest wage rates are paid in the leather and leather products industry, an industry which is a more significant component of the economy of New England than of the national economy.

The remainder of the wage gap is due to the fact that within specific industries, wage rates in New England are generally below the national average. The manufacturing industry with the greatest share of New England employment is electrical machinery. The New England average wage rates in that industry range from $4.98 to $6.13, considerably below the national average of $6.31. (Table XVIII)

Productivity Of The Labor Force: Unionization and Work Stoppages

An often-mentioned determinant of the economic development of a region is the productivity and volatility of the labor force as demonstrated by unionization and strikes. This factor has often been used to explain the migration of industry from the North to the South — that firms move to "right to work" states with weak unions and few strikes.

Although none of the New England states has a right to work law, New England compares favorably with the rest of the country in terms of unionization and time lost through work stoppages. The percent of non-agricultural employees that is unionized in New England is slightly lower than the national average, although there is a wide fluctuation among states. (Table XIX) Thus the extent of unionization in New England cannot be considered a negative factor in the economic development of the Region.

Time lost through work stoppages in a region, due to strikes or walkouts, has negative implications for the Region's economic development. It implies a substantial loss of income to the Region as well as a lack of harmony between the Region's business and labor communities.

Table XVII

Average Hourly Earnings In Manufacturing
New England and the United States (Dollars/Hour)

	1949	1959	1969	1970	1971	1972	1973	1974	1975	1976	1977	1978	1979
U.S.	1.38	2.24	2.29	3.46	3.70	3.98	4.24	4.68	5.03	5.46	5.92	6.47	6.69
MA	NA	2.03	3.04	3.23	3.42	3.65	3.89	4.16	4.48	4.79	5.13	5.54	6.05
CT	1.37	2.26	3.28	3.43	3.61	3.87	4.14	4.42	4.78	5.12	5.56	5.96	6.43
ME	1.15	1.70	2.55	2.71	2.86	3.03	3.23	3.51	3.81	4.16	4.52	4.91	5.42
RI	1.23	1.82	2.69	2.85	2.99	3.15	3.37	3.62	3.84	4.15	4.39	4.71	5.10
NH	1.18	1.71	2.61	2.81	3.03	3.20	3.39	3.65	3.97	4.26	4.56	4.93	5.39
VT	1.14	1.78	2.76	2.93	3.12	3.26	3.50	3.78	4.07	4.40	4.70	5.10	5.53

Source: U.S. Department of Labor, Bureau of Labor Statistics   NA - not available

Table XVIII

1979 Manufacturing Wages By Industry

New England and the United States (Dollars Per Hour)

		US	MA	CT	ME	RI	NH	VT
20	Food	6.272	6.128	6.666	4.654	5.657	6.386	5.183
21	Tobacco	6.702	NA	NA	NA	NA	NA	NA
22	Textiles	4.658	4.984	4.975	4.401	4.648	4.489	NA
23	Apparel	4.240	4.632	4.213	4.152	4.293	4.171	4.014
24	Lumber & Wood Products	6.083	4.773	4.944[1]	5.482	5.627[1]	4.928	4.357
25	Furniture	5.061	4.972	4.944[1]	NA	5.627[1]	4.921	4.532
26	Paper	7.116	6.126	6.645	7.437	4.920	6.368	6.042
27	Printing & Publishing	6.904	6.809	6.507	NA	6.818	6.012	6.055
28	Chemicals	7.590	7.242	7.034	NA	6.895	5.483[4]	NA
29	Petroleum Refining	9.364	5.042[3]	NA	NA	NA	NA	NA
30	Rubber & Plastics	5.962	5.806	5.753	NA	NA	5.483[4]	4.700
31	Leather	4.225	4.428	NA	4.230	3.519	4.251	NA
32	Stone, Clay & Glass	6.841	7.070	NA	NA	5.760	5.689	5.871
33	Primary Metals	8.977	6.323	7.259	5.268[2]	5.840	5.482	NA
34	Fabricated Metals	6.817	6.367	6.005	NA	5.192	5.357	NA
35	Machinery, Except Electrical	7.327	6.366	7.056	NA	NA	5.744	6.482
36	Electrical Machinery	6.308	6.131	5.323	5.268[2]	4.983	5.436	6.073
37	Transportation Equipment	8.524	7.653	7.800	NA	6.372	5.763[5]	NA
38	Instruments	6.168	6.612	5.902	NA	5.238	5.763[5]	NA
39	Miscellaneous Manufacturing	5.034	5.042[3]	NA	NA	4.218[6]	NA	NA
	All Manufacturing	6.688	6.046	6.426	5.413	5.101	5.386	5.525

[1]Data for SIC 24 (Lumber & Wood Products) and SIC 25 (Furniture) combined
[2]Data for SIC 33 (Primary Metals) and SIC 36 (Electrical) combined
[3]Data for SIC 29 (Petroleum Refining) and SIC 39 (Miscellaneous Manufacturing) combined
[4]Data for SIC 28 (Chemicals) and SIC 30 (Rubber and Plastics) combined
[5]Data for SIC 37 (Transportation Equipment) and SIC 38 (Instruments) combined
[6]Includes only SIC 39 (Jewelry, Silverware and Platedware)

Source: U.S. Department of Labor, Bureau of Labor Statistics   NA - not available

Work stoppages consumed a smaller percentage of working time in New England than in the U.S. Statistics for 1959, 1969 and 1978 indicate that the percentage of time lost to work stoppages has been substantially lower in New England than in the U.S. (Table XX)

The Educational Attainment Of The New England Labor Force

New England's public and private colleges are considered major assets, and both students and employers come to the Region to take advantage of the benefits of educational institutions. A skilled and educated labor force is considered one of the Region's most important locational advantages and has contributed to the rapid growth of high technology and other knowledge based industries, and has sustained employment in other important sectors.

The average levels of educational attainment in New England's population are higher than for the United States. The percentage of persons 18 years and older who graduated from high school and college is substantially higher in New England than the nationwide average. Over 70 percent of adult New Englanders are high school graduates and one out of six of them were graduated from college.

The Mismatch Between New Industrial Demands and the Regional Labor Supply

Despite the fact that employment in New England is at an all time high, the unemployment rate for the Region is significantly higher than it was at the beginning of the 1970s. Furthermore, this unemployment is disproportionately felt among blue collar workers and, to a lesser degree, service workers; the 1978 unemployment rate for white collar workers was a very low 3.4

percent. As Table XXII indicates, blue-collar unemployment is double that of white-collar workers.

Within the Region, access to job opportunities is not shared equally for all geographic locations. Rural communities of the Northern Tier traditionally lead the Region in unemployment. During the period between July 1977 and June 1979, six counties in New England had unemployment rates more than one and one-half times the national average: two in Northern Vermont and four in Northern Maine. Many individual cities and towns of Southeastern New England also experience high unemployment. Large cities including Boston, Providence and Hartford have pockets of severe unemployment. Smaller cities throughout the Region have suffered unemployment in recent years as a result of an erosion of the local economic base.

The minority and female populations of New England have traditionally suffered significantly higher rates of unemployment than the rest of the population, although in 1978 the gap was much smaller than that prevailing nationally. Higher unemployment and lower income for women and minorities reflect the fact that these populations have been concentrated in lower paying, less stable jobs because of lack of access and/or lack of skills.

Unemployment generally, and in particular geographic locations and population groups specifically, has several causes. Women and minority groups have been chronically under-utilized in both the Region and the Nation. Structural unemployment in rural communities of the Northern Tier has resulted from a lack of economic activity. These long-term issues have been exacerbated by the changes in industrial structure which have affected the entire Region

Table XIX

Unionization
New England and the United States: 1978

	Number of Members (000)	Percent Unionization of Non-Agricultural Employees
New England	1,371	26.2
United States	23,306	26.8
Massachusetts	692	27.7
Connecticut	356	26.4
Maine	100	24.7
Rhode Island	119	29.9
New Hampshire	61	16.8
Vermont	43	22.7

Source: U.S. Department of Labor, Bureau of Labor Statistics, *"Directory of National Unions and Employee association"*, Sept. 1980.

Table XX

Work Stoppages in New England and the United States
1959-1978

	Number of Work Stoppages	Workers Involved
1959		
New England	264	73,000
United States	3,708	1,880,000
Massachusetts	134	43,000
Connecticut	68	20,500
Maine	19	1,280
Rhode Island	20	5,430
New Hampshire	14	1,250
Vermont	9	1,640
1969		
New England	373	155,900
United States	5,700	2,481,000
Massachusetts	172	85,400
Connecticut	99	47,200
Maine	18	2,100
Rhode Island	52	15,700
New Hamphire	23	3,100
Vermont	9	2,400
1978		
New England	246	52,400
United States	4,230	1,622,600
Massachusetts	117	25,200
Connecticut	55	8,400
Maine	24	7,600
Rhode Island	36	7,200
New Hampshire	15	3,100
Vermont	11	900

Source: U.S. Department of Labor, Bureau of Labor Statistics, *"Work Stoppages"*

TABLE XXI

Educational Attainment
of Persons Aged 18 and Over
New England and the United States
Percent Completing Years of School

	Cumulative Distribution						Median School Years Completed
	Elementary		High School		College		
	0-4	5-8	1-3	4	1-3	4+	
Massachusetts	100.0	97.6	86.4	72.3	35.1	16.8	12.6
Connecticut	100.0	97.9	84.7	70.3	35.3	18.3	12.6
Maine	100.0	98.0	84.6	67.8	29.0	13.6	12.5
Rhode Island	100.0	96.5	80.1	61.8	28.9	14.9	12.4
New Hampshire	100.0	98.7	85.2	70.3	34.0	15.3	12.6
Vermont	100.0	98.4	82.8	69.4	33.1	15.6	12.5
New England	100.0	97.8	85.2	70.4	34.0	16.6	12.6
United States	100.0	96.6	82.5	66.6	30.6	13.9	12.5

SOURCE: U.S. Census, 1976 Population Estimates, Series P 25

over the last decade. Emerging industries have labor shortages, while declining industries have left in their wake unemployed people whose skills are no longer appropriate. Strategies must be developed to aid the unemployed members of the labor force in accessing new job opportunities.

New England Growth Industries and the New England Labor Force
The need for the maintenance of a skilled labor supply has been singled out as critical to the continued growth of the Region. The important growth industries in New England, including high technology manufacturing and high grade professional and business services, need employees in a range of occupations in these industries. Government and industry should cooperate and use the various institutions and mechanisms available for education and training to create programs that meet these needs. Since unemployment among blue collar workers is about twice that of white collar workers, special efforts should be made to retrain the blue collar workers who have skills that are no longer in demand. To encourage industry to take a lead in the training and retraining of the workforce, public policymakers should consider providing various incentives to industries.

Labor Market Forecasting
In order for the various mechanisms designed to facilitate the workings of the labor market to operate effectively, a firm basis of information about the supply and demand of labor is required. It is necessary to help new entrants and reentrants into the labor force, as well as chronically unemployed workers, make long-term educational and career decisions. This is a dilemma that is faced by all individuals, affluent as well as disadvantaged. A good labor market forecasting system would be of tremendous

assistance, and should be distributed to high school counselors and local public libraries so as to be readily available.

There currently exist several sources of projections of occupational demand prepared by various agencies and organizations. The states are required to prepare five year occupational demand forecasts to guide the various CETA manpower training programs. Other occupational demand projections are done by several industry and trade groups as well as various educational institutions.

Although these projections all have their limitations, they do provide a base of information on current and projected occupational demand. There is no such comparable base of information on the supply of labor because there is no complete system of information on the supply of labor generated by the educational and training institutions and their capacity to generate this supply. Thus the information base against which the effectiveness and usefulness of the various institutions and programs can be measured is inadequate.

State Occupational Information Coordinating Committees (SOICCs) were established for the purpose of developing a comprehensive labor market data resource for planning and evaluating the various manpower training programs. They collect and distribute data for manpower planning purposes. Most SOICCs are in the process of developing labor market supply and demand information and forecasting systems. The committees are made up of representatives of various state agencies that impact the labor market such as Employment Security, Occupational Education, Manpower Affairs etc. Therefore, as their name suggests, they also function as mechanisms of coordination.

The SOICCs operate under guidelines of the

Table XXII

Labor Force Status by Occupation

1979 Average (Numbers in Thousands)

	Total	White Collar Workers	Blue Collar Workers	Service Workers
United States				
Employment	96,945	49,342	32,065	12,834
Unemployment Rate	5.8	3.3	6.9	7.1
New England				
Employment	5,765	3,083	1,856	781
Unemployment Rate	5.4	3.1*	6.7*	6.5*
Massachusetts				
Employment	2,731	1,502	830	388
Unemployment Rate	5.5	3.6	7.1	5.3
Connecticut				
Employment	1,500	834	473	187
Unemployment Rate	5.1	2.8	5.7	6.7
Maine				
Employment	453	202	178	64
Unemployment Rate	7.2	3.6	9.0	8.4
Rhode Island				
Employment	420	212	149	59
Unemployment Rate	6.6	4.4	8.6	6.9
New Hampshire				
Employment	431	224	155	48
Unemployment Rate	3.1	2.1	3.7	5.5
Vermont				
Employment	228	108	70	35
Unemployment Rate	5.1	3.0	6.9	7.3

Source: *Geographic Profile of Employment: States*, 1979, U.S. Department of Labor, Bureau of Labor Statistics

*NERCOM Estimates

National Occupation Information and Coordinating Committee. The data base is therefore consistent among different states. The intent is to eventually develop a national data base that can be used for national manpower planning.

Future Occupational Needs of New England

Despite the shortcomings of the various labor market demand forecasts, certain general conclusions can be drawn from those projections and from the NERCOM analysis of growth industries in New England. It can be concluded, for example, that occupations in the high technology industries, such as engineers, technicians, and computer software specialists, will grow rapidly. In the service sector, rapid growth in holding companies and insurance agencies suggests a growth in demand in occupations in these industries, such as insurance agents, accountants and financial analysts. The rapid growth projected for medical services indicates continued heavy demand for doctors, nurses, paramedics and physicians' assistants. All other occupations in these fields, including clerical and managerial occupations, can be expected to grow. At the same time, declines can be expected for occupations in declining industries such as sewers and stitchers and shoemaking machine operatives, and for occupations such as teaching that are being adversely impacted by general economic or demographic conditions.

Institutions Which Influence the Quality and Flexibility of the New England Labor Force

In order to maximize the economic and social benefits of economic growth, the labor force must be skilled and flexible to adapt to the changes in the economy. The labor force should be able to shift smoothly from occupations in declining and stagnant industries to occupations in rapid growth industries.

The educational institutions of New England are the major influences on the quality and flexibility of the labor force. These same institutions are also important in improving the overall quality of life of the Region's inhabitants. The educational institutions are essential in meeting the special needs of groups that have not participated in the economic growth of New England.

Primary and Secondary Education System

The most important institutions in terms of influencing the quality of the Region's labor force are the primary and secondary schools. It is the responsibility of these institutions to provide basic learning skills which are necessary to develop any further employment related skills. More importantly, however, it is the task of the school system to transmit the knowledge and skills of society to new generations so that these individuals will be able to participate in and make a contribution to society.

There has been much discussion in recent years about the alleged deterioration of the schools in this country. This deterioration, whether measured quantitatively through such factors as SAT scores or rate of high school dropouts, or subjectively, as by the increased desire of parents to find alternatives to their communities' public school systems, is evident. This phenomenon can be partly explained in financial terms. The percentage of funding that comes from local sources is significantly higher for New England's schools than the national average. This implies greater fiscal disparities among the Region's school districts, with the poorer ones unable to provide many needed programs. There are also important causes that are related to complex social issues with no apparent easy solutions. However, it is the responsibility of government to take action to actively promote

improvement of the primary educational system.

Higher Education

One of the reasons that New England is a prime source of innovation and invention is that the Region is the home of some of the most highly respected colleges and universities in the world. From these colleges and universities come the scientists, engineers, financiers and businessmen whose innovations are an important generator of economic growth in the Region. Graduates of these institutions are among those principally responsible for managing the Region's economy. The Region's colleges and universities are both privately and state operated and funded. In recent years, colleges have devoted much more emphasis to educating older students on a part-time basis for career advancement or change than was previously the case. There has also been a shift in the courses of study chosen by college students from liberal arts to more career-oriented fields. Both these trends reflect the increasing degree to which students view a college degree as preparation for meaningful employment. Although liberal arts should and will remain important, both as a course of study and to round out the education of students in career-oriented fields, this trend is consistent with economic realities and should not be discouraged.

The future role of the colleges and universities of New England in the Region's economic development process should be to improve the standards of quality education and to refine the means of providing access to this education to the disadvantaged groups of the Region.

Comprehensive Employment and Training Act (CETA)

The Comprehensive Employment and Training Act of 1973, as amended, is the Nation's primary initiative to deal with the problems of those members of the population for whom the labor market works the least effectively; those people who are chronically underemployed or unemployed. CETA's principal aim is to provide job training and employment opportunities for economically disadvantaged, unemployed and underemployed persons so as to enable them to secure self-sustaining, unsubsidized employment.

CETA is designed to enhance the employability of structurally unemployed persons so that through participation in a CETA program, they will have improved prospects for obtaining and holding regular jobs with decent incomes. Since it is aimed at disadvantaged portions of the population, CETA cannot be relied upon as a general skills training economic development tool.

To accomplish this goal, three major program efforts were authorized: 1 / a system of comprehensive services encompassing skills training, remedial education, employment and counseling for the economically disadvantaged people, including programs for special groups with particular labor market disadvantages (Titles II, III and VII); 2 / a program of transitional public service employment (PSE) and other employment services for areas of high unemployment, designed to deal with both structural and cyclical unemployment (Titles II and VI); 3 / programs designed to deal with the special employment and skills training programs of disadvantaged youth.

Manpower training funds are administered as special purpose revenue sharing. While the funds come from the federal government, they are spent by "local prime sponsors," which may be local governments, consortiums of local governments, or state governments, who adminis-

ter the program to areas of the state not covered by other local prime sponsors. The Department of Labor, Office of Comprehensive Employment Development, evaluates proposals initiated through the local prime sponsor and monitors their performance. The prime sponsor may run some of the programs directly, but may also engage in subcontracting with community based organizations (CBOs) and public and private training organizations.

Public Service Employment claims the largest share of CETA funds. In 1978, 36 percent of the enrollees of CETA were in PSE and 50 percent of the total funding went to PSE. It is intended to give the enrollees new skills through participation in employment in the public sector. Observation indicates that, in effect, its primary function is as a counter-cyclical revenue sharing program for local governments, by allowing them to fill necessary positions with CETA workers.

Comprehensive employment training services are provided through Title I. These services encompass classroom training, skills development and on the job training. Providers of these services are reimbursed by the local prime sponsor. The OJT program is an outgrowth of the Work Incentive Program (WIN). Employers are reimbursed for up to 50 percent of the employees' salaries while they are enrolled in the program.

There are many CETA programs that are aimed at disadvantaged youth. In 1978, the Employment and Training Administration established the Office of Youth Programs to administer programs authorized by the Youth Employment and Demonstration Projects Act. These programs are generally designed to provide skills and attitudinal training as well as income maintenance. Among other things, these pro-

grams often provide income to the clients through subsidized employment as an incentive to participate in the training or to stay in high school.

The Job Corps is a national program authorized by Title IV of CETA. The program is designed to provide comprehensive services, vocational skills training, basic education, health care and residential support for disadvantaged youth. Its focus is intended to be the provision of skills that will enhance the long term employability of the participant.

A problem with CETA has been that the graduates of its programs have not been well suited for meaningful and well-paying employment in the private sector. This has led to a growing recognition of the importance of involving the private sector at all stages of the process, from designing the training programs, through screening the enrollees, sponsoring on the job training, to contracting for placement. Therefore, what has emerged is a greater emphasis on pivate sector participation in the various aspects of job development through the establishment of Private Industry Councils (PICs) and the Skills Training Improvement Program.

The Skills Training Improvement Program (STIP) is a Title III demonstration program which provides funds to selected prime sponsors to establish advanced skill training programs in the private sector for the long term unemployed, underemployed and low income persons.

The Skills Training Improvement has four objectives: 1 / to provide training and employment for the targetted population, 2 / to improve the quality of CETA training; 3 / to meet the needs of the private sector for skilled workers; and 4 / to increase the participation of the private sector in CETA programs. To achieve these objectives, prime sponsors work with local private sector employers in developing training programs, consisting of either classroom or a combination of classroom and on the job training, lasting from six to eighteen months, and including attitudinal as well as skill training. The program, therefore, is more oriented towards the needs of private employers than previous CETA programs.

PICs were established as a result of the Private Sector Initiative Program which was incorporated by the Congress in the 1978 CETA amendments as a new Title VII. Its primary purpose was to provide a vehicle for shifting CETA's emphasis from subsidized employment to the absorption of the unemployed into the private sector. Private Industry Councils were initially established with 39 prime sponsors as a demonstration program which has been expanded to all prime sponsors. The councils are composed primarily of local business representatives, with representatives of organized labor also serving. The principal function of the councils is to relate the needs of local private employers to the employment and training activities of CETA. They also function as an outreach mechanism to generate interest among local employers in CETA programs and activities. A variety of approaches to secure local business participation are being used including a comprehensive marketing strategy, designed to identify and reach private employers who potentially could utilize the program. This marketing strategy includes a targeted jobs tax credit (TJTC) established by the Revenue Act of 1978.

Occupational Education
While CETA is designed specifically for the economically disadvantaged members of society, occupational education is more broadly based. Its purpose is to provide students with the appropriate skills and attitudes required for entry level employment in a given occupation. Programs are available to all segments of the population with some special programs targeted to groups with special occupational educational needs, such as disadvantaged youth, displaced homemakers, the physically handicapped and adults seeking to upgrade their employment skills or acquire new ones. The occupational education institutions generally emphasize attitudinal development and basic education, as well as skills training.

Occupational education, as defined broadly, is performed by several groups of providers on a variety of levels, both publicly and privately and on the secondary, post secondary and adult levels.

Most occupational education students are enrolled in public institutions. As with general education, the states are the fundamental providers. They are responsible for establishing standards and guidelines for the programs as well as evaluating these programs on a periodic basis. The states are also responsible for the preparation of an annual program plan and accountability report.

In New England all occupational education programs are administered by the state Boards of Education. The specific programs are provided on the local level through the local school districts or regional groupings of districts with the aid of Local Advisory Councils. The advisory councils are composed of representatives of local businesses and labor groups. They provide input into the design and operation of the programs. Where appropriate, new programs are also initiated on the local level through the advisory council.

The Federal government is also involved in occupational education through the establishment of planning and evaluation requirements and the provision of funds. This stems from Title II of the Educational Ammendments of 1976-P.L. 94-482. The basic purpose of the acts, as stated, is to assist states in:

1 / Improving planning in the use of all resources for vocational education and human resources training involving a wide range of agencies and individuals.

2 / Extending, improving, and maintaining, where necessary, existing programs and developing new programs as needed.

3 / Developing and carrying out such programs so as to overcome sex discrimination and sex stereotyping in vocational education.

4 / Providing part-time employment for youth who need earnings to continue or enter a vocational program.

The legislation also requires that states develop the annual plans which are approved by the Department of Education.

Federal funding through Title II generally accounts for less than 20 percent of the total cost, with the state and local governments providing the bulk of the funding. CETA funds are also available for certain special programs.

Occupational education is provided on the secondary level through a variety of institutions. Comprehensive high schools offer industrial, business and vocational training, as well as academic programs. Vocational technical schools offer a greater concentration of effort on occupational training and employment skills development. Regional skill centers offer vocational programs to students from district high schools in the eleventh and twelfth grades.

Cooperative education is a concept that is used extensively in secondary occupational training. It is a program of vocational education for persons who, through written cooperative agreements between school and employees, receive both academic and vocational instruction by alternating study in school with a job.

Post secondary occupational education is provided by community/junior/technical colleges. Most of these institutions are public. Often they offer transfer programs for a baccalaureate degree as well as occupational education. The occupational education is generally for careers more technical in nature than those offered by secondary institutions.

Private or proprietary institutions are significant providers of occupational education. They are generally heavily oriented toward skills training with little attitudinal development. They are licensed by the state and sometimes receive public funds for specific programs. A CETA demonstration program is providing vouchers for use in proprietary occupational education institutions.

Training for adults seeking to upgrade their employment skills or acquire new ones is done by all of the above mentioned institutions. This is perhaps the most rapidly growing program in occupational education as it services people with skills that are either obsolete or no longer in demand.

In recent years, there has been a recognition of the commonality of function between CETA and occupational education and a push to coordinate these activities. CETA 112 grants are often used to set up coordination mechanisms and to fund certain eligible occupational education programs. In addition, the CETA PICs and occupational education local advisory councils now use a common data base.

Apprenticeship Programs

Apprenticeship programs are formalized on-the-job training which is usually operated through an agreement of business and labor. The federal agency that is involved with these programs is the Bureau of Apprenticeship and Training (BAT) of the Employment and Training Administration. BAT has three roles: (1) to formulate labor standards to safeguard the welfare of the apprentices; (2) to bring employers and labor together to set up programs of apprenticeship; and (3) to provide equal employment opportunities in apprenticeships to minorities and women. In addition, there are state apprenticeship councils which cooperate with labor and employers in developing apprenticeship programs with the state in conformance with BAT guidelines.

There are special programs available to members of the military, veterans and inmates in correctional institutions. There were approximately 362,000 people enrolled in apprenticeship programs in 1977.

Conclusions

1 / *New England's comparative advantage lies in its skilled, innovative workforce.* In order to continue to prosper and to provide good, well-paying employment to all residents of the Region, New England needs to continue to produce a skilled, well-educated workforce and to ensure that these desirable characteristics prevail even more widely among the labor force.

2 / *A Flexible, well-educated labor force is also important to meet the needs of industries that are growing in the Region.* These industries need employees with certain levels of skills and training to continue to expand within the Region. Since a fundamental component of the New England economy is innovation, a

highly skilled labor force is vital for the continued economic health of the Region.

The preceding overview indicates that New England has a comparative advantage in terms of a skilled labor force, but there are some important needs that must be addressed. There is still a fundamental problem in the Region's labor market; the apparent contradiction of the existence of both labor shortages in emerging industries and a large number of unemployed people.

There are institutions designed to address this mismatch through education and skills training; primary and secondary education, higher education, CETA, occupational education and apprenticeships. Each of these institutions is designed to serve specific needs or client groups, and each has its limitations. These institutions must be strengthened and improved to collectively serve the entire labor force and enhance the economic growth potential of the Region.

Basic Strategies Aimed at Improving Employment Opportunities and Industrial Desirability of the Region's Labor Force

1 / The quality of the New England labor force must be maintained and improved. The institutions designed to provide skills training and flexibility to the labor force must be strengthened, providing training and skills development in the emerging occupations. Recognizing that the needs of the disadvantaged continue to be of major importance, the prime focus of a regional labor policy shoud be the quality of the labor force as a whole.

2 / Employment skills training and general economic development have a common purpose, the creation of employment

opportunities for residents of a certain area. Generally there has been a lack of coordination between these activities. The commonality of purpose makes it imperative that there be greater coordination between these functions on the national, state and local levels. For example, skills centers should be located in industrial parks to train people for employment in nearby industries.

Public Policy Recommendations

The following program and policy recommendations are designed to increase the skills and flexibility of New England's labor force:

1 / The most important determinant of the quality and flexibility of the Region's labor force is the population's level of basic educational skills, both verbal and mathematical. These skills are necessary for the development of any other employment-related skills. The primary and secondary educational institutions have the critical responsibility to improve the schools so as to raise the basic educational level of the population. The school systems must find a way to educate the people of the Region without substantial new investments.

2 / Occupational education institutions are the principal mechanisms through which the pre-college general population can obtain employment skills for emerging occupations. These institutions should be strengthened through such measures as greater emphasis on career counseling, a strong outreach program to make people aware of the opportunities for employment skill development, and greater

attention to skills training for emerging occupations.

3 / The retraining of workers whose specific skills are obsolete or not in demand in the current labor market is an important means of addressing the mismatch of demand and supply for labor in New England. The Region's occupational education institutions, colleges, and CETA must work with private industry to design new programs and improve old ones to meet this need. To encourage industry to take a lead in the retraining of the labor force, incentives to industries should be considered.

4 / A comprehenive regional employment and training planning function should be instituted to assist in the coordination and development of the various manpower development programs. This could be done in conjunction with the substate regional planning agencies and economic development districts with representation from business, labor, CETA, occupational education and states' Departments of Employment Security. This would also serve to better coordinate employment skills training activities with the economic development function on the local level.

5 / A good data base containing information on the supply and demand of labor in New England is needed in order for the various occupational skills training programs to be more effective. Since the New England labor market crosses state boundaries, a data base should be developed on

a regional level. The SOICCs are an ideal mechanism to assemble the state information. NERCOM, in cooperation with the Department of Labor should aid and encourage the SOICCs in the formulation of a forecasting system, and should bring them together to develop a regional system. This system should include an assessment of the actual supply of labor produced by the various educational and training institutions as well as their capacity to produce the needed supply.

6 / In recent years, there has been a strong push to involve the private sector in employment skills training activities. A prime example is the establishment of Private Industry Councils as part of CETA. This trend should be expanded to involve the private sector in all phases of employment skills training, from program development to direct employment of graduates, so that programs can better meet employment needs.

7 / Special efforts are needed to bring people into the labor force who would not otherwise be included. CETA, the primary response to the problem, should be strengthened to operate more effectively. CETA should be reauthorized in 1982 with a stronger emphasis on on-the-job training in skills that are useful in private sector employment. In addition, the CETA 112 Discretionary Program should be expanded to allow the introduction of experimental programs that better fit the needs of the state and community and to foster coordination with the occupational education function.

8 / Higher education in New England is very important to the economy of the Region. Its presence has provided a great deal of support for the growth of the high technology and high grade service industries. The colleges and universities also serve as a stimulus for the research and development taking place in the Region. There should be continued strong support for the institutions of higher education in New England.

9 / The state Departments of Employment Security should run more effective job placement activities, offering job counseling as well as placement. Better coordination with the private sector is also needed in this effort.

10 / Stronger efforts should be made by both the public and private sectors to grant equal opportunity to jobs and training to all groups of people in New England through enforcement of affirmative action regulations and through voluntary programs of firms not subject to regulations.

Financing Regional Economic Growth

Throughout the history of our country, those proper men of Boston have been in the fore-front of that great American pastime of making money. And Boston money has almost as consistently been in the vanguard of American economic life.

Russell B. Adams, Jr., in *The Boston Money Tree*

New England's strengths include a broad base of innovative, technological know-how, a skilled, stable labor supply, a regional pool of risk capital and a record of Yankee ingenuity and self-reliance. These ought to be the ingredients for entrepreneurial success. That they have been less than adequate to date seems to be due, at least in part, to problems raising risk capital.

William E. Wetzel, Jr., in *Risk Capital Research*

New England is a national financial center. Based in Boston and Hartford, the Region's financial sector is among the most highly developed in the Nation, particularly in the areas of insurance and venture capital. Yet despite its size and capabilities, the Region's conventional, private financial institutions have been unable to meet all of the capital needs of New England. In this, New England's financial institutions are not alone: the issue of capital availability as it affects economic development has a substantial and complex history on the national level.

Years of discussion as to how public policy can promote balanced economic growth have produced a variety of public-sector programs to influence economic development through the channelling of financial capital. The state of current thinking on the design of such programs reflects the consensus that public funds alone cannot alter the configuration of economic growth but can work as an incentive to leverage private investment in target areas and industries.

In New England, the issue has ranged from charges that some or all local financial institutions discriminate against New England to academic studies of existing sources of financing against capital needs. In 1975, the New England Regional Commission sponsored a major effort to identify capital gaps in New England and made specific recommendations on

The issue of financing local development with private money is marked by controversy and even some historically rooted myths. Nevertheless, public policy, carefully targeted, can act as an important guide and incentive to private investment.

how to address them which included a Regional risk capital corporation.

The issue of capital availability remains very controversial, partly because it is impossible under existing disclosure laws to discover the complete picture of Regional sources and uses of funds.

Without establishing definitively whether capital "gaps" exist, it is possible to focus on the most constructive issue in this area: how public policy can best promote balanced economic growth, and, more specifically, how public policy toward capital availability can further the goals of the New England Regional Development Plan.

The New England Capital Market
New England has a well-developed mix of conventional private financial institutions, including commercial banks, life insurance companies, pension and endowment funds, venture capitalists and venture capital corporations, and mechanisms for the issuance of stocks and bonds, which can service industries seeking to locate or expand in New England. Such private-sector institutions and mechanisms provide the bulk of business financing, regionally as well as nationally. New England firms must compete for these funds with alternative investments and firms from other regions.

New England's commercial banks include five or more major regional banks, based primarily in Boston with correspondent relationships to banks throughout the Region, as well as one major international commercial bank. The volume of commercial and industrial loans outstanding issued by New England commercial banks totalled more than $9 billion in June 1978, while the total issued by all commercial banks nationwide exceeded $224 billion.

Although commercial banks in New England hold only 3.6 percent of the Nation's commercial bank deposits,* they provide 4.0 percent of the C & I loans made by such banks nationwide. The ratio of commercial and industrial loans to deposits — sometimes used as a measure of willingness to take risk — is higher (26.4 percent) for New England's commercial banks than for the Nation's as a whole (23.5 percent). New England's firms also have access to and make considerable use of New York banks.
*Federal Deposit Insurance Corporation Annual Reports

Commercial banks constitute the primary source of short-term debt and almost the only source of capital for smaller sized businesses in New England. Although long-term commercial and industrial loans are not generally available through commercial banks, there frequently exist "gentlemen's agreements" to roll over medium-term loans at the rate current at the time of roll-over. Banks' short-term commercial and industrial loans (three months) are generally used for inventory and cash flow, while longer term loans (usually about four years) are typically used for corporate development and equipment. In addition, construction and land development loans (average term: 10 months) provide initial financing for construction projects.

Financial assets held by life insurance companies nationwide were nearly $400 billion in 1978. New England has a disproportionately large share of the Nation's life insurance companies, employing about 2.6 percent of the Region's labor force, while nationally they employ 1.6 percent of the total. Corporate bonds are the largest asset group (40 percent) held by life insurance companies and the fastest growing. They represent a major source of capital for large scale corporate development and serve as

loans to businesses for capital purchases. In addition, life insurance companies finance business and development by investing in stocks (9 percent of assets), both commercial and residential mortgages (27 percent of assets) and real estate loans for development projects such as apartment complexes and industrial parks. (Source: American Council of Life Insurance and B.E.A.)

Venture capital from the Nation's major venture capital centers, Boston, New York, Chicago, and California, is available to New England companies. The pool of capital managed by Boston-based venture capital corporations totalled $150 million in 1979, about double 1978's total. Of this, 40–50 percent was invested in New England. Venture capitalists finance risky later-stage expansions. Only 15–20 percent of the investment of New England's venture capital corporations is for start-up firms. California's venture capitalists tend to be less conservative, with 25–30 percent of their investment deals in start-ups.*
* Stanley Pratt, Venture Capital Magazine

Mechanisms Addressing Unmet Capital Needs In New England
New England's mix of private financial institutions is important to the economic growth of the Region both as a major employer and as a provider of capital. But despite its size and capabilities, the Region's conventional, private financial institutions have been unable to meet all of the capital needs of New England. Over the recent past, a mix of public and private non-profit vehicles have been developed to meet special capital needs of the Region. The public sector and non-conventional private lending corporations provide financial capital in certain instances as a response to imperfections in the capital market; and in order to attract

financial capital to businesses in distressed areas; or to finance industries that are too risky for conventional private investment. Public and non-conventional private investments are directed principally at the following situations:

Start-Up and Young High Technology Firms

Information about new and young firms and innovative products is difficult and expensive to obtain. Small and new firms tend to lack attachable assets. As a result, the risk involved in financing start-ups is often too great for conventional lenders. In order to direct capital to new ventures, public risk-sharing with private investors is useful. For example:

- Connecticut Product Development Corporation (CPDC) supplies money for risk capital specifically for the development of new innovative products. CPDC provides 60 percent of the cost of product development with private sources providing the remaining 40 percent. In 1979, CPDC aided five projects for a total of $570,999 in public and private investments.

- Massachusetts Technology Development Corporation (MTDC) finances start-up and young high technology firms. It uses a grant from the U.S. Economic Development Administration (EDA) as a revolving loan fund to leverage $4 of other public and private financing for every $1 of MTDC investment. In 1979, MTDC financed five projects, totalling $4.1 million in public and private investments.

Geographic Targeting

Firms in distressed rural and urban areas are perceived as being high risk because bankers are not always knowledgeable about their potential for profitability. Geographic isolation from banks can also preclude such firms from

accessing private sources of capital. In order to provide jobs and adequate incomes in distressed areas, the public sector or non-profit corporations provide non-traditional funding sources. For example:

- The Northern Community Investment Corporation (NCIC) is a non-profit private capital corporation that invests in northern rural Vermont and New Hampshire. Its investments are in the form of equity and subordinated debt. In 1979, NCIC made fourteen investments totalling $1.3 million in NCIC financing and $5.9 million in other public and private financing.

- Connecticut, Maine, New Hampshire and Vermont all have revolving loan funds financed by EDA and state funds. These have target geographic areas and provide loan guarantees and direct financing through secured, subordinated, junior mortgages for working capital and real estate.

- Massachusetts Community Development Finance Corporation (CDFC) provides funds to new and existing ventures in the form of debt or equity, in economically depressed areas of the State. A local non-profit community development corporation must be involved in the business to ensure that its benefits accrue to the target area. CDFC made eleven investments in 1979, totalling $1.6 million in other public and private funding.

- Federal business loan programs through Urban Development Action Grants (UDAGs) from the U.S. Department of Housing and Urban Development (HUD) and loans from EDA and U.S. Farmers Home Administration (FmHA) are in New England to target distressed areas. New England received

10.5 percent of EDA's business development loans, 12 percent of HUD's UDAGs, and 7 percent of FmHA's rural industrialization loans in 1979.

Minority Entrepreneurship

Racial discrimination in lending is a long standing issue that affects the ability of minority businessmen to obtain financial capital. Public and non-conventional private financing has been developed to provide for the capital needs of firms owned by minorities.

Expansions and Move-Ins

The provision of capital with special terms and/or lower costs has traditionally been a public policy instrument for attracting and retaining industry. Each of the New England states has various forms of financial assistance for firms that want to expand, or move into the state. Industrial revenue bonds and loan guarantees are made available for the purchase and development of land; construction, purchase or remodeling of buildings; purchase of machinery and equipment; installation of pollution control equipment; and working capital. In total, the six states issued $643.6 million in industrial revenue bonds and $13.03 million in loan guarantees for 395 projects in 1979. Maine and Vermont also make direct loans for these purposes. Together, they made 52 loans totalling $5.2 million in 1979.

Each state also has private corporations, capitalized by banks, insurance companies, and other private conventional lenders. They invest in riskier ventures than the lenders would individually finance. They either take first mortgages themselves or leverage conventional first mortgages by taking second mortgages. These corporations augment the private capital market by pooling and spreading risks, and by reducing information and transactions costs. In 1979, they made 86 loans for a total of $31.12 million.

Capital Availability In The Context Of The Regional Growth Strategy

New England has a diverse and innovative mix of public and private financing mechanisms to provide capital for growth and to influence location. Many of the vehicles are relatively new, developed since the recession of 73-74 and since the New England Regional Commission capital markets report of 1975. The first objective of any regional financial strategy should be to assess the performance of these institutions and to review regional capital needs against what those institutions can provide.

The capital availability issue, however, must be addressed in context. Capital availability is related to the profitability of a firm and the profitability of doing business in New England. Profitability is a function of productivity, entrepreneurial skills, labor costs, which are discussed elsewhere; and it is a function of government tax and regulatory policies.

Since most firms, especially smaller firms, grow on retained earnings, the federal corporate income tax has a direct impact on the ability of smaller indigenous companies to expand. New England is a Region whose growth is disproportionately tied to the incubation and expansion of home grown industries and therefore the individual income tax on capital gains is of particular concern. Similarly, business depreciation allowances, particularly for retrofitting and reuse, are important to New England businesses.

It is important to note that creative financial mechanisms cannot alone produce the conditions for firm expansion. A good loan will not rescue a bad deal and favorable terms will not significantly affect plant location except at the margin, all other factors being equal. Governments in New England must consider the impacts of all tax and regulatory activities on the costs of doing business, and public officials should be sensitive to the limitations of public lending vehicles. The availabilty of capital at appropriate terms is an important component, however, of a growth strategy for New England.

The Region's high-growth industries are not easy to lend to. High-grade services and high technology manufacturing lack attachable assets that would make them attractive to conventional lenders. Certain of these companies are growing or can grow so rapidly that their need for funds consistently overreaches their cash flow. Smaller firms, both in high-technology and in more traditional businesses always have greater difficulty in raising capital than large firms because they are too small to be attractive to institutional investors.

More traditional industries — transportation equipment, lumber and paper — are attractive to conventional lenders. In fact, the paper industry in New England has recently undergone a period of massive reinvestment. Other traditional industries — leather, jewelry — can be stabilized and can grow with investment in new technologies. But capital for "declining industries" is more difficult to come by and government has taken steps to make use of Federal EDA loans, Trade Adjustment Assistance and other mechanisms to augment the private market.

The capital requirements of businesses in target distressed rural and urban communities remain a concern because of the history of underinvestment by conventional institutions and the limited resources of Federal and State alternative mechanisms. This problem is being mitigated through voluntary private investment as areas are revitalized and through the mandate of the Community Reinvestment Act.

Remaining Unmet Capital-Related Needs In New England

As Belden Daniels and others have pointed out, the major remaining unmet capital-related needs in the Region, even in the presence of a plethora of public-sector financing mechanisms are:

- Information Exchange — Perhaps the most significant failure of the New England capital market is the interchange of information about sources of capital. Commercial lending officers are unfamiliar with existing Federal, state and special-purpose financing vehicles. Federal loan guarantee programs are underutilized in New England. The resources of the larger regional banks are not always understood in smaller, more remote communities. An ongoing regional information exchange is perhaps the most immediate and important component of a regional capital strategy.

- Long Term Debt Financing for Small and Medium Size Firms — Existing conventional and non-traditional institutions should be monitored against needs before any new mechanisms are proposed. Federal loan mechanisms should be more fully utilized and targeted at those industries which have good growth potential but are unable to secure capital from conventional sources.

- Equity Capital for New and Expanding Firms — This is perhaps the most significant form of capital for New England's industrial mix. Governments should encourage equity formation through tax and regulatory policy and should work closely with private institutions to develop new equity funding vehicles. Projects like the Connecticut Product Development Corporation should be monitored, and if successful, replicated in other parts of the Region.

- Reduced Transactions Costs — Loan packaging costs do not vary proportionately with the size of the project. Transactions costs limit the ability of banks and institutional investors to work with small firms. The ability of the public and private sectors to develop means to share or reduce transactions costs would allow for a significant increase in conventional resources available to a wide variety of small businesses.

- Risk Pooling — Since transactions costs can be prohibitive for certain kinds of companies, and since the Region's most significant growth potential is associated with higher risk industries, new risk-pooling vehicles should be explored on a regional basis to supplement public and private mechanisms now in place.

The channeling of capital to target areas, industries and groups is a major vehicle by which public policymakers can influence the nature and extent of economic growth. In order to use this tool with maximum effectiveness the public sector must establish a substantive dialogue with the private sector, where the institutions and expertise for raising and channeling financial capital already exist. Without genuine cooperation between the public and private sectors in this critical area, public attempts to use financial capital flows as a means to influence development are destined to prove inadequate.

Basic Strategies To Improve The Flow Of Capital To Business And Economic Development in New England

1 / Public policymakers in the Region should design tax and regulatory policies so as to create a favorable environment for private investment.

2 / Public financial mechanisms (federal, state and local) should supplement conventional private market mechanisms to compensate for market imperfections, including imperfect information and high transactions costs. NERCOM should increase awareness on the part of the financial community of the increasingly favorable investment climate in New England.

3 / Recognizing that the Region's new and high growth industries face exceptional difficulties securing long term financing (because of size and industry structure), public policy makers must focus special attention on the availabilty of debt and equity capital for the small firms, start-ups, new technology products and specialty services which are so important to the sustained growth of New England.

4 / Public policy-makers should promote balanced economic growth by channelling funds to geographic areas and individual projects which would be perceived as too risky or insufficiently profitable by conventional private financing sources but which are essential to the economic health of target communities. Federal loan and loan guarantee mechanisms should be better coordinated and targeted to serve these regional priorities.

Public Policy Recommendations

1 / Recognizing that tax policies significantly affect the availability of firms to operate profitably and generate equity for expansion, federal and state tax legislation should be designed so as to encourage investment from retained earnings. Specifically, liberalized depreciation allowances and lower corporate income tax schedules would facilitate such equity financing, especially critical for firms without access to the public equity markets. In addition, capital gains roll-over provisions would stimulate direct investment.

2 / The Regional Commission, in conjunction with state development officials, should monitor the effectiveness of existing unconventional and public financing mechanisms, many of which are funded at low levels, in meeting the special capital needs of the Region.

3 / The Commission, in coordination with state development agencies, should play a lead role in disseminating information throughout the Region concerning federal, state and special purpose financing mechanisms, convening an ongoing dialogue between conventional lenders, equity investors and the public sector to maximize access to existing resources for development.

4 / Congress should not make modifications in the federal tax code that would eliminate tax exempt industrial revenue bonds.

5 / States should take a leadership position in developing innovative mechanisms to spur capital formation in the private sector.

6 / The private financial community should be encouraged to increase access to insurance company finance, through creation of mechanisms such as the Massachusetts Capital Resource Corporation.

7 / The Public Works and Economic Development Act amended to include a development financing program should be passed and implemented in such a way as to facilitate growth of target industries and distressed communities in the New England Region.

Yankee Ingenuity:
The Entrepreneurial Edge

. . . the industries with staying power in New England have been ones characterized by high skill and high value relative to weight or volume, factors which helped New England compete despite its distance from the center of the growing American market . . . Present-day New England is thus much more a product of man-made invention than it is of natural or evolutionary industrial forces. A recitation of New England's leading corporations bears scant relationship to New England's early industrial origins. Rather, New England's modern strengths are companies and industries which depend more on skill and know-how, not natural gifts. In a sense, New England has been, and remains, the "Japan" of the United States, bereft of many resources and dependent on her people.

Roger W. Schmenner, in *The Manufacturing Location Decision: Evidence From Cincinnati and New England*

The work of Roger Schmenner and John Hekman, among others, has shown that New England's comparative advantage lies in its technological know-how, creativity and highly-skilled labor force. The Region has traditionally prospered by incubating new firms, products, and processes and by using specialized skills to nurture them in their early stages of development. With relatively scarce mineral and other natural resources, the Region needs to ensure a continuing ability to capitalize on its skilled, innovative work force. This has implications for most of the major topics that the Plan addresses, most obviously labor and capital. In addition, the Region's innovative and entrepreneurial productiveness is dependent on maintaining a favorable climate for business. Small firms require special attention, especially with respect to their need for research and development funding and their participation in federal procurement, particularly for defense-related and other high-technology goods and services.

High-technology firms are a key source of the Region's current prosperity. Technology based industries are significant employment generators in New England. They are also a highly productive and price-stabilizing sector of the economy and produce products that are especially attractive to foreign buyers. In order for the Region to remain economically healthy, it must continue to generate new ideas and offer a receptive environment in which new firms —

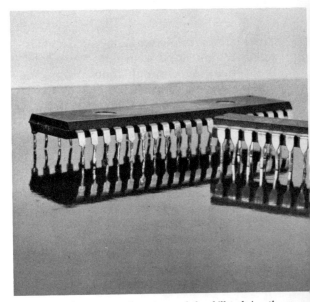

Ideas for new products and services and the skill to bring those ideas to fruition in the marketplace are among the most important building blocks of New England's prosperity.

high tech or other — can start, flourish and grow.

The Importance Of Small Business To The Economy Of New England

Small businesses play a vital role in the economic life of the Nation and of the Region. The need to maintain and strengthen New England's traditional comparative advantage in innovation makes it particularly important that the Regional Plan address the issues that affect small business. Small firms are the principal vehicle for the introduction of new products and technologies. They are the principal source of new jobs and a major source of employment. Small business provides entrepreneurial and employment opportunities among members of disadvantaged groups and in distressed parts of the Region. In rural areas, small firms are often the most appropriate scale of economic activity.

Small business plays an important role in the development and commercialization of new technologies. Technology development often leads to the growth of new industries or the rapid expansion of smaller technology based companies into larger firms. This is especially important to New England, which has a concentration of home-grown high technology industries. Professor William E. Wetzel, Jr. of the University of New Hampshire, made the following findings on the relationship of firm size to technology innovation:*

Risk Capital Research

- In the 1946-1955 decade, over two-thirds of the major inventions resulted from the work of independent inventors.

- On the basis of a sample of major innovations introduced to the market between 1953 and 1973, small firms with up to 1,000 employees were found to produce about 24 times as many innovations per R&D dollar as large firms

(over 10,000 employees).

- The contributions of large firms were largely in the area of improvement innovations.

David L. Birch, a Senior Research Scientist at M.I.T. and a pioneer in quantifying the importance of small business using Dun and Bradstreet data, has made the following observations:

- Very small businesses (with one to nineteen employees) accounted for 88 percent of all establishments in 1976, and small businesses (one to ninety-nine employees) accounted for about 98 percent. In this regard, New England is very similar to the United States as a whole.

- The great majority of smaller establishments tend to be independent, with very small businesses accounting for over 75 percent of all establishments in New England.

Birch found* new job creation, in the form of firm births and expansions, to be the key determinant of differential regional economic growth. Firm death rates were found to be relatively constant across regions and physical migration of firms played an insignificant role. In identifying the source of new job creation, Birch found the following:

- 66 percent of all new jobs generated in the U.S. between 1960 and 1976 were from firms with 19 employees or fewer.

- All net new jobs generated in New England during that period were generated by firms with fewer than 50 employees, with 91.7 percent from firms with 19 employees or fewer.

In addition to providing a major source of new jobs, small businesses provide a large share of total employment. In New England headquar-

* "The Job Generation Process"

Table XXIII

Employment In New England-Headquartered Firms:

Small-Firm* Employment As A Percent Of Industry

Industry	% of Employment in New England Headquartered Firms With 99 Employees or Fewer
Auto Repair, Services, and Garages	93.1
Fisheries	83.7
General Building Contractors	71.4
Insurance Agents and Brokers	70.2
Lumber and Wood Products	66.3
Wholesale Trade	57.8
Miscellaneous Business Services	45.1
Holding and other Investment Companies	30.4
Miscellaneous Manufacturing	30.2

Source: Dunn & Bradstreet data, July 1980.

*99 Employees or Fewer

tered firms, 22.9 percent of employees in all industries are employed by firms with 99 employees or fewer. In addition, employees of small businesses make up large shares of total employment in many industries identified as rapidly growing in New England, as shown in Table I.

Beyond its role as a major employment generator, small business has the potential to provide economic opportunities to disadvantaged groups and geographic areas where general economic growth does not normally occur.

Small business plays an important role in keeping our economy competitive. The innovative small firms which prosper and grow play an important role in introducing new technologies into the marketplace, thereby forcing larger businesses to produce efficiently in order to remain competitive.

Small-scale enterprises are often more appropriate to smaller communities. In addition, a small locally-controlled firm is likely to be more sensitive to the needs of the community than a firm which is controlled from outside. Locally-owned firms tend to expand and reinvest in the community. Firms that are controlled from elsewhere are more likely to consider investments outside of the community.

Technology And Innovation

Innovation is a key to economic growth in New England. The Region's comparative advantage lies in its technological know-how, creativity, and highly skilled work force. New England has traditionally prospered by incubating new firms and ideas and by using specialized skills to nurture those firms in their early stages. New products and new processes for doing business are designed and introduced here.

New England's technology based creativity is well documented. The Region has received more patents per capita than any other region. And, while comprising only 6 percent of total U.S. population, New England has generated 15 percent of the energy-related innovations recommended for development by the National Bureau of Standards.*

Innovative and high technology firms are significant employment generators with high rates of employment growth. Technology-based firms are highly productive and contribute to productivity in other industries by developing better products and more efficient processes. Innovative firms design and develop new technologies that enhance New England's international trade position.

Research and Development

Research and development (R&D) is important to maintaining the flow of innovation. Its special importance to New England is shown by the high proportion of R&D funding characteristic of the five industries that provide over half of the Region's manufacturing employment. Three of these industries — instruments, electrical equipment, and nonelectrical machinery — are among New England's most rapidly growing manufacturing industries. Furthermore, these industries supply rapidly-growing and increasingly sophisticated service industries in New England such as medicine and business services.

Federal government funding can enhance the ability of R&D to contribute to economic growth. However, federal expenditures in New England for non-defense related research are

* William E. Wetzel, Jr., *University of New Hampshire*

Table XXIV

Industry	% NE Manufacturing Employment (1978)	% Total R & D Dollars Nationwide (1977)
Electrical Equipment	13.0	19.9
Nonelectrical Machinery	12.5	13.3
Fabricated Metals	9.5	1.3
Transportation Equipment	8.5	11.4
Instruments	6.5	4.5

Source: BEA Data, N.S.F.

low. While the Region comprised 5.6 percent of U.S. population in 1979, it received only 4 percent of federal expenditures for general science, space, and technology.*

Federal Procurement
Federal spending represented 21 percent of GNP in 1979. The geographic distribution of this spending significantly impacts regional economies. New England receives its "fair share" of total direct federal expenditures on a per capita basis. The Region received 6.1 percent of total direct federal expenditures in fiscal 1979.* Defense expenditures are an important component of the New England economy. Many of these expenditures go to the Region's high-technology industries. In 1979, the Region received 13.3 percent of defense prime contracts.**

The high level of defense expenditures in New England has both positive and negative implications for the regional economy. It is a source of many jobs and is a major support of certain important industries in New England. For example, the transportation equipment industry of Connecticut is significantly dependent upon defense contracts. However, the high level of defense expenditures can negatively affect the Region because defense spending is cyclical and subject to political considerations. Although defense expenditures are increasing at the present time, this trend cannot be expected to continue indefinitely. This leaves many geographic areas and economic sectors of the Region vulnerable to national policy shifts. The State of Connecticut

* Geographic Distribution of Federal Funds in (Each of New England State): Fiscal 1979, compiled for the Executive Office of the President by the Community Services Administration, published by NTIS

** U.S. Department of Defense

has recognized this issue and is developing policies to encourage diversification away from defense dependency.

The high level of defense spending for high-technology industries also promotes technological innovation, particularly through Research, Development, Testing and Evaluation (RDT&E) Prime Contract Awards. These innovations often lead to "spin off" products that can create new industries in the Region. New England receives a very high proportion of the Defense RDT&E prime contract awards (12.6 percent in fiscal 1978*) although its share has been expanding at a slower rate than the national totals. (18.9 percent in 1975-78 versus a 37.7 percent rate nationally)

Strategies Aimed At Enhancing The Climate For Entrepreneurship And Small Business In New England
1 / Public policy makers in New England should foster a fiscal and regulatory environment that encourages the formation and growth of small business. Small business is of special importance to the economic growth prospects of the Region as the incubator of new products and technologies and as a major source of new job generation. Problems with capital availability and compliance with government regulations can disproportionately impact smaller business. Government in the Region should address these issues without driving a wedge between small and large businesses.

2 / Cooperation among high technology companies, universities, government laboratories and financiers is essential if the Region is to take full advantage of its ability to commercialize its innovations. Public policy

* U.S. Department of Defense

should support measures designed to encourage cooperative ventures among the Region's various private and public institutions, aimed at commercializing new technologies.

3 / Federal investment in research and development has fallen steadily from 6.6 percent of GNP in 1960 to 2.6 percent in 1977, affecting national innovation and producivity. Since New England traditionally is a leader in R&D, the Region's governors should take the lead in urging a new national effort in R&D expenditures with special reference to energy resource development.

Public Policy Recommendations
1 / In order to promote the commercialization of new technologies on a regional basis, a regional mechanism, modeled after the Massachusetts Technology Development Corporation (MTDC), which finances start-ups and young high-technology firms, should be established to bring together innovators who lack financial experience and venture capitalists who lack technical expertise.

2 / The states should strengthen their commitment to small business assistance centers as a vehicle for offering management training to business people, especially those from small firms and, where appropriate, link them to university centers.

3 / The utilization of Federal business loan programs through revolving loan programs operated at the state and substate level should be promoted as an effective vehicle for extending Federal programs to small businesses in target communities.

4 / Consideration should be given to amend-
ing the Securities and Exchange Act of 1933
to raise the exemption level on bond
issues.

5 / Since regulations severely impact small
business, states should assess the impact of
their regulatory and paperwork requirements on small business operations.

6 / Congress recently passed the Stevenson-
Wydler Act, creating an Office of Industrial
Technology within the Department of
Commerce and authorizing the establishment of centers for industrial technology
affiliated with universities or other non-
profit organizations. The legislation author-
izes funding of $19 million in fiscal 1981,
$40 million in fiscal 1982, $50 million in fiscal 1983, and $60 million in fiscal 1984 and
1985 for grants to establish these centers.
The actual level appropriated for fiscal 1981
was $5 million. Congress should appropri-
ate monies for this legslation at the full authorized funding level.

Export Trade:
Tapping Foreign Markets

International trade is becoming increasingly important to the U.S. economy and to the New England Region. The recent decline in the value of the dollar has accentuated the world-wide demand for U.S. goods, particularly high-technology machinery and other capital goods. New England has a natural advantage in international trade because of its good port facilities, proximity to European and Canadian markets, and its leadership in innovative and high-technology industries. Because New England has limited natural resources, an expanding export account is essential to the growth of employment and the income of the Region. Because of these same advantages plus proximity to the U.S. population centers, New England is a good candidate for foreign investment and the location of foreign manufacturing facilities.

New England's need to import primary goods, particularly energy, can be offset by increased international exports of manufactured goods as well as by exports of the Region's highly-sophisticated educational, professional and business services, and tourism. In the primary sector, the Region's forest products, both lumber and paper have significant export potential. Besides contributing to the Region's trade balance, export production can stabilize periods of economic slack and supplement periods of prosperity. New England's high-tech goods and services are very desirable on world markets and are becoming more exportable as telecom-

The importance of encouraging vigorous international trade cannot be underestimated. Major factors are the promotion of a wide-ranging export pattern and the local establishment of foreign investment and foreign manufacturing facilities.

Table XXV

New England's Leading Export Industries in Manufacturing: 1976

Ranked By Value of Exports

Industry	New England Export-Related Shipments ($ millions)		Value of Export Related Shipments As Percent of Industry Shipments New England		Value of Export Related Shipments As Percent of Total Manufacturing Exports from New England
	Direct & Supporting	Direct	Direct & Supporting	Direct	
1. Machinery	1542.6	1146.5	21.6	16.0	18.8
2. Transportation Equipment	1367.8	1143.6	25.2	21.1	16.7
3. Electrical Equipment	1017.3	729.7	19.6	14.1	12.4
4. Instruments	700.2	607.7	19.6	17.1	8.6
5. Chemicals	593.6	448.1	20.4	15.4	7.3
6. Fabricated Metals	555.8	306.6	11.0	6.1	6.8
7. Paper	493.0	248.8	11.5	5.8	6.0
8. Miscellaneous Manufactures	232.9	195.5	8.7	7.3	2.8
Total: Leading Industries	6503.2	4826.5	17.9	13.3	79.4

Source: Bureau of Census, Annual Survey of Manufacturers, 1976, *Origins of Manufacturing Establishments*

munications networks link diverse areas of the globe. Because of its desirable product mix, New England is in a good position to capitalize on the increased competitiveness of U.S. products, resulting from recent weakness of the dollar on world currency markets. Promoting exports to world markets is a crucial part of New England's regional growth strategy.

Manufacturing Exports

Manufacturing remains a cornerstone of New England's economic base. As demonstrated earlier, the manufacturing sector continues to comprise a larger share of the Region's economy than of the Nation.

Within manufacturing, exports comprise a larger share of total employment and output in New England than nationally. Over $8 billion worth of export and export-related goods were shipped from New England in 1976, representing 13.7 percent of the Region's total manufacturing shipments. Nationally, exports comprised 11.6 percent of manufacturing shipments in 1976. In terms of employment, export-related jobs comprised nearly 170,000 jobs in 1976, or 12.7 percent of the Region's manufacturing employment, compared to 11.3 percent of the Nation.*

Other data from the Census Bureau, measuring exports by port of origin (*Highlights of U.S. Export and Import Trade*), suggest that the importance of trade to New England has increased dramatically in the recovery period. Exports from New England ports and airports increased by 49 percent between 1975 and 1978, by 23 percent between 1977 and 1978. Boston and St. Albans were the two leading ports in the Region. These data provide only a general indica-

* Bureau of Census, Annual Survey of Manufacturers, 1976, *Origins of Exports of Manufacturing Establishments*

tion of a trend. However, it appears that less than half of New England's manufactured goods by value are shipped abroad from New England's ports.

The Region's greatest strength in manufactured exports is in capital goods: The most important export and export-related industries — machinery, transportation equipment, electrical and electronic products, instruments, chemicals, fabricated metals, paper and miscellaneous manufacturing — are, with the exception of chemicals and paper, among those industries already identified as having rapid-growth potential in the Region. The paper industry has a bright future as measured by current and planned reinvestment in the industry.

As Tables XXV and XXVI illustrate, the Region's leading eight export industries in the manufacturing sector comprise nearly 80 percent of all manufacturing exports for the Region, both in terms of value of shipments and in terms of number of jobs. On average, roughly one-sixth of the value of total manufacturing shipments by these leading industries is export-related, as are approximately one-sixth of these industries' jobs. In nearly all of these industries New England is more export-intensive than the Nation. On average, direct export and export-related jobs in these industries comprise 17.2 percent of total in New England versus 15.8 percent nationally. In terms of value of shipments, direct and supporting export shipments comprise 17.9 percent of total New England shipments by these industries versus 15.9 percent nationwide.

Service-Sector Exports

Manufacturing exports are the easiest to measure and therefore receive considerable attention. However, New England's private sector

Table XXVI

New England's Leading Export Industries in Manufacturing: 1976

Ranked By Employment

Industry	Export-Related Manufacturing Employment (persons)		Export-Related Employment as Percent of Industry Employment New England		Export-Related Employment as Percent of Total Export-Related Employment in New England Manufacturing
	Direct & Supporting	Direct	Direct & Supporting	Direct	
1. Machinery	33,100	24,000	20.5	14.9	19.5
2. Electrical Equipment	27,200	19,000	20.5	14.3	16.0
3. Transportation Equipment	23,400	19,500	22.9	19.9	13.8
4. Instruments	15,000	12,900	19.3	16.6	8.8
5. Fabricated Metals	11,800	6,200	9.9	5.2	6.9
6. Miscellaneous Manufactures	6,600	5,600	9.2	7.8	3.9
7. Chemicals	5,800	4,100	19.1	13.5	3.4
8. Paper	7,200	3,400	11.3	5.3	4.2
Total: Leading Industries	130,000	94,000	17.2	12.5	76.6

Source: Bureau of the Census, Annual Survey of Manufacturers, 1976, *Origins of Exports of Manufacturing Establishments*

services which are larger and growing faster than the nation's may be of equal or greater importance in terms of international trade. New England's service sector industries, exclusive of government, account for 49% of all employment in the Region. Among these, finance, insurance, tourism, education, medicine and other professional services have important export potential and should be given equal weight in the development of international trade strategies despite the lack of specific data measuring current performance.

The U.S. Commerce Department estimates that some 65,000 jobs in the service (i.e. finances, transportation and communications) and primary sectors support the 170,000 export-related manufacturing jobs. This statistic refers only to jobs directly related to the export of manufactured products of which the preponderance are in the service producing industries.

Within the service producing sector, such industries as education, professional services, and medical and other health services have been identified as growth industries in New England and important exporters. Employment shares analysis indicates that these New England industries are important exporters to the rest of the country. The Region's preeminence in high grade services also suggests that these services are exported internationally. Since the growth of these industries is a major factor in the development of the regional economy, the international export of services deserves special attention in a regional growth strategy.

International services account for a significant share of business transacted in the management, architectural, engineering and other consulting industries. The overall amount of international business in these firms is unobtainable. However, an estimate from Arthur D. Little

Company of Cambridge, Massachusetts, one of the Nation's leading management consulting firms, is that between 10 and 20 percent of the activity in the Cambridge office alone is devoted to international business. There is reason to believe that the situation in other large consulting firms in New England is similar.

The Region's outstanding medical services industry also is deserving of special mention. New England's health-related facilities draw patients from all parts of the world. As advances occur in medical technology and research, so too will the flow of foreign patients into the Region increase.

Educational services represents another major export industry for the Region. According to data published by the Institute of International Education, an estimated 18,643 foreign students attended institutions of higher education in New England in the 1978-1979 academic year. These students represented 7.0 percent of the national total for the period, and 2.7 percent of all students enrolled in a New England institution of higher learning. The share represented by foreign students in some of the more prestigious colleges and universities is even higher. For example, foreign students make up almost 20 percent of the student body at the Massachusetts Institute of Technology. Based on the estimated $10,000 expenditure per student, foreign students in New England in higher education alone contribute $186.4 million to the Region's export account.

Tourism is another important export industry. Many foreigners come to New England not only to vacation, but also to visit educational institutions and to learn latest techniques and product development from high technology industries. Current data on foreign visits is

sparse, though the United States Travel Service of the U.S. Department of Commerce is beginning to collect such information. In 1978, the Service published a summary of foreign trips to the United States by region. According to this source, 3.2 million foreign visitors came to New England in 1977 and spent approximately $435 million in the Region, or 6.3 percent of the Nation's total. Tourism exports are comparable to chemicals, the fifth largest manufacturing export, in terms of impact on the Region's export account.

Primary-Sector Exports
Natural-resource-based industries account for a small share of economic activity in New England, due to the relative scarcity of natural resources in the Region. However, certain primary-sector industries do produce exportable products.

New England agricultural exports consist of fresh and processed fruits and vegetables and agricultural by-products such as animal feeds. In comparison to the Nation, the Region's agricultural exports are very small. In 1978, the Region's agricultural exports represented 2 percent of the Nation's total.

Exports of New England agricultural commodities to foreign markets amounted to $53 million in 1978, up 67 percent from the 1976 level. The national increase was 20 percent during the same period. Higher prices for agricultural commodities accounted for about three quarters of the increase in value according to the Federal Reserve Board.

An estimated $30.2 million of fish and fish products were exported from New England in 1978 according to estimates based on Census and National Maritime Administration information. This represents 3.3 percent of national fisheries exports, a sharp rise in share from New England's 1976 share (1.4 percent). Recent efforts to increase fisheries' exports have included large-scale export of underutilized species; future efforts will probably include increasing shipments of fish by-products for animal feeds and fertilizers. As more foreign markets are found, the Fisheries industry will become an increasingly important contributor to the Region's export activities.

There is strong potential for expanded development in the forest products industries through growth in export activity. In 1976, 10.4 percent of New England's total shipments of lumber and wood products were directed to export markets as compared with 11.4 percent for the Nation. Realizing the untapped export potential in New England's natural resource industries would increase economic stability in periods of fluctuating demand and contribute to the prosperity of the Region.

Foreign Investment In The New England Economy

Changes in international conditions plus the size of the U.S. market have made the U.S. and New England in particular attractive to foreign investment and, more importantly, to the location of manufacturing and service facilities. Foreign investment is smaller than exports in terms of employment and income in the Region, but it is an issue of increasing public policy attention for New England.

Foreign owned assets in New England including land, plant and equipment amounted to $1.8 billion in 1977, about $1.6 billion in plant and equipment. New England affiliates of foreign companies employed more than 70,000 residents in various jobs. These jobs represented 6.2 percent of total jobs created by foreign

owned affiliates in the U.S. and accounted for 1.3 percent of the Region's employment.

Current Public Policy Toward Trade

Balance Of Payments deficits due principally to the cost of imported oil have led to a federal emphasis on export promotion. One result has been the structuring of the International Trade Administration of the U.S. Department of Commerce to facilitate trade expansion. These changes are recent and have not included significant funding increases. Legislation pending in Congress would provide public sector incentives and reduce regulations on private sector trading activities to encourage increased exports.

The Tokyo Round Of The Multilateral Trade Negotiations completed in 1979 was designed to reduce tariff barriers and other obstacles to freer trade. The Tokyo Round will benefit the Region's stronger growth industries including tourism. Regional policy makers should monitor the MTN to identify industries and nations for expanded export opportunities, and to watch for adverse impacts on less competitive regional industries.

State And Regional International Trade Programs Promotion of exports by state and regional institutions has not been a high priority for government attention. International Trade offices exist in each of the six New England states, and some states have increased their emphasis on exports through trade missions and other activities, but their greater priority is the promotion of industrial location of foreign businesses. NERCOM has a small but successful small business export program which serves as an information center and sponsors participation in foreign trade shows. The Massport /SBANE small business program helps exporters through trade missions.

TABLE XXVII

Employment, Plant and Equipment of U.S. Affiliates of Foreign Owned Companies: 1977

New England and the U.S.

	Value of Plant and Equipment ($ Millions)	Employment[1]
U.S. Total	53,792	1,122,207
New England	**1,629**	**70,097**
Massachusetts	457	21,540
Connecticut	193	4,706
Maine	552	27,646
Rhode Island	160	8,318
New Hampshire	155	3,542
Vermont	111	4,345

[1] Average number of full-time and part-time employees during the year.

Source: Bureau of Economic Analysis, U.S. Department of Commerce

International Trade In The Context Of The Regional Growth Strategy

Capitalizing on New England's strengths in international markets and identifying industries with potential for export development will benefit both the economy as a whole and individual firms within the Region. Exporting to foreign markets can generate and maintain employment, foster industrial expansion and augment the quality of life in New England.

- Export sales broaden a firm's sales base, making possible support of a larger volume of research and development spending, which is crucial to the continued economic growth of the Region.

- Industries which predominate in economically distressed areas of the Region and have untapped export potential, such as fisheries and forest products, can be targeted for export growth.

- Industries which experience seasonal or cyclical sales fluctuations, such as metalworking or machine tools, can stabilize demand through market diversification.

- Continued expansion of the Region's high-technology manufacturing and high-grade services exports should be encouraged as part of the Regional Growth Strategy.

- Tourism is an export of increasing importance regionwide and has special significance to employment in target communities.

- New England's small businesses, the Region's principal employment generators, represent a vast, unrealized source of export potential. According to Dun and Bradstreet, April, 1980, 90 percent of the manufacturing firms headquartered in New England employ fewer than 100 workers. The

U.S. Department of Commerce estimates that 20,000 small and medium sized firms have strong export potential, yet 80 percent of the Nation's exporting is done by the Nation's 200 largest companies, and the same is generally true for New England.

Many small New England firms produce goods or services which are in great demand by foreign buyers, yet the products are sold solely to domestic purchasers. Facilitating the entry of small business into international markets would expand the Region's export account, increase employment and income and offset the Region's need to import primary materials.

International Trade Strategies For New England

Recognizing the significance of international trade to the overall strategies of the New England Development Plan, the Commission and the New England governors should devote more attention to national export policy and to the promotion of exports from the New England Region. In addition to increasing the volume of New England's exports, public policy should encourage expansion of New England small business exports and increased utilization of New England ports and airports.

To take full advantage of the jobs and income potential from exports and to increase regional exports directly, the Region's leaders should act collectively to insure the adequacy of international port and airport and facility development. Since a disproportionate quantity of the Region's exports exit from non-New England ports, it is probable that current facilities are inadequate. Since much of the Region's exports are high-value-added manufacturing and high grade services, the importance of airports for both freight and passenger service should be given special attention.

Public Policy Recommendations

1 / The States and the New England Regional Commission should devote more attention to export promotion. The States should consider establishing one stop offices for exporters to guide them from the initial stage of obtaining leads to the loading of the commodities destined for export.

2 / The Multilateral Trade Negotiations will play an important role in the near future. As many products manufactured in the Region are affected positively or negatively, NERCOM should monitor MTN and its effects on New England products. New opportunities for exports should be investigated.

3 / The Commission's sponsorship of trade missions and shows should be expanded. Many small firms with no previous export experience can develop foreign business contacts for present and future business at minimal public cost.

4 / The Commission, and the states and private sector leadership should closely monitor proposed national export promotion legislation, particularly those bills calling for the establishment of trading companies, to insure that legislation which is enacted will benefit both manufacturers and banking and other export support services in New England.

5 / The Commission should play an advocacy role in working with the CAB and the Region's airports to insure the competitiveness of international flight (both passenger and freight) service.

6 / Expansion of air and seaport facilities is essential. Ongoing port facility planning should be strengthened and public funds for port expansion should be identified.

Meeting Regional
Energy Needs

Now is the time . . . to come to terms with the realities of the energy problem, not with romanticisms, but with pragmatism and reason. And not out of altruism, but for pressing reasons of self-interest.

Robert Stobaugh and Daniel Yergin in
Energy Future

Hiqh energy prices and potential energy supply shortages are nationai and global problems that affect the cost of living, the ability to operate businesses, and the availability of capital for economic development. In New England, these problems are especially significant because of the Region's high consumption of imported foreign oil and the fact that New England's winters are colder than winters in most other regions of the country. However, New England does have opportunities to lessen the negative effects of its energy problems. The Region has proven that it can continue to grow even while it conserves energy. New England has the potential to become a leader in developing alternative energy sources; a course of action that would capitalize on the Region's natural resources and technological innovation. Energy resource management and planning are essential to provide for a mix of conventional and new energy sources to meet the needs of the regional economy.

Energy Issues For New England
New England currently pays higher prices for energy and spends a greater portion of its income on energy despite lower per capita consumption. Gas and coal prices are significantly higher in New England than in the Nation as a whole because the Region is at the end of the pipeline for domestic energy supplies and must pay higher transportation costs. In 1979, the Region paid approximately $17 billion for energy. This expenditure comprised more than 20 per-

It is now clear that a mix of conventional and new energy sources is essential to solving New England's unique energy problems. Effective energy resource management and planning with an eye toward long-range effects will help determine how that mix will be weighted.

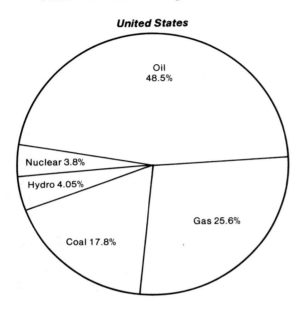

FIGURE XI
**1978 Total Energy Consumption By Source
United States and New England — % of Total**

United States

Oil 48.5%

Nuclear 3.8%

Hydro 4.05%

Coal 17.8%

Gas 25.6%

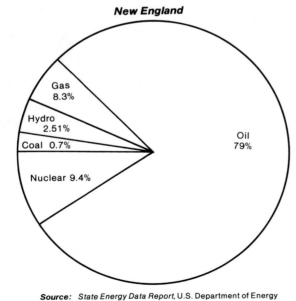

New England

Gas 8.3%

Hydro 2.51%

Coal 0.7%

Nuclear 9.4%

Oil 79%

Source: State Energy Data Report, U.S. Department of Energy

cent of New England's total personal income. Since the Region imports most of its energy supply, these expenditures result in a substantial outflow of capital from New England.

- In 1979, the weighted average price of energy to the end user on a comparable BTU basis was 40 percent higher in New England than in the U.S. This differential will continue to increase as long as natural gas and coal prices increase more slowly than oil prices.

- On a per capita basis New England spent $1,463 per person on energy in 1979, 5.9 percent above the national average of $1,381, even though the Region's per capita consumption of energy was lower than the Nation's.

The possibility of an interrupted fuel supply is a factor that was introduced into economic decision-making only during the last two decades. In the future, the perceptions of regional fuel availability will increasingly influence industrial decisions to remain or locate in the Region. New England is more vulnerable to supply interruptions and to sharp price increases than the Nation as a whole because the Region has little indigenous fossil fuel and its energy supply mix relies disproportionately on foreign oil.

- Approximately 84 percent of the petroleum consumed in New England is supplied from foreign oil.

- Petroleum provides about 79 percent of the Region's total energy, compared to 48 percent for the U.S. Figure XI compares New England's energy consumption by source to that of the U.S.

In addition to higher energy costs and more supply uncertainty, the Region faces problems that result from energy use and supply in other

parts of the Nation. Prevailing wind patterns carry air pollution generated outside of the Region into New England. Because of this pollution, the Region requires more stringent pollution control requirements to meet ambient air quality standards. Severance taxes on oil drilling and coal mining go directly into the general funds of oil and coal producing states. As a result, not only can these states offer existing and potential businesses a more secure energy supply, but they can also offer lower taxes than states that are net energy consumers.

Energy Needs For Economic Growth In New England
Increasingly high energy costs significantly add to the cost of doing business and subtract from the disposable income of consumers. Further, the uncertainty of supply and higher energy costs in New England are deterrents to industries planning to locate or expand here.

Energy Impacts on New England Consumers
Energy costs lower consumers' disposable income and thus affect the quality of life in the Region. Compared to the national average of 16 percent, the average New England household currently spends 18 percent of its income on energy. Energy consumption in low-income households comprises over 36 percent of income. Since the Region imports almost all of its energy, every 10 percent increase in the cost of energy effectively moves another billion dollars out of the Region. Households have to meet increases in the price of energy by decreasing consumption of other goods. Figure XII shows residential energy consumption by source in New England and the United States.

Energy Impacts on Business
Increasing energy costs and uncertainty about energy availability are critical to New England

industries. Energy costs adversely impact industry by raising production costs and transportation costs and by affecting consumer income. Certain New England industries, especially those that do not require resources in which New England has a strong locational advantage, but do require large amounts of energy in their production, are extremely vulnerable to sharp energy cost increases. Many industries and firms located in remote rural parts of the Region depend on existing transportation and storage networks which are economically viable at current energy costs but may not be at higher costs. New England firms which sell within the Region are adversely affected by relatively lower consumer disposable income available for non-energy purposes. Relatively higher consumer prices affect the ability and desire of valuable labor to reside in New England. Tourism and recreation, industries for which New England has a natural advantage, depend on easy accessibility from large population centers and are therefore particularly vulnerable to disruption of gasoline supplies. Firms which use computers, including the Region's growing high technology and service industries, require a reliable electricity supply and cannot operate with supply interruptions. Figures XIII and XIV show energy consumption by source in the industrial and commercial sectors of New England and the United States.

An Evolving Economy With Less Energy Use
New England has proven that it can conserve energy without sacrificing economic growth or the quality of life.

Despite the Region's energy problems, its economy has grown. New England's industrial mix has evolved in a direction which is less energy-intensive than that of the Nation. Although New England contains 5.6 percent of the Na-

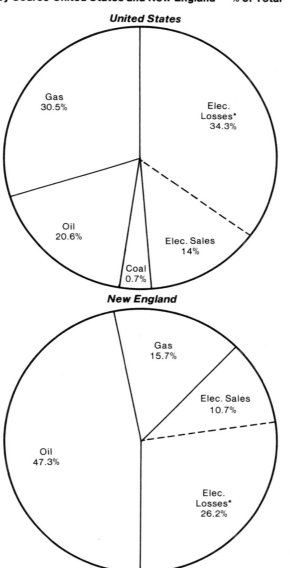

FIGURE XII
1978 Total Energy Consumption for Residential Sector by Source United States and New England — % of Total

United States

Gas 30.5%
Elec. Losses* 34.3%
Oil 20.6%
Elec. Sales 14%
Coal 0.7%

New England

Gas 15.7%
Elec. Sales 10.7%
Oil 47.3%
Elec. Losses* 26.2%

* Energy losses in generation and transmission are included to reflect total energy consumed for electric generation.

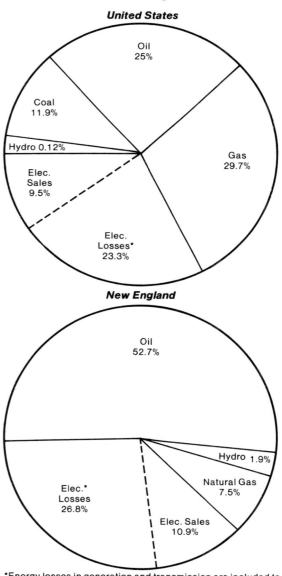

FIGURE XIII
1978 Total Energy Consumption for Industries by Source United States and New England — % of Total

United States

Oil 25%
Coal 11.9%
Hydro 0.12%
Elec. Sales 9.5%
Gas 29.7%
Elec. Losses* 23.3%

New England

Oil 52.7%
Hydro 1.9%
Natural Gas 7.5%
Elec.* Losses 26.8%
Elec. Sales 10.9%

*Energy losses in generation and transmission are included to reflect total energy consumed for electric generation.

Source: *State Energy Data Report,* U.S. Department of Energy

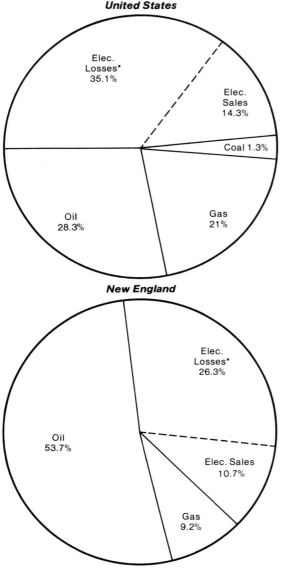

FIGURE XIV
**1978 Total Energy Consumption for Commercial Sector
by Source United States and New England — % of Total**

United States

Elec. Losses* 35.1%

Elec. Sales 14.3%

Coal 1.3%

Oil 28.3%

Gas 21%

New England

Elec. Losses* 26.3%

Oil 53.7%

Elec. Sales 10.7%

Gas 9.2%

*Energy losses in generation and transmission are included to reflect total energy consumed for electric generation.

Source: *State Energy Data Report*, U.S. Department of Energy

tion's population, the Region consumes 3.9 percent of the Nation's energy. U.S. energy consumption increased by 2.5 percent between 1973 and 1977 while New England energy consumption decreased by 3.9 percent over the same period.

Between 1973 and 1977, U.S. consumption of petroleum products increased by 6.7 percent while New England petroleum consumption decreased by 8.8 percent. Currently, about two million cords of wood are consumed in the residential sector of New England, displacing 8.6 million barrels of oil per year. It is estimated that 60 percent of the homes in Maine, New Hampshire, and Vermont use wood as supplemental heating fuel. In the industrial sector, it is estimated that wood is displacing 6.8 million barrels of oil annually.

New England's energy use for industrial production, per real dollar of output, fell 5 percent between 1973 and 1977. The energy intensity of New England manufacturing is significantly less than in the U.S. as a whole. In 1976, the U.S. manufacturing sector used 2.27 times as much energy per dollar of value added as New England manufacturers. New England's industrial sector accounts for about 21 percent of the Region's total energy consumption, while industrial users consume 37 percent of energy nationwide.

Potential For Alternative Energy Development
New England can decrease its dependence on foreign energy imports and provide regional benefits by maximizing the use of its own resources. The Region currently imports all of its coal, natural gas, and oil as well as nuclear fuel used in nuclear power plants. New England's indigenous resources can provide alternative sources of energy. Rivers, woods, sun, wind, ocean tides, peat and solid waste are all renew-

able resources that can provide the Region with energy to meet some of its demand.

The New England Energy Congress has projected that 25 percent of our energy demand could be met by these renewables by the year 2000. Although the development of alternative sources cannot be expected to supplant our dependence on conventional resources in the near future, investment in alternative energy would enhance the use of the Region's natural resources and take advantage of New England's innovative and high technology expertise.

Substituting indigenous energy resources for imported energy would reduce the flow of funds that currently leaves the Region to pay for fuel produced elsewhere. Retaining these funds in the Region would allow for their investment in New England's economy.

Conventional Energy Facilities
Conventional fossil fuels and nuclear power will continue to provide the majority of energy to the Region in the near term. However, dwindling supplies and potential interruptions, rapidly increasing prices, potential environmental problems, and the constant drain on the Region's economy are characteristic of many of these energy resources. Diversification of the Region's fuel mix and sources of supply are necessary to create greater dependability and stability of conventional energy resources.

The only major energy facilities located in New England are electrical generating plants. More than 92 percent of the electricity from these facilities is generated by using resources that are exogenous to the Region: oil, natural gas, coal, and nuclear fuel. Figure XV shows the fuel sources used to generate electric power in the United States and in New England.

Potential conventional energy facilities in New England other than electrical power plants include co-generation facilities, oil refineries, and offshore oil and gas rigs.

Presently, the long lead time required to build new generating facilities, the uncertainty about new technology, and the Region's high dependence on unpredictable oil supplies for electricity generation make development of new facilities difficult. However, energy facility planning must take place to meet future needs. Within such planning, a consensus must be reached on the appropriate conventional fuel mix for the future, weighing the costs, supply, and environmental effects of coal, nuclear power, oil, and natural gas.

Delays that could be avoided by a more effective energy facility siting process make inherently long siting and construction times even longer. The resulting long lead times make accurate capacity planning more difficult. They also unnecessarily tie up capital, thereby vastly increasing costs, particularly in an inflationary environment. For example, the lead time on a nuclear power plant is now twelve years. However, electricity demand has changed dramatically over the past decade.

From 1972 to 1978 the annual growth rate of electricity demand fell from 7.6 percent to 2.2 percent. Thus, a plant which becomes operative in twelve years may be unnecessary if the growth rate of demand continues to fall. On the other hand, unforeseen increases in demand may make for insufficient capacity in newly constructed facilities. Improvements in siting procedures could avoid massive waste of capital and inappropriately sized facilities.

Basic Energy Strategies

1 / A diversification of energy sources (including solar, wind, and other alternative sources, coal, nuclear, and Canadian natural gas and hydro) is necessary for balanced regional growth.

2 / Building a public consensus on energy and a framework for long-range decision-making to plan for future energy facilities is an essential part of the Region's energy resource development.

3 / Increased conservation must remain a cornerstone of New England's energy strategy. Conservation reduces the burden of increasing energy costs, which directly affect disposable income.

4 / Public policymakers should encourage production and use of energy by means that are consistent with environmental safeguards necessary to protect the quality of life important to many of New England's industries. Trade-offs between energy and environmental goals must be made within the framework of the Region's total economic development strategy.

5 / Policymakers should move to develop increased capacity within the regional infrastructure to allow for greater use of conventional and indigenous fuels other than oil, and develop the sources and markets for these fuels.

6 / Energy officials should develop contingency plans so the Region and its various energy sectors will be able to respond to supply interruptions, sudden increases in the cost of energy, and new developments in technology.

FIGURE XV

**Fuel Sources for Electric Power
United States and New England — % of Total**

United States

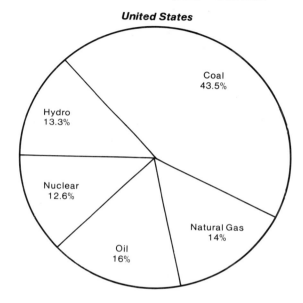

New England

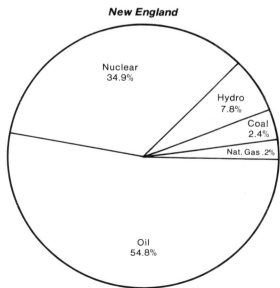

Source: *State Energy Data Report,* U.S. Department of Energy

7 / New England should encourage industries that are not energy intensive, or are basically energy self-sufficient, such as those related to forest products.

Public Policy Recommendations

1 / A broad based understanding of the Region's energy needs and supply options is necessary for facility development. In coordination with the other regional organizations, the Commission should make a major effort to build a region-wide consensus on long-range energy needs and the appropriate mix of conventional and alternative energy sources. State and local decision-making processes for new energy facilities should be expedited to reduce the time, uncertainties, and costs of facility siting once siting decisions are made.

2 / Investment in energy conservation is an essential investment in the productivity and growth of New England and the Nation. Federal and state tax incentives, a continuation of existing federal conservation programs, and new conservation initiatives should be supported.

3 / The rapid progress made in the industrial and residential use of wood, hydropower, and solar energy underscores the importance of alternative energy sources to New England. The market for these resources, still in its early stage of development, necessitates infrastructure and implementation assistance. Continued attention, in the form of research and development, should be paid to other applications of alternative energy.

4 / A Regional Petroleum Reserve, as a component of the Strategic Petroleum Reserve, should be supported. This will guarantee short-term oil supply in the event of an unexpected emergency and thus reduce economic dislocation in our Region.

5 / As our Nation's most plentiful nonrenewable fuel, coal deserves careful, steady development. Incentives for New England utilities to convert to coal are a high priority. This should be pursued with air quality safeguards.

6 / Oil and gas deregulation, whatever its merits as a spur to increased domestic production, has severe effects on the ability of lower- and middle-income families to pay their fuel bills. New England's reliance on oil for heating homes necessitates that fuel assistance, low-income weatherization programs, and similar projects be in place.

7 / All levels of government, especially the United States Department of Energy, should facilitate the continued, safe operation of nuclear power plants by requiring safe waste disposal, operator training, maintenance, and contingency planning.

8 / NERCOM should work to expedite the purchase of hydropower from Canada.

9 / U.S. Department of Energy and the States should cooperate with Canada to develop United States markets for Canadian natural gas.

10 / State severance taxes on oil drilling and coal mining create severely unequal tax environments in energy producing states relative to energy consuming states. Federal grant-in-aid programs should mitigate the adverse effects that severance taxes in energy producing states have on states that do not produce energy. In determining state revenue efforts, the aid formulas in federal programs should preclude state severance taxes and royalties on oil and coal production.

The Transportation Network: Keeping Pace with a Changing Economy

⑨

. . . I guess you can't get there from here.

Marshall Dodge in "Which Way to East Vassalboro?" from *Bert and I and Other Stories From Down East*

The movement of goods, supplies, and people to, from, and around New England is an essential component of the regional economy. New England has to confront the challenge of distance from national markets, older transportation infrastructure, deregulation, and the high cost of short hauls within the Region. The Region's transportation services and facilities must provide for intra and interregional mobility in order for New England to remain competitive with other regions. Transportation infrastructure should reflect New England's changing economic activity and living patterns by being flexible enough to provide new service as dictated by new demands. Of particular importance is the continued ability of the transportation network to move goods such as pulp and paper, chemicals, and electronics out of the Region; and to bring foodstuffs, steel and grains into the Region without allowing the costs of such movements to decrease the competitive position of New England. This is an important consideration in foreign as well as domestic markets. Geographically, New England is well-situated for exporting and importing large quantities of commodities through its gateways. A major inhibitor of growth in exports is the lack of capacity in transportation infrastructure, services, and facilities, which encourages the use of ports and airport facilities outside of the Region.

Transportation infrastructure should reflect New England's changing economic activity and living patterns by being flexible enough to provide new service as dictated by new demands.

Transportation Issues For New England

Presently, several issues confronting New England will require imagination, initiative, and long-term commitment on the part of the consumers and providers of transportation services. Of primary importance is the simple fact that New England is dependent on the import of food, fuel and other materials, and is the final leg of domestic freight movements.

Moving primary and finished products in and out of New England is often more costly than shipments to and from other parts of the country. The additional cost must be added to the price of finished goods imported and consumed here, or exported and sold in markets elsewhere. This factor contributes to a poorer competitive position of New England manufacturers relative to manufacturers elsewhere.

New England' transportation infrastructure is old. The Region's transportation system was in place before systems were created elsewhere. Being older, New England's systems are in greater need of immediate repair, incur larger maintenance costs, and require large capital expenditures for both new equipment and modernization. Introducing new technologies in one mode usually requires further complementary changes in interchanging modes, new training, new marketing approaches, and new operational procedures. In short, modernization of the existing infrastructure involves investment of considerable magnitude, the return on which may take many years to realize.

Fuel consumption for both freight and passenger transportation purposes is now 28 percent of total energy consumed in New England and is likely to increase. Freight currently accounts for 23 percent of transportation energy use. If freight transportation's demand for energy continues without significant conservation measures,

consumption levels will reach 43.75 billion gallons per year nationally by 1985.* Conservation efforts currently in place would reduce the increase by about 16 percent but, regardless of conservation efforts, freight's share of the total transportation fuel demand is projected to grow to 29 percent in 1985. Energy use in the passenger transportation sector is equally critical.

The adequacy and cost of passenger transportation throughout the Region will affect both the cost of living and working in New England and the locational decisions of new and expanding businesses. Higher fuel costs plus the almost total dependence of many sections of the region on the automobile will have an increasing impact on the disposable income of the workforce. At the same time, high capital costs and living and working patterns make mass transit investments very difficult.

Efficient transportation access by air, highway, and rail will affect the locational decisions of industry in the region. The transportation of goods and supplies is essential to economic development. Industrial location decisions are closely tied to the freight transportation network connecting suppliers, producers, and markets.

* Maio, Dominic J., *Freight Transportation Petroleum Conservation Opportunities-Viability Evaluation*, U.S. Department of Transportation Research & Special Programs Administration, Transportation Systems Center, March 1979.

The adequacy of intra-regional air service is of particular importance to expanding high-tech industries and high grade services. Ground transportation between work centers and population centers will impact each and every business expansion decision.

Deregulation of transportation modes can have a far-reaching, long-term impact on New England's economy and competitive position rela-

tive to other regions. Truck and rail deregulation became law very recently and have not yet been fully implemented, and potential impact in this region is very difficult to assess. The example of airline deregulation portends that parts of New England will be adversely affected by a fully deregulated transportation environment.

- The purpose of airline deregulation was to provide improved and increased air service, greater competition, and lower prices through the workings of a free market. In transcontinental, trans-Atlantic and inter-regional flights, it has been successful. However, service in rural parts of New England has markedly declined with fewer cities served, fewer carriers, lower flight frequency and higher prices. Deregulation has impacted small communities the most. With limited transportation alternatives, rural areas become less accessible and less attractive for industry location and a diversified economic base.

- Figure XVI shows the decline of air service in New England's small communities. With increased fuel costs and more freedom to leave less profitable markets, truckers may be less capable or willing to serve small and rural communities under deregulation.

- Amendments to the rail deregulation bill may have a particularly serious impact on rail service in Southern New England. The legislation allows for increased rates on branch lines as well as abandonment or supplemental transfer of branch line service under a variety of circumstances. As a result, future freight service may be interrupted, become less reliable, or be discontinued in certain areas. In combination with deregulation, the restructuring of CON-

RAIL's route system in Southern New England could have significant deleterious effects on the economic viability of that portion of the Region.

Access to foreign markets via increased export trade through the Region's gateways is of interest to private and public sectors. In New England, this issue must be addressed by both sectors because access to foreign markets will require expansion and modernization of the Region's port and harbor facilities. Judicious planning and investment can lead to balanced port growth which would improve New England's competitive position relative to New York and Montreal and reduce transportation costs and ultimately consumer costs of imported goods.

Because New England is smaller geographically than other regions and centers of population are much closer together, intra-regional goods movements here tend to be much more short-haul. As a result, the cost per mile of in-region goods shipment is higher. Short hauls are frequently run at less than full load. They also are terminal intensive, so they require a disproportionately higher amount of transferring and loading operations than do long hauls.

High quality management capability facilitates an effective and useful transportation network. Developing more cooperative and coordinated efforts among modes would create a balance in operations and an equitable sharing of available markets, emphasizing fuel efficiency and cost effectiveness.

Transportation Needs For Economic Growth In New England
In order to contribute to economic development in New England, the Region's transportation network must respond to both freight and passenger transportation requirements.

Figure XVI
Changes in Service at New England Airports

% Change (1/79 vs. 1/80)	New England Non Hub Airports	New England Hub Airports	Total N.E. Airports	Total U.S. Airports
Departures	-11%	2%	0%	-2%
Capacity	-7%	2.5%	1%	1%

Loss in Departures (1/79 vs. 1/80)		Loss in Capacity (1/79 vs. 1/80)	
● Block Island	74%	● New Bedford	71%
● New Bedford	54%	● Rockland	55%
● Martha's Vineyard	43%	● Martha's Vineyard	49%
● Lebanon	26%	● Presque Isle	38%
● Keene	24%	● Montpelier	25%
● Presque Isle	14%	● Rutland	18%

Departures

Capacity

Source: Civil Aeronautics Board, NERCOM calculations

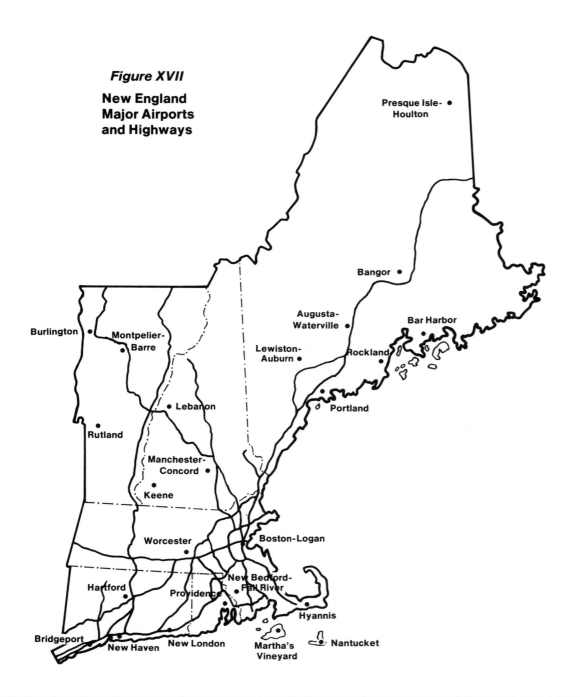

Figure XVII

**New England
Major Airports
and Highways**

Presque Isle-
Houlton •   •

Bangor •

Augusta-
Waterville •
Bar Harbor •

Burlington •
Montpelier-
Barre •

Lewiston-
Auburn •
Rockland

Lebanon •

Rutland •

Portland •

Manchester-
Concord •

Keene •

Worcester •
Boston-Logan •

Hartford •
New Bedford-
Fall River •
Providence •

Hyannis •

Bridgeport •
New Haven   New London   Martha's
Vineyard   Nantucket

Materials Movement Into And Out Of The Region

The balance of truck, rail, and air service required for fast and reliable freight movement to and from the Region depends on the type and value of commodity moved, the time sensitivity of the move, and the additional infrastructure maintenance, repair and upgrading costs of such moves.

Bulk shipments of low value commodities, whose delivery is not primarily time sensitive, are often best shipped by rail. Economies of scale are achieved in certain cases by moving large amounts of a single commodity to a single destination in unit trains. Such a strategy would also avoid highway repair costs running into the billions of dollars if significant quantities of such commodities were moved by truck. Such movements by rail would also be a long haul for New England and, as such, would be more fuel efficient than movements by truck.

This is not the case for low bulk, higher value commodities, especially if they require special care or attention. For example, because of the special care requirements of foodstuffs; their fragility, and need for refrigeration and quick movement, trucks are the most likely mode selected by shippers. At some point, foodstuffs may move by rail or air. Considerable opportunity for combined truck/rail movements could exist in New England. However, physical impediments to the use of "Trailer-On-Flat Car" (TOFC) technology, especially in Southern New England, currently preclude this. Such a combined system would offer fuel efficiency with rapid, reliable delivery, resulting in lower costs and higher quality foodstuffs in New England.

Low bulk, high value, time sensitive commodities move primarily by air to national and foreign markets. Air shipment, while more costly, generally assures shippers of same day or next day service and minimizes possible damage or loss during transit. Air freight service relies upon local delivery by truck. This intermodal relationship has considerable expansion potential, especially as high technology and service industries expand in New England.

International Exports And Port Development
Access to international markets is a basic requirement for New England's economic growth. The Region can export commodities that originate here such as paper and high technology products, as well as commodities that originate outside of New England but could exit through the Region's ports.

Currently, 15% of imports and exports originating or terminating in New England move through Montreal and 32% move through New York. This unfortunate condition is primarily due to shipper preference and reliability of service through the other gateways. Capturing even a portion of that 47% total that either originates or terminates in the Region but does not go through New England ports, would increase jobs and incomes. To capture that traffic, the Region's port facilities must be modernized and intermodal port connections must be improved so that New England is more competitive with ports north and south of the Region. One danger in regional port development, however, is that over-capacity may occur. If all New England ports develop and expand their capacity to handle containerized freight, for example, they may reach a point at which the levels of containerized traffic generated are insufficient to sustain the viability of all ports. Coordination of port management is essential in any modernization efforts. Coordination in the management of ports would also assist in balanced development. Centralized management for New England ports is unwarranted and impossible, but

inter-port as well as private and public sector coordination are necessary to improve the attractiveness of the Region's export gateways. Figure XVIII shows current activity at major New England ports.

Coal represents a major potential for export expansion in New England. Because the ports of Philadelphia, Baltimore and Hampton Roads are highly congested, shallow, or not readily expandable, they are seen as being unable to handle the projected magnitude of coal exports via Atlantic ports. New England's deepwater ports are considered feasible for such a purpose. Massive coal exports would require huge capital investments for transloading equipment, storage facilities and shipping vessels. The economic feasibility of moving coal by rail to New England ports from mines in Pennsylvania, Ohio and West Virginia must be determined. Although this constitutes a longer haul from the mines, expedited transloading and avoidance of extended layovers might more than compensate for higher transportation costs. If New England ports can capture part of the projected volume of export coal, then investment and new jobs would be created not only at the ports but also within the Region's railroad industry.

Intra-regional Goods Movement
In order for New England to prosper, it is essential that transportation and distribution networks link the Region's remote areas to its economic centers. The patterns of goods movement within New England are changing, in part, as a reflection of the changing composition of the economy. The "New England Rail Study," recently completed by NERCOM and the United States Railway Association, concluded that demand for short-haul rail has decreased with the decrease in production of bulk

goods in the Region. At the same time, the maintenance of freight rail is imperative to the continued growth of the lumber and paper industries and the transshipment of industrial fuels, particularly coal. Trucking is emerging as a more important short-haul carrier. But trucking also needs special attention in terms of its impact on the rail industry and in terms of high costs per mile in New England due to the shorter-haul, terminal intensive nature of goods movement in the Region.

Deregulation of airlines has seriously limited access to small communities and sharply increased the cost of transportation to remote areas of the Region. The same problems may also arise with rail and truck deregulation since New England has mostly branch lines to remote areas, characterized by high costs, and short haul, terminal intensive operations.

Mobility Of Persons In High-Grade Service Industries
A major part of the Region's economic expansion will depend on the ability of air carriers to provide quick and reliable intra- and interregional movement of people for business purposes. The issue of mobility is critical for the future of New England's economy, and this mobility must be by air. Quality air service, connecting company headquarters in urban hubs such as Boston, New York and San Francisco and satellite facilities or production plants based in smaller, less accessible areas of the Region must be guaranteed for balanced development and increased employment opportunities. Many communities in New England are inaccessible by modes other than air. Rail or bus service either does not exist, or is too time consuming, as is travel by automobile. However, since the implementation of the Airline Deregulation Act of 1978, air service in New England has deteriorated.

Transportation Of The Labor Force

Outside of metropolitan areas, the work force, particularly potential new workers, has few transportation options. In small communities dominated by one car families, economic activity depends on the movement of people to the marketplace and to the workplace. If the primary wage earner uses the family's only car to travel to and from work each day, the other members of the family do not have access to shopping centers, health services or cultural or recreational activities. If specially fashioned mass transportation systems were developed for those areas, then additional economic growth could result. The primary wage earner could use the systems to travel to and from the workplace, leaving the car for family use. A second wage earner in a family could also use mass transportation to get to and from the workplace. In either case, comparatively moderate expenditures for transportation systems such as vanpooling or busing could be catalytic to the growth and development of small communities. In urban areas, mass transit systems have long been recognized as the most effective means of transporting people.

The Inter-Relationship Of Transportation Modes

New England has external links with other regions and internal links among its cities and smaller communities, through various transportation systems. These modal systems, in the composite, need to create a competitive and complementary transportation network which provides the services necessary for the Region to carry on its business. Any growth of the Region's economy or enhancement of its growth potential depends on the improvement of the transportation services and facilities now in place. Determining how to best modify the current network requires that existing capacities be fully employed and future investments be planned in concert with growth industries. This planning should involve the assessment of costs and benefits to both the private and public sectors.

Modal viability and competitiveness are not related simply to how one mode operates compared to another. Rather, they reflect the Region's predominant economic activities and trends. In New England, there will always be a need for a variety of modes but the costs of maintaining all modes must be minimized and proportionally shared. Intermodal cooperation and integration of services should be guided by efforts to achieve greater fuel efficiency and cost effectiveness. In this way, investments in transloading and multimodal depot facilities could eventually lead to reductions in transportation costs and therefore lower consumer costs.

Similarly the inter-relationship between air and surface transportation services, and water-borne and surface transportation services must be understood and assessed correctly if the Region's economy is to continue expanding. For example, surface transportation serves as the collector of freight or passengers within the region — bringing cargo to a centralized facility for movment by another mode. The modal systems operating in this Region are interdependent. A weakness or failure in one system weakens the entire network. Transportation symbiosis must characterize the Region for economic expansion to take place.

Relationship Of Transportation To The Regional Growth Strategy

Growth Industries

Much of New England's current growth is based upon the rapidly expanding high technology and service sectors. Professional employment in these sectors is increasing rapidly and the mobility of this segment of the work force is critical for its continued growth. In most cases, their mobility within and outside of this region requires convenient reliable service by air because of the time constraints under which they operate. In responding to clients' needs, conducting training sessions, or attending general business meetings and consulting assignments, minimal time must be expended for transit purposes. As a result, rail, bus and automobile are not satisfactory substitutes for air service. The decline in air service resulting from deregulation will adversely affect these growth industries, especially in small communities.

Maintaining Employment In Existing Industries

For those industries which do not have a national locational advantage for being in New England, transportation costs can seriously impact their ability to compete with industry in other parts of the U.S. In transportation equipment and machinery, among others, the costs associated with importing materials (particularly steel) and exporting finished products directly affect the long-term viability of doing business in the Region. Transportation policies must be concerned with the cost of transportation for these industries, including the impacts of fuel costs, decreasing demand, and deregulation.

The forest product related goods are New England's second fastest growing industry. Continued expansion requires special transportation services. Almost all of the lumber and paper related commodities are moved by rail to regional and non-regional markets. By 1988, the volume of paper commodities moving by rail is projected to increase 39 percent over 1977 totals, from 6.5 million tons to 9.0 million tons. This expansion and the new jobs and economic activity that it would generate will only be possible if rail service is available. Trucks are neither fuel efficient nor cost effective for moving paper, particularly in the long-haul markets which exist.

Improving the passenger transportation infrastructure would make the Region a more attractive place for tourists. The recent inception of additional Boston-London air service has not only created approximately 100 new jobs, but will also bring in up to 56,000 European tourists' using Boston as their U.S. gateway, and spending time in New England before travelling on. It is also projected that these tourists will spend approximately $311 each in New England, totalling $17.5 million per year. Additional gains could be expected from American and Canadian tourists using new rail or bus services and special fares to travel to and around New England. Such gains would require service improvements and upgrading of facilities but are certainly realistic goals for the transportation industry.

Targeting To Rural Needs

The targeting strategy of the Regional Plan requires special attention to the needs of rural communities. Good transportation service, for both passengers and freight, is essential to the economic viability of New England's rural areas. Firms operating in rural New England need to be able to ship in supplies and ship out products to regional and national markets. Because they are remote from major markets and population centers, these firms face high shipping costs and the unintended adverse effects of transportation deregulation. Low population density in rural communities results in homes, workplaces, and markets being far from one another. Rural residents must have access to their places of work and to goods and services in order for employment and income opportunites to accrue to rural communities.

Figure XVIII
Major New England Ports

	Main Channel Depth (in feet)	Dry and Liquid Bulk Terminals	General Cargo Terminals	Number of Petroleum Storage Tanks	Capacity of Petroleum Storage in 1,000's of bbls. Petroleum	Percentage of Total Cargo Tonnage*	Major Non-Petroleum Cargoes Handled**
Searsport	35	3	1	14	1,454	83	salt, potatoes, chemical products, newsprint
Portland	40	10	1	136	8,898	99	fish and shellfish, woodpulp, fresh and frozen vegetables
Portsmouth	35	11	1	37	1,683	88	salt, limestone, scrap metal, steel cable
Boston	40	33	3	387	17,534	73	general cargo, sugar, salt, limestone, lumber, motor vehicles, liquefied natural gas
New Bedford	30	2	1	14	1,450	63	fresh fish, lumber
Fall River	35	10	1	112	6,054	98	crude rubber/allied gums, coal
Narragansett Bay, RI	40	15	2	467	11,931	83	cement, scrap metal, lumber, liquefied natural gas
New London	36	13	1	38	1,640	88	molasses, woodpulp, sulphuric acid, chemicals
New Haven	35	19	1	914	10,045	91	chemicals, cement, scrap metal, steel products, seafood
Bridgeport	35	12	1	54	2,599	82	steel products, scrap metal, paper products

* Does not include liquefied gases
** Relative to each port

Sources: U.S. Army Corps of Engineers Port Series No. 1 (Rev. 1976)   Port Series No. 4 (Rev. 1976)
Port Series No. 3 (Rev. 1979)   Waterborne Commerce of the United States, 1977

Basic Transportation Strategies

Both freight and passenger transportation services are essential to linking the various economic sectors of the Region and enabling the economy to expand. The regional transportation network must provide fuel efficient and cost effective means for interregional and international shipments and travel. It should also facilitate the mobility of people, goods and services around New England.

Since the Region ships and demands a wide variety of commodities from high-bulk, low-value to low-bulk, high-value items, a balanced variety of services and modes must be available. Currently, some of these modes are out of balance and services overlap in some markets while underserving others. In some cases, modes are not well coordinated with national and international networks, resulting in higher regional transportation costs and a weakening of New England's competitive position.

The Region's passenger transportation needs also necessitate balance and variety. This modal mix, including the private automobile, should be fashioned to extend individual mobility in all parts of the Region for regular commuter and business purposes as well as for tourism. Lack of service, inhibiting the mobility of people in the Region, would negatively impact the quality of life and the development potential of those areas that are underserved. Government policies such as deregulation, and fuel price and availability impact all modes and purposes of transportation and must be monitored carefully to avoid unanticipated negative impacts.

Development of a strategy to address the major transportation issues of the Region should be undertaken on a regional basis because the network is regional and the effects of a weakness in that network extend beyond state boundaries. The strategy should include closer coordination of the modes operating in the freight and passenger sectors. Its purpose should be to create a balanced, integrated, fuel efficient, and cost effective network that will contribute to improving the quality of life and economic vitality of New England.

Public Policy Recommendations

1 / The Commission should continue to monitor the economic impacts of airline industry deregulation on New England, begin to evaluate the effect of rail and truck deregulation on the Region, and report on these effects so that the Governors and the New England Congressional Delegation can support remedial action in the interest of regional growth.

2 / The states should work with NERCOM and the New England River Basins Commission to coordinate port and harbor development policy, developing new ports in New England and making ports more attractive as freight gateways by improving connections to them and developing their trans-loading facilities.

3 / State and local governments should take action to provide the means to move people in a cost effective, fuel efficient manner by encouraging vanpooling, carpooling, and other cost and fuel saving initiatives and by offering additional mass transportation services where justified.

4 / In order to enhance the economic viability and accessibility of small communities and to improve labor force mobility in rural areas, the states should work with the providers of transportation services so that levels of freight and passenger service sufficient for their individual developmental needs will be assured.

5 / The Commission should encourage, initiate, and coordinate a New England wide effort to identify and modify state and federal regulations and conditions which obstruct or inhibit the use of modern transportation technologies.

6 / NERCOM should convene a regional transportation task force which would provide an ongoing forum for dialogue among the different modes with the intended results being intermodal cooperation, coordination of services and operations, and greater balance in and efficiency of transportation services.

7 / The Commission should analyze the significance of rail service in Southern New England. In the event that CONRAIL discontinues operation, or substantially alters its service patterns, NERCOM should coordinate a regional position on restructuring the rail system to provide uninterrupted service for rail dependent industries in Southern New England.

8 / NERCOM should coordinate the efforts of the states, the Federal Regional Council, and the New England Congressional Delegation to guarantee an equitable share of federal funding for upgrading, maintaining, and adding to New England's transportation infrastructure.

The Physical Framework for Development

A good part of the capital structure of northern cities was put in place between 1880 and 1930. The bridges, streets and even some of the sewer and water lines of that era have begun to reach the end of their normal life span.

George E. Peterson, *The Urban Institute*

Time makes the high building costs of one generation the bargains of a following generation. Time pays off original capital costs, and this depreciation can be reflected in the yields required from a building. Time makes certain structures obsolete for some enterprises, and they become available to others.

Jane Jacobs, in *The Death and Life of Great American Cities*

The vast network of highways, rivers, power plants, sewer and water lines, industrial parks, and old mill buildings across New England serves as the underlying framework for the Region's development. This network, often hidden below ground, has both natural and man-made components, and includes such diverse systems as sewerage treatment, water supply, airports and even cable television lines. "Infrastructure" is the term used to describe this network of facilities which is so necessary for the support of the Region's economy.

Although transportation systems and energy facilities are very much a part of this infrastructure, the scope and implications of these issues are discussed fully in separate chapters. In this chapter, the focus is narrowed to address three infrastructure areas which are not only important to New England, but also present an opportunity for regional action.

- *Pollution Control,* especially sorely needed hazardous waste management facilities, response to the acid rain threat, air emission offsetting and similar programs, and water pollution facilities.

- *Water Supply,* with special emphasis on source protection, urban system rehabilitation, conservation and the linkage to economic development.

- *Housing, Commercial and Industrial Structures,* particularly the reuse of old mill buildings and the cost and availability of housing.

Historically, buildings like this one have been recognized as representative of a once-thriving New England economy. After seeing hard times through most of the twentieth century, these grand old structures are having new life breathed into them as a result of a regional economy on the re-bound.

In addressing each of these, discussions will focus on how New England's infrastructure compares with that available in other regions. The challenge in ensuring that New England's infrastructure is adequate for economic growth is to determine how older infrastructure can be reused and revitalized, and where new infrastructure is appropriate.

The Public Sector's Role in Infrastructure

Government's role in infrastructure has evolved in many ways over the years. It now includes direct construction as well as incentives or disincentives to private projects. Regulations and public subsidy programs that encourage and mandate private investments have greatly expanded in recent years while direct public expenditure on construction has been deemphasized. Literally dozens of federal and state agencies now have significant infrastructure programs. The New England Regional Commission itself has spent an estimated $34 million on a wide variety of infrastructure projects since 1967.

The public sector's role in infrastructure provision began with essential services such as roads, (discussed in the transportation section) and sewers, which were necessary for purposes of commerce and public health. In recent years, however, government's activities have also addressed problems of equity and environmental quality. Environmental legislation has required the construction of new pollution-control facilities. Numerous urban programs concentrate on housing and development projects in depressed cities. Publicly-sponsored infrastructure projects have also been used for countercyclical stimulation and job creation.

Provision of appropriate infrastructure may be government's single most important role in targeting economic activity to specific places. It may be an even more critical tool in promoting growth than the development financing mechanisms previously discussed. In fact, many economic development "strategies" consist of little more than elaborate lists of infrastructure improvement projects necessary for industrial development.

Government's ability to provide streets and sewers to support the growth of a community has long been considered a factor in economic development. The ability of state and local governments to provide timely and tailored infrastructure investments to meet the needs of prospective industrial or commercial firms has now become a key tool for development officials in attracting and retaining industries. Government builds industrial parks and shell buildings and provides site improvements, streets, and sewers to influence industrial location.

New England's Aging Infrastructure

New England's infrastructure is among the oldest in the Nation because of early industrial development and because, in many cases, these investments have not been modernized or rehabilitated. Declining tax bases and escalating government costs, especially in urban areas, have forced local officials to cut back on funds intended for capital maintenance. Despite large federal expenditure for construction of new capital projects over the past decades, there is little funding available for rehabilitation and maintenance. As a result, streets, bridges, sewers, water lines and other facilities are in decay. Infrastructure age is even used by several federal agencies as a measurement of economic distress. New England states invested much more in infrastructure in previous decades than they are investing today.

To accurately determine infrastructure needs is difficult and expensive. Several major studies of infrastructure requirements have recently been initiated by the U.S. Department of Housing and Urban Development, the Farmers Home Administration, and the U. S. Department of Commerce. The Department of Commerce study, the only one completed so far, examined the pattern of public works investment and found that the annual rate of investment rose until 1968 and has declined thereafter.

The extent of New England's infrastructure, however, can be seen as an advantage. Given the rate of inflation, modernization of existing structures and systems can be substantially less expensive than new construction. For example, New England's 19th Century industrial buildings, sometimes located near reusable hydroelectric facilities, represent assets that are potentially valuable for regional growth through adaptation for reuse with cheap energy. Likewise, with declining school enrollments, underutilized educational facilities have presented excellent opportunities for innovative reuse.

New England's older infrastructure is also clustered. While in recent decades it was cost effective to build new and sprawling developments, today's high energy and material costs make clustered development and re-use of existing infrastructure often more cost effective.

The character of different regions of the country clearly influences the need for, and type of, infrastructure projects undertaken. On a per capita basis, federal distribution of funds for infrastructure varies significantly by region, and to New England's disadvantage. For example, the Mountain Region received $97 per capita in 1977 (current dollars) while the New England Region received $3 per capita. (source: U.S. Department of Commerce, Consad 1980). As Figure XX shows, in 1957 New England was the highest spending region in terms of state public works expenditures; however, twenty years later the Region is tied for last place with the Pacific Region. This illustrates the decline in overall expenditures and highlights the regional differences in terms of infrastructure age.

Infrastructure and the Regional Strategy

The quality of the Region's infrastructure will play a key role in fullfilling the goals of New England's economic development strategy: improving employment opportunities and income; improving the standard of living and quality of life; and distributing the benefits of growth throughout the Region.

Adequate infrastructure is a necessity for industrial expansion and retention in many sectors. The absence of hazardous waste management facilities in New England, for example, presents a threat to an estimated 4,600 waste generators, many within the jewelry industry. The lack of such facilities can deter expansion and result in layoffs, plant closing or relocation. New waste facilities could serve as an incentive to attract new industry.

Industrial and commercial expansion requires adequate factory and commercial space. The structural resources left behind by declining industries can be reused by new growth industries, but public policies and programs must also be designed to meet new construction needs where appropriate.

Infrastructure is important to maintaining and increasing employment opportunities in the Region, especially in less competitive sectors of the economy and parts of the Region. Our older facilities need not be a liability. Older, deteriorated housing and public facilities and systems can be retrofitted to make currently distressed areas more attractive, more livable, and more competitive with areas that have newer infrastructure.

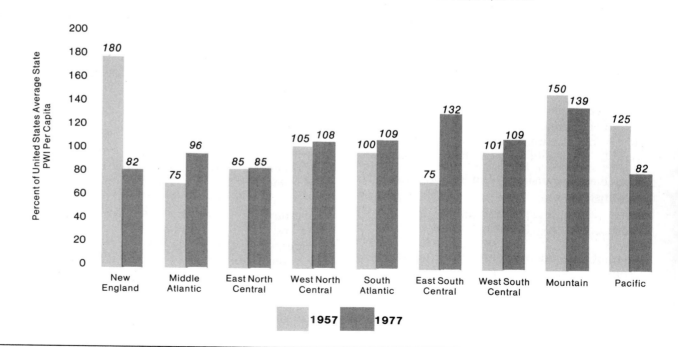

Figure XX

State Public Works Investments by Region
(Per Capita Percent of U.S. Average Constant 1972 Dollars)

Source: "A Study Of Public Works Investment In The United States,"
U.S. Department Of Commerce/Consad Research Corp., April 1980

1957   1977

The proposed growth strategy suggests the targeting of scarce resources to those communities which would not normally benefit from the growth of the regional economy. For many of these communities, economic expansion and diversification are impossible without new or improved infrastructure investments. In fact, infrastructure can often direct specific types of growth to particular locations. Existing infrastructure tends to have greater shortcomings in fiscally distressed areas because of the burden of capital maintenance or replacement on the tax structure of the community. The significance of infrastructure investment in disadvantaged urban and rural communities is discussed in the Targeting chapter.

New England has a reputation for a clean and safe environment. The Region's diverse natural resources are directly linked to tourism-related industries, for example, but environmental quality in general is also important to attract and hold a skilled labor force. The varied geography and distinct seasons have a dramatic effect on the desire to protect the environment and strengthen the overall quality of life.

Infrastructure Strategies and Overall Recommendations

Public infrastructure programs and policies should be consistent with the following goals:

- facilitate expansion of the Region's growth industries

- maintain and expand employment in existing industries

- target investment to those geographic areas of the Region which are economically distressed, and

- maintain and enhance environmental quality.

Public policy should be directed at maximizing the utility of existing capital stock through better maintenance, upgrading, and adaptive reuse.

Recognizing that the scale and location of infrastructure influence private investments, states should take a more sophisticated view of the growth and economic implications of new public capital investments and plan so as to:

- encourage investment in already developed areas

- encourage clustering of new economic development and minimization of sprawl, and

- design investments to be sensitive to the character and scale of affected communities.

NERCOM should monitor ongoing national studies on the federal role in infrastructure to ensure that they include the New England perspective and provide information for addressing the problems of rehabilitation and maintenance.

Federal tax legislation should encourage renovation and revitalization of structures for all uses by liberalizing tax depreciation allowances on the costs of improvements.

A / Pollution Control

The volume and scope of federal and state legislation passed in the 1970s to protect the environment have tremendous implications for economic development. Pollution control increases costs to businesses, consumers, and governments. However, it also provides for a safe and clean environment for the Region's residents and labor force, and protects the quality of our natural resources needed for production in many industries. Without a clean environment, health problems will occur, industries that depend on high quality natural resources will be unable to operate, and tourism

and its related industries will suffer. Most important, the quality of life which attracts and holds a skilled labor force to the Region is dependent on environmental quality.

The Council on Environmental Quality (CEQ) estimates that the cost of complying with all existing federal pollution control and environmental programs nationally in 1978 was $26.9 billion. CEQ, however, also found that pollution control programs have raised the real GNP between 1970 and 1977, lowered the rate of unemployment and added slightly more than .3 percentage point to the rate of increase in the Consumer Price Index. (*Source: CEQ 10th Annual Report*).

Hazardous Waste

Hazardous waste is fast becoming the biggest environmental issue of the 1980s. The problem can be viewed from three perspectives: proper regulation, the need for safe facilities, and the clean-up of past illegal dumping.

The Federal Resource Conservation and Recovery Act of 1975 (RCRA) provides for a strict new "cradle-to-grave" regulatory system for the management of so-called "hazardous waste." Hazardous waste is defined as any waste which is toxic, corrosive, flamable, or explosive, and therefore requires special handling to protect human health and the environment. The regulatory system established by RCRA was put in place in November 1980.

Currently, hazardous waste is disposed of in ordinary landfills or shipped out of the Region to disposal facilities in New York, New Jersey and even farther away. EPA estimates that 90 percent of hazardous waste is now improperly managed — poured down sewers or illegally disposed of by so-called "midnight dumpers." The Region's most serious problem is the lack of proper facilities. New England does not have a single approved chemical landfill, yet the Region generates an estimated 230–330 million gallons of hazardous waste annually (see Figure XXI).

Another critical problem relating to hazardous waste involves past illegal practices or so-called "midnight dumping". Almost 100 uncontrolled sites have been found in the six states and the containment and clean-up costs are estimated to be in the millions of dollars. The so-called superfund bill, recently passed in compromise version by the Congress and about to be signed by the President, will establish a $1.6 billion fund to finance emergency response, clean-up and containment and limited compensation to state and local governments for damages to trees, lakes, parks and other natural resources. $1.38 billion will come from a special tax on the chemical and oil industries and $220 million from appropriations of general revenue over a five-year period in fiscal 1981-85. The tax would be collected from approximately 1,000 oil, inorganic and petrochemical firms, and these firms would then pass the cost on to all industrial sectors.

The New England Regional Commission has had an active hazardous waste program for over two years now, concentrating on three areas: the promotion of safe treatment storage and disposal facilities; public education with an emphasis on solutions; and compatible state regulations, most notably a regional waste tracking system. Government, business, and the general public all work cooperatively on this program and a great deal of progress has been made to date. The Commission also adopted a resolution supporting the overall concept of a superfund.

Hazardous waste has a very direct impact on the overall economy and on employment.

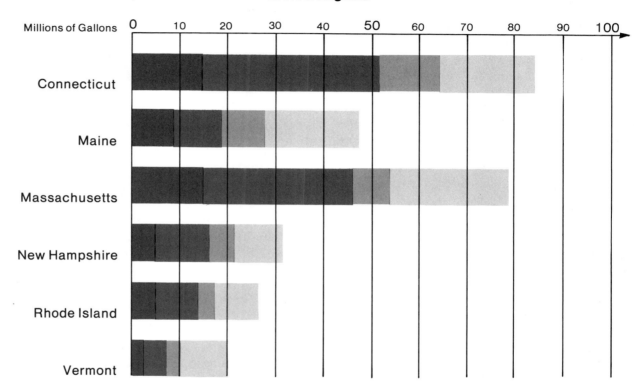

Figure XXI

Management of Hazardous Waste In New England

Source: *A Plan for Development of Hazardous Waste Management Facilities in the New England Region,* prepared for NERCOM by Arthur D. Little, Inc.

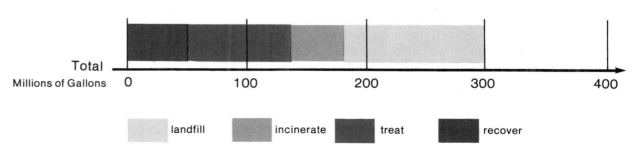

***Total* Management of Hazardous Waste in New England**

landfill   incinerate   treat   recover

Approximately 4,600 of the Region's manufacturing firms generate hazardous waste. These firms employ 310,000 people and produce an estimated $21 billion in annual sales. Strict new RCRA regulations will significantly impact these firms, their sales, and their employees. EPA recently studied the impacts of the regulations on 4,600 plants in six industries nationwide. EPA expects the regulations to cause a price increase in these industries of one percent, and result in 86 plant closings with a loss of 5,300 jobs. In New England, 80 percent of the manufacturing firms which generate hazardous waste are small businesses employing fewer than 100 people. These firms are least able to afford increased treatment, shipping, and disposal costs.

Solid Waste

Ordinary solid waste is not as serious a problem as hazardous waste, but it is a changing area and offers some energy-related opportunities. New England generates an estimated 30.7 million pounds of solid waste every day. Increasing amounts of waste, a shortage of disposal sites, and more stringent regulations have forced local governments to consider alternatives to dumping and incineration. The two most promising alternatives are source separations (sorting trash in the home or business) and centralized source recovery (burning trash at a central facility for its energy value). Central resource recovery facilities can recover energy and materials and drastically reduce the volume of material that has to be landfilled. EPA estimated that the energy yield from burning trash in the U.S. would be enough to meet the home and office lighting needs of the entire nation. (Source: CEQ) Strong home rule in New England, however, makes inter-municipal resource recovery systems difficult to arrange. The advantages of inter-municipal cooperation are nonetheless compelling and many regional solid waste projects such as the Landprey Solid Waste Cooperative in Durham, New Hampshire have proved successful. Meanwhile, interstate arrangements are also being explored by 25 communities from Vermont and New Hampshire. Solid waste impacts the economy through high management and disposal costs to municipalities. If resource recovery becomes widespread, the energy that it generates may enable solid waste management to pay for itself, or even become profitable.

Air Quality

Air quality regulations and standards are a result of the federal Clean Air Act of 1970 which is up for renewal in 1981. Under the Clean Air Act, states administer air quality programs through a state implementation plan (SIP). The business community has become increasingly involved in developing these SIPs and assessing the economic implications. These strategies address indirect sources such as shopping malls, transportation control plans, new sources covering the heaviest polluters and air quality maintenance areas (AQMAs). Approved SIPs are necessary before new construction of major pollution sources is permitted in "non-attainment areas". A non-attainment area is a region or community which already exceeds air quality standards and new sources can only be allowed if existing emissions are reduced.

Transportation, especially by automobiles, is responsible for 99 percent of carbon monoxide and 50 percent of the smog in New England's air. Certain industries such as paper, rubber, chemicals, and metal production also contribute to the Region's smog problem. Smog is a mixture of gases and particles oxidized by the sun.

Air quality affects the overall environmental quality of the Region both for the labor force and for firms located in New England. There are two specific issues, however, which are especially important to New England's economy, namely equity between regions of the country and economic development in non-attainment areas.

Acid rain is perhaps the best example of the regional equity issue. The trend towards coal conversion may very well intensify this problem. Lumber-related industries which have been rapidly growing in recent years are adversely affected by acid rain. Acid rain reduces tree growth productivity and thus affects the lumber-related industries, furniture and paper. Acid rain can also damage agricultural crops and fresh water fish. New England's efforts to deal with this problem must address the high sulphur/low sulphur issue (See the Energy chapter) and work toward a national solution rather than fostering regional conflict.

In violating or non-attainment air quality areas, measures must not only control new sources, but further reduce emissions from existing sources. These pollution control goals, however, must also be weighed against continued economic well-being. The concept of trading off or "offsetting" emissions is one promising method of ensuring continued economic growth. For new major emission sources, offsetting will allow new pollutants in non-attainment areas if existing sources are reduced. The air quality could improve and economic growth could still take place. Two pilot projects are now underway in Boston and Bridgeport/Waterbury to manage air quality growth increments. These Air Quality Technical Assistance Demonstrations (AQTAD) projects are designed to integrate the goals of environmental quality and economic development.

Water Quality

Historically, the treatment and disposal of

wastewater and sewage in the United States have been strictly government functions. The 1972 Water Pollution Control Act Amendments launched a major pollution control program by providing large scale funding for the construction of sewage treatment plants and related facilities. Between FY 1973 and 1979, $1.8 billion was obligated in New England for the construction of sewers and treatment plants under this program. In this Region, however, 35 percent of the households are unsewered, using septic systems instead; therefore, approaches which are not construction oriented are also important.

Despite the availability of these water pollution control programs and the funds that have been put into pollution control facilities, the goal of obtaining fishable and swimmable water quality standards by 1982 remains an elusive one. In 1978 the Environmental Protection Agency conducted a water pollution control needs assessment, and determined $16 billion was needed in New England in order to meet the mandate of the Clean Water Act. With double digit inflation and increasing needs as old systems deteriorate, it is doubtful that sufficient funds will be available to meet the fishable/swimmable standard.

Water pollution grant programs have been criticized not only because of insufficient funds but also because of a bias toward large scale construction projects. Even with the federal government providing up to 80 percent of the funds, the local capital share is still high for these expensive plants, as are ongoing operational/maintenance costs. Non-structural pollution approaches such as zoning, road salting regulations, subdivision regulation, septic tanks and land application of sludge are all potential alternatives to massive construction projects.

New England has historically had good quality water which has helped to make the Region attractive for individuals and water dependent firms. In order to attract, expand, and maintain industry, sewer lines and treatment plants must be adequate to meet environmental standards and maintain the Region's high quality water. Like so many other parts of New England's infrastructure, our sewer lines are old and in need of major repair. Furthermore, these older systems are often combined sewers, handling both sanitary waste and street runoff in the same pipes. Federal funds are scarce for expensive sewer separation projects necessary to correct this problem, which threatens the safe operation of treatment plants. In contrast, our clean lakes and streams present a diversity of landscape and recreational opportunities that fosters tourism and the quality of life in the Region.

The location and capacity of new sewers and treatment plants can also have a direct influence on the level and type of growth and economic development. A new sewer line which is constructed to serve a remote industrial area, for example, could in fact be an incentive for new development along the sewer line, especially if it is built with excess capacity. Likewise, existing industry can more easily expand or new industry be attracted if a new treatment plant is able to handle wastewater which results from that expansion or addition.

Basic Pollution Control Strategies
Hazardous Waste
1 / Federal and state programs should continue to encourage recycling, recovery and neutralization of hazardous waste while recognizing that this may be more expensive than the last resort option of land disposal.

2 / Government, industry and the general public must continue to work together to promote the establishment of environmentally sound hazardous waste treatment, storage, and disposal facilities through:

- public education and awareness
- the development of sensible site selection processes in each state
- the development of compatible state regulations among the states (such as a common manifest tracking system).

Solid Waste
3 / Public policy should encourage environmentally sound central resource recovery facilities which can generate energy and serve as an alternative to landfills.

4 / Public policy should encourage cooperation among municipalities and among states in addressing solid waste management problems.

Air Quality
5 / Regional leaders should endorse the reauthorization of the Clean Air Act with provisions which are sensitive to acid rain and other air quality issues in the region.

6 / Public policymakers should develop mechanisms, such as emissions offsetting, that will permit growth while protecting the overall air quality in non-attainment areas.

7 / The states should continue to collectively assess air quality problems which result from pollution outside of the Region and participate in the development of national solutions.

Water Quality

8 / States should recognize and plan for the impact that the location and scale of sewer and waste water treatment projects have on overall growth and development.

9 / Water pollution control programs should encourage appropriate technology and non-structural solutions especially in smaller, rural communities.

Public Policy Recommendations

Hazardous Waste

1 / NERCOM should continue to assist the states in a regional approach to waste management with special emphasis on siting new facilities.

2 / NERCOM should take the lead in developing programs which provide technical and financial assistance to smaller firms that generate hazardous waste to mitigate the economic impact of compliance with the strict new regulations which took effect in November 1980.

3 / The states should continue to work with the Congressional Delegation to support the passage of a superfund-type bill which will help pay for the cost of cleaning up illegal dump sites.

Air Quality

4 / The states should continue to work through NERCOM and NESCAUM (Northeast States for Coordinated Air Use Management) on regional air quality issues in an effort to ensure regional equity in terms of the cost and impact of acid rain and other regional pollutants.

5 / The states should encourage research and development efforts which would provide alternatives to burning high sulphur fuels.

6 / The Clean Air Act should be reauthorized.

Water Quality

7 / Economic development considerations should be given more weight when water pollution control projects are prioritized by states, including the ability of the community to finance its share of the project.

8 / The states should document and publicize the magnitude of the need for water pollution control projects in order to promote adequate funding for EPA's construction grant and loan program (Section 201 of the Water Pollution Control Act).

9 / The states should examine the economic implications of water pollution control regulations and assess the need for flexibility in environmental standards.

B / Water Supply

With an average annual precipitation of 42 inches, New England has abundant water resources. Water has not been a major factor of production in most of the Region's newer industries, but it continues to be an important part of the production process in some manufacturing industries and other important sectors such as forest products and agriculture.

Potable water is supplied by a number of purveyors in New England including municipal water departments, water districts, and private water companies. Approximately eighty-four percent of the New England population is served by public water systems (those with 15 or more hook-ups) while 16 percent is served by individual wells. Seventy-four percent of the population is served by surface water and 16 percent by groundwater. Water must be protected from pollution not only to ensure that it is adequate for personal consumption, but also for industrial use.

A major economic advantage of New England is its ample supply of fresh water. This is often taken for granted, but in contrast to arid regions of the country abundant water is indeed a significant asset. Agriculture and tourism are, perhaps, most directly impacted by the availability of water. In Vermont, agricultural employment is quite significant (4.6 percent of state employment) and tourism employs an estimated 5.2 percent of the Region's labor force. Farming and water recreation activities are highly dependent upon water supply potential. Growth industries, such as jewelry and lumber, also require water as an essential part of their operation.

The 1974 Safe Drinking Water Act charges the Environmental Protection Agency with safeguarding public drinking water supplies. In some cases, the Act, administered by the states, will require substantial investments in water treatment plants. Massachusetts has estimated its cost of complying with the Act at $132.8 million. Connecticut has estimated its cost at $192 million.

While the Safe Drinking Water Act specifies standards for water quality, it does not provide funds to attain these standards. Although there are a few small state programs, there is no federal EPA construction grants program for drinking water programs as there is for water pollution control.

Northeasterners have maintained for some time that when it comes to federal water supply programs, this region is treated unequally. For example, the West received the highest per capita allowment of federal funds between 1950 and 1975 with $377, while the Northeast received only $47. The Northeast, however, has fewer federal dollars largely because major water projects like those built in the arid West or the flood prone South have not been needed in the Northeast.

More importantly, the water supply needs that the Region does have, namely protection and system rehabilitation, are not eligible for federal programs. The Army Corps of Engineers, for example, can only develop water supply programs if they are a part of a flood control project. There is no comprehensive needs assessment for water supply, except for the above cited estimated costs of complying with the Safe Drinking Water Act. However, a scattering of studies does address three areas which are vital to both personal consumption and industrial use in the Region.

Source Protection
New England's most serious water supply problem is the protection of both surface and groundwater supplies. The EPA has documented 57 cases of source contamination in New England caused by road salting operations and leachate from landfills. Recently, a polluting solvent used in adhering plastic coatings to water supply pipes has been discovered in 1,000 miles of pipe in approximately 135 communities in New England. Urban run-off and improperly located landfills have also contributed to this pollution problem. Acid rain that is threatening the Region's lakes and rivers also poses a threat to sources of drinking water by raising the level of dissolved heavy metal ions.

Urban Systems
Concern has been expressed by officials in the Northeast that urban water supply systems are in a state of serious disrepair and that local and state agencies do not have sufficient resources to correct the situation. Throughout the Northeast, many of what were model water delivery systems earlier in the century have been the victims of neglect, inadequate maintenance and insufficient capital expenditures. In some systems, large volumes of water go unaccounted for due primarily to leaks and a lack of metering.

A Massachusetts survey of 24 select urban water systems reveals a financial need of $441 million for system rehabilitation, while current expenditures total only $9 million.

Conservation — Water Use Efficiency
Opponents to river diversion projects object to making major ecological changes when, as they claim, increased efficiency in the use of water, as in the repair of leaks, increased metering and increased water rates, would result in a decreased demand, obviating the need for major diversions. Aside from the diversion-related argument, water conservation can be an important means of maintaining our water-rich status. The New England River Basins Commission is now undertaking a major water conservation study which will help to identify the true potential of conservation in water supply planning. There is wide-spread agreement that conservation is an important element in any supply strategy. Water is a real bargain in New England and the current pricing system does not encourage necessary conservation.

Unlike other parts of the country, New England is a water rich region in terms of annual precipitation; however, potable water must still be piped great distances. For example, Greater Boston, the largest importer of water in New England, depends on the diverted waters of the Connecticut River Basin. The controversial Northfield Diversion Project calls for the importation of an additional 72 million gallons per day from the Connecticut River. Other New England states have plans for major new source development including the Big River Reservoir project in Rhode Island.

New England's water supply situation is changing and as the supply is threatened so is the economic activity tied to it. Federal funds are going to "water-short" regions and few large scale water projects are pending in New England. Social and environmental issues have figured prominently in the rejection or delay of proposed water projects such as the Dickey-Lincoln hydropower project. For New England however, massive projects have never dominated the water supply picture. Programs for conservation, repair and upgrading have traditionally complemented smaller projects to meet our water resource needs.

Basic Strategies For Water Supply
1 / The New England States should develop a regional water supply strategy which recognizes the economic implications of water resources as well as the special problems of maintenance and rehabilitation.

2 / Water conservation and source protection should be the cornerstone of all water supply programs and activities in the Region and should be clearly articulated as federal policy.

3 / Existing federal water resource programs should be coordinated and targeted to meet the needs of the New England Region.

Public Policy Recommendations
1 / The New England River Basins Commission in cooperation with NERCOM should continue to play the lead role in developing a regional water resources strategy. This strategy should include development of statewide water resource plans.

2 / The states should work with the Congressional Delegation to promote new legisla-

Table XXVIII
Average Number Of Persons Per Dwelling Unit 1970 And 1980, States And New England*

	Average Persons Per Household in 1970	Average Persons Per Household in 1980
New England	2.94	2.54
Connecticut	3.10	2.67
Maine	2.50	2.24
Massachusetts	3.00	2.60
New Hampshire	2.63	2.38
Rhode Island	2.98	2.54
Vermont	2.69	2.30

Source: U.S. Census

* 1980 figures are based on preliminary Census information and are subject to change.

Table XXIX
Percentage Change, Population And Dwelling Units, 1970-1980, New England And States*

	% Change in Population	% Change in Dwelling Units
New England	4.0	20.0
Connecticut	2.1	18.0
Maine	13.1	26.1
Massachusetts	0.6	16.7
New Hampshire	24.6	37.5
Rhode Island	0.4	16.6
Vermont	14.8	35.2

Source: U.S. Census

* 1980 figures are based on preliminary Census information and are subject to change.

tive initiatives which will provide financial assistance for the cost of rehabilitation and maintenance of our older water supply systems, using existing programs if possible.

3 / HUD's Community Development Block Grant Program and FmHA's Community Facility Program, and similar federal programs which can be used for water supply projects, should require that conservation measures be included and that water rates reflect the true cost of service.

C / Housing, Commercial and Industrial Facilities

The adequacy and cost of housing for the Region's workers, and the quality and availability of space for industrial and commercial activities are essential factors in New England's economy. Housing availability, quality, and cost affect the mobility of New England's labor force and the willingness of skilled workers to move into and around the Region. New England's commercial and industrial sectors require a variety of facilities that can adequately house their activities with easy access to the transportation network, energy supplies, waste disposal facilities, and natural resources.

Because of the age of New England and the evolution of its economy, the space that once adequately served the Region's needs cannot fully provide for the changing modern mix of people and industries. New England's growing economy needs a mix of old and renovated structures, as well as new construction and development. While older housing and structures for commercial and industrial use were once considered a liability to the Region, recent trends to renovate housing, recycle old mill buildings, and revitalize downtowns, prove that already existing structures are an asset to New England.

Cost structures have changed in the past decade so that it is no longer always cost effective to build new facilities rather than reuse existing ones. High costs of energy and construction materials can make retrofitting older buildings more cost effective than new development. However, existing structures cannot be renovated to meet all of today's needs. New construction and development are necessary to meet the needs of New England's modern economy and should be undertaken to complement, and capitalize on, existing development.

Housing in New England

Housing is a key component of the "quality of life" in New England. An adequate supply of all kinds of housing, at affordable prices, and in diverse locations throughout the Region is necessary for economic development: to attract highly skilled labor into the Region, to retain valuable employees and entrepreneurs, and to ensure the availability of a full range of labor skills throughout New England. The size of the average household in New England is smaller than it was a decade ago. In 1970, average household size in the Region was 2.94 persons. Today it is 2.54 persons.* Table XXVIII shows the change in average household size for each New England state from 1970 to 1980. *1980 figures are based on preliminary Census information and are subject to change.

While New England's population increased by 4 percent between 1970 and 1980,* the number of dwelling units increased by 20 percent. Table XXIX shows the percentage change in population and number of dwelling units between 1970 and 1980 for New England and the States.

Although the Region generated over 800,000 additional dwelling units during the past ten years, New England's housing stock tends to be older than housing stock nationwide. While about 43 percent of the Region's housing was built before 1940, only 33 percent of the national housing stock is this old. (Source: NEEMIS, U.S. Census Estimates)

Despite the generation of housing units to meet growing population and lifestyle changes that create smaller households, housing costs nationwide and in New England are high and are rapidly increasing. In at least six out of the past ten years, the percentage increase in the national consumer price index of housing has been higher than the consumer price index of food, clothing, transportation, and medical care.

In 1979, housing costs in Boston were 6 percent higher than the national average and 4 percent higher than the average for all metropolitan areas. (Source: Bureau of Labor Statistics). However, housing costs vary as much within New England as they do among different regions of the Country. Construction costs are an indicator of housing costs. An index of construction costs in cities throughout the United States illustrates the variability both within and between Regions. Table XXX shows construction costs in selected areas.

Three issues are inherent in the problem of high housing costs: (1) Housing is a human necessity yet high costs preclude low income people from obtaining good quality housing. A shortage of adequate affordable housing for low income residents exists in New England's rural and urban areas. (2) A diversity of housing at various costs is necessary throughout the Region so that locating or expanding industries can be assured of available housing for diverse labor requirements. (3) "Quality of life" is a large factor in the employment decisions of

highly skilled, mobile professionals; since housing is an important component of "quality of life," New England's housing supply and costs must be able to attract and retain skilled labor for New England's high growth industries.

In many other Regions experiencing rapid growth in high tech industries, housing costs are as high, or higher, than they are in New England's technology growth centers. For example, in comparing the cost of living in centers for electronics manufacturing, a senior engineer in Sunnyvale, California (part of the "Silicon Valley") could expect to pay $22,224 annually for housing, transportation and taxes. However, he would pay $12,883 in Burlington, Vermont; $15,798 in Nashua, New Hampshire; $17,898 in Waltham, Massachusetts; and $18,968 in Norwood, Massachusetts (Source: Runzheimer Co.).

High mortgage interest rates and the high cost of labor, materials, land, road and utility installation, and state and local regulatory and permitting requirements weaken the demand for and supply of a diversity of both new and renovated housing. In addition, rapid economic growth in various parts of the Region, such as Southern New Hampshire and Southwestern Connecticut, and tourist areas, such as coastal Maine and Rhode Island causes further pressure on housing and land markets, driving up prices. The effects of these situations have been (1) to restrict the supply of housing that traditionally "filters down" to moderate and low income families; and (2) to depress activity in the housing construction industry.

Commercial and Industrial Facilities In New England

In order to meet the needs of New England's changing economy, a strong network of commercial and industrial facilities must be de-

Table XXX
Variations in Housing Construction Costs Within Regions (October 1979)
Base = 1.00 (Average for Selected Areas)

Mid-Atlantic

Eastern Maryland	0.81
Vicinity of Reading, Pennsylvania	0.91
Southern New Jersey	1.01
Vicinity of District of Columbia	1.04

Midwest

Upper Penninsula, Michigan	0.93
Central Wisconsin	0.95
Vicinity of Milwaukee, Wisconsin	1.07
Vicinity of Detroit, Michigan	1.14

New England

Vicinity of Brattleboro, Vermont	0.87
Vicinity of Providence, Rhode Island	0.99
Vicinity of Boston, Massachusetts	1.03

Pacific West

Southeastern Washington	1.04
Vicinity of San Bernardino, California	1.12
Vicinity of Seattle, Washington	1.12
Vicinity of San Jose, California	1.22

Southeast

Vicinity of Greenville, South Carolina	0.75
Southeastern Alabama	0.83
Vicinity of Birmingham, Alabama	0.92
Vicinity of Memphis, Tennessee	0.95

Southwest

Central Texas	0.85
Central New Mexico	0.91
Vicinity of Houston, Texas	1.03
Vicinity of Phoenix, Arizona	1.05

West

Central Utah	0.91
Vicinity of Salt Lake City, Utah	0.96
Northeastern Colorado	1.01
Vicinity of Denver, Colorado	1.03

Source: E. H. Boeckn Co.

veloped which combines the re-use of older facilities with new construction and development. New England's numerous mill buildings are a good example of innovative re-use. They can be adapted not only for industrial, but also for commercial and even residential use. As a complement, new industrial parks, housing, and retail centers which encourage reinvestment and clustering and respect the character and scale of a community can be developed. It is this type of adaptation, combining the old and new, that can provide the necessary facilities to serve New England's commercial and industrial needs.

Fuller utilization of commercial and industrial space can result in better local fiscal health and employment retention and growth in the Region. New England's changing industrial mix and a maturation of production processes has resulted in under utilized industrial space in communities throughout the Region. If this space remains underused, it cannot generate adequate taxes for localities or house numerous jobs for residents of the Region. Underutilized space can be renovated to better accomodate today's commercial or industrial needs.

Industrial parks are designed specifically to meet the needs of industry. Suburban areas have long been able to develop industrial parks because of their adequate land parcels and highway access. But industrial parks can also be developed (1) on urban land that currently has severely underutilized structures; (2) on cleared land that is not being utilized for the purpose intended after clearance; or (3) on publicly owned land such as closed state hospitals or Naval shipyards.

The Region has more than 35 million square feet of vacant industrial space in old mill buildings. Although these buildings may be obsolete in terms of their original functions, they are, in many cases, structurally sound and very suitable for conversion to productive re-uses. In contrast, development of new commercial and industrial space is costly because it is so time consuming.

- Inflation of construction costs, a shortage of lending dollars, and a scarcity of energy and materials encourage adaptive re-use as an alternative to new construction.

- Rehab and adaptive re-use are more labor intensive than new construction so they are not influenced by the skyrocketing costs of building material needed for new construction.

New England's older commercial and industrial areas are efficiently developed because proximity among housing, work, and shopping was so important when the Region's industrial economy was originally developing. Such clustering is once again important. Gasoline costs make commuting patterns and sprawling development expensive. Because of their central location, old city and town centers can capitalize on their unique historical and locational characteristics such as canals or 18th and 19th century architecture.

Rehabilitation of older buildings is clearly important for New England, but practical limitations on re-use exist. The Region's need for commercial and industrial facilities must also be met with new construction. Older industrial and commercial structures may be unsuitable for modern industrial production technologies and contemporary commercial needs. New development must be well planned and complementary to existing space in order to provide for a full range of economic activities.

Basic Strategies For Housing, Commercial and Industrial Space

Housing

1 / Public programs should encourage the conversion of vacant non-residential structures to residential uses as an alternative to new construction, where appropriate.

2 / State and federal programs should continue to make decent quality, scattered site housing available to low-income people through rent subsidies, rehabilitation assistance, and mortgage and down payment assistance.

3 / In both new construction and re-use, mixed developments should be permitted where feasible.

Commercial and Industrial Space

4 / Federal programs such as UDAGs, Public Works and Urban Systems Grants, Economic Development Loans and Guarantees, and CDBGs should continue to be used to provide physical capital and amenities in order to leverage private investments.

5 / Government should work to ensure that new commercial development does not adversely impact the viability of existing commercial centers.

6 / States should expedite the conveyance of underutilized state land (except for open space, parks, reserves or prime agricultural land, etc.) to local or substate industrial development agencies or sell such property to private developers through a public bidding system, for preparation as industrial parks where there is a demonstrated need for industrial space.

7 / Public investment in site preparation for new construction and re-use should maxi-

mize private investment to create and retain jobs.

Public Policy Recommendations

Housing

1 / States and local governments should review existing laws and regulations and remove constraints to rehabilitation and adaptive re-use of older buildings for residential purposes.

2 / NERCOM should evaluate and disseminate information on the impact of federal housing assistance formulas on the New England states.

3 / Federal legislation on tax exempt bond issues for housing should allow for state targeting to reasonable housing market needs.

Commercial and Industrial Space

4 / Local government should take full advantage of federal grant and loan programs to provide physical capital and amenities in support of new private construction and rehabilitation of commercial and industrial space.

5 / States should review building codes and other regulations to ensure that they allow for the re-use of older commercial and industrial buildings.

Spreading the Gains:
Targeting Development to Distressed Communities

11

Government action is . . . necessary not only to maintain an environment favorable to economic growth, but also to deal with special problems in communities and industries suffering from economic dislocations and to help those who, through unemployment, are bearing an unfair burden . . .

John F. Kennedy, Speech, February 2, 1961

Introduction

While New England's overall economy is in a good position relative to the Nation, certain population groups, occupational and industry groups, and geographic areas do not share fully in the benefits of the Region's economic health. Poverty and unemployment persist in the Region's inner cities, older industrial "mill towns" and rural communities. Underemployment in the North Country and chronic unemployment of the disadvantaged have been exacerbated by problems resulting from the rapidity of economic change.

Target Populations

Women, youth and members of minority groups have lower incomes, higher unemployment, and a higher incidence of poverty than the Region's population as a whole. Unemployment among women in New England was 6.4 percent in 1978, while among men it was 5.3 percent; unemployment among the youth population was 15.6 percent. While information by race is unavailable for all of New England, unemployment in Connecticut among non-whites was 11.2 percent compared to 4.8 percent among whites. In Massachusetts it was 9.8 percent for non-whites and 5.9 percent for whites. (Source for all unemployment data: U.S. Department of Labor, Bureau of Labor Statistics Report 571, September 1979.)

As can be seen in Table XXXI, the median income of full-time working women in New Eng-

In the midst of a generally improving regional economy, a special effort must be made to extend the benefits to every group of people and to be sure the scale and nature of that development is appropriate to each group's needs and desires.

land is only 59% of the median income of full-time working men. Black males working full-time have a median income that is 15 percent lower than that of full-time working white men.

Entrepreneurship among women and minorities is low. While women comprise 51 percent of U.S. population, they own only 5 percent of business establishments. Blacks, comprising 11 percent of U.S. population, own only 2 percent of business establishments.

Occupation and Industry

Underemployment and low income are also closely associated with certain industries. Unemployment among blue collar workers in New England was 7.0 percent in 1978, among service workers it was 6.4 percent, and it was only 3.4 percent among white collar workers. Low wages are prevalent among workers in specific industries. In New England in 1979, the average wage was 18 percent lower in textiles, 23 percent lower in apparel and 27 percent lower in leather, than for manufacturing in general. (Source of information U.S. Department of Labor, Bureau of Labor Statistics)

Geographic Distress

In New England's rural and urban areas and older small cities, a higher proportion of people are poorer, and underemployed and unemployed than in the Region as a whole. The median income of families in rural parts of New England is 8 percent lower than the median income of all families in the Region. While 7.8 percent of all persons in the Region live below poverty level, 9 percent of rural New Englanders are poor.

The median income of central city families is $2,500 lower than the median income of all New England families. While 25 percent of all persons in the Region live in central cities, 79

Table XXXI
Median Income of Full-Time New England Workers By Race and Sex: 1975 and 1978

	All Races		Whites			Blacks		Hispanics	
	Men	Women	Men	Women		Men	Women	Men	Women
1975	$11,350	$6,531	$11,247	$6,543	1975	$ 9,726	$6,621	$9,102	$5,090
1978	$15,745	$9,602	$15,830	$9,632	1978	$12,960	NA	NA	NA

Source: U.S. Census P-60, No. 110, March 1978   NA - not available

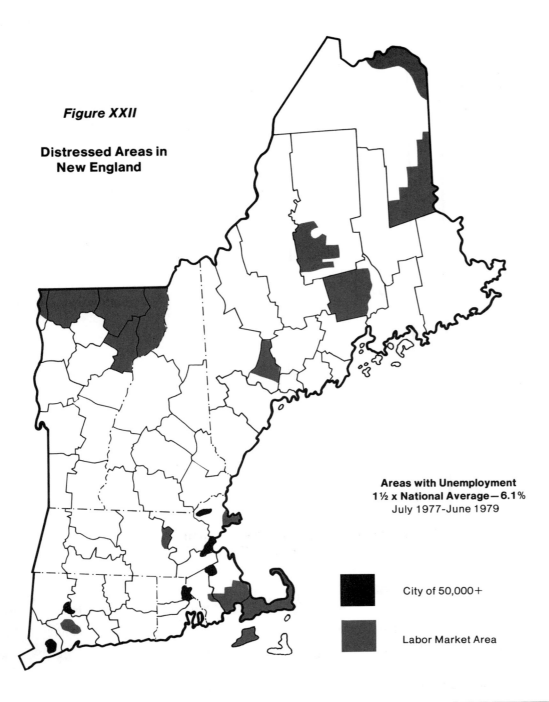

Figure XXII

Distressed Areas in New England

Areas with Unemployment
1½ x National Average—6.1%
July 1977-June 1979

City of 50,000+

Labor Market Area

percent of all Blacks, 60 percent of all Hispanics, and 38 percent of all persons below poverty level are central city residents. In the U.S., while 27 percent of all families live in central cities, 42 percent of all female-headed families reside in central cities (figures for New England are unavailable.)

Poverty and unemployment are problems not just in large central cities. Many of the Region's medium-sized cities are also economically distressed. Table XXXII shows that the unemployment rates in many medium-sized cities (with populations 10,000 to 49,999) are higher than the regional average.

Since members of those population and occupation groups that are not sharing in the benefits of the Region's economic growth are concentrated in rural areas and both large and medium-sized cities, further discussion about the special needs of distressed urban and rural areas follows.

A / DISTRESSED URBAN AREAS

Introduction
Throughout the 1960's and mid 1970's New England was identified as a region facing severe economic dislocation based largely on the perception of decline of its urban areas. High unemployment, social unrest, physical deterioration and the outmigration of manufacturing were most manifest in older American cities including both large and smaller cities of New England. New England and its urban communities were particularly impacted by the recessions of the early 1970's and cities were specifically disrupted by the structural shifts which altered the composition of the regional economy.

Some problems that are traditionally associated with large central cities are also prevalent among New England's older, small and medium-sized cities, especially those whose economies were originally mill-based, and whose current employment is concentrated in low-wage manufacturing industries such as textiles, apparel, and leather.

Despite an overall economic downturn in cities in the early 1970's, the urban areas of the Region have begun to reflect the same general optimism as the Region as a whole. The Region's rapidly expanding service sector, including both technology and related services as well as finance and insurance, is based largely in cities. Manufacturing activities which require these support services or which emerge from university based technology innovation are locating in urban areas. Because of available low-cost older infrastructure and labor supply, cities in New England have new prospects for growth in employment, income and tax base. The principal issue in developing an urban targeting strategy is not to simply increase the economic base of cities, but to ensure that the benefits of urban economic development accrue to urban residents who face higher unemployment and lower income than the Region's population in general. Secondarily, there is concern that urban residents not be displaced by returning suburbanites, as desirable reinvestment in cities continues.

Targeting

Efforts to distribute the benefits of economic development to urban areas should focus on distressed city neighborhoods. Concern is with those neighborhoods where residents have low incomes and high under- and unemployment, where residents are not currently sharing in the benefits of economic growth occurring in the rest of their city or in the Region as a whole.

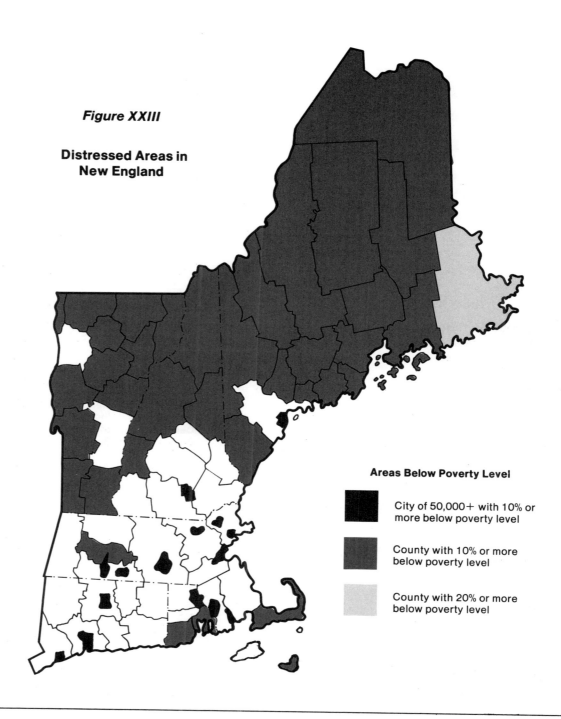

Figure XXIII

Distressed Areas in New England

Areas Below Poverty Level

City of 50,000+ with 10% or more below poverty level

County with 10% or more below poverty level

County with 20% or more below poverty level

Table XXXII

Unemployment Rates in Selected Medium-Size Cities and New England: 1979

(Percent)

New England	**5.4**
Torrington, CT	8.5
Norwich, CT	7.1
Willimantic, CT	5.8
Bangor, ME	7.6
Auburn, ME	7.2
Methuen, MA	7.1
North Adams, MA	8.9
Taunton, MA	7.2
Berlin, NH	8.2
East Providence, RI	7.5
Tiverton, RI	6.4
Woonsocket, RI	6.6

Source: State Departments of Employment Security

Table XXXIII

Median Income in Central Cities and Suburbs* (1976)

New England and U.S. Average

	Median Income of Central City Population	Median Income of Suburban Population	Percent Difference Between Central City and Suburban Median Incomes
U.S.	$13,280	$16,376	19
N.E.	$12,564	$17,238	27
Conn.	$13,412	$18,124	26
Me.	$11,881	$14,936	20
Mass.	$11,857	$17,336	32
N.H.	$15,838	$18,510	24
R.I.	$13,814	$14,865	7
Vt.**	NA	NA	NA

Source: U.S. Census, Series P-60, No. 110

* "Suburbs" refers to localities in SMSAs, but excludes the central cities

** Vermont has no SMSAs   NA = not available

Residents of distressed city neighborhoods have historically been hit hardest by inflation and unemployment. On one hand, they have been prevented, by poverty, racial discrimination, and inadequate education, from moving to places in which they could readily participate in the benefits of growth. On the other hand, when the areas in which they are living become revitalized, they can no longer afford to remain. They tend to have less access to capital and job opportunities, poorer quality schools and other services, and a severe lack of job skills. Since their housing tends to be old and deteriorated, fuel costs hit them the hardest.

Economic development that occurs within the Region frequently bypasses the resources available in more distressed urban places. Labor, existing structures, and other infrastructure tend to be underutilized.

Urban Distress In New England

While data on New England's distressed urban neighborhoods would best illustrate the situation of the urban poor, up-to-date information for neighborhoods is unavailable until the outcome of the 1980 census. Data on cities as a whole do, however, show how New England's cities compare with cities nationwide.

- While New England's median income regionwide is higher than the national average, the median central city income is lower than the median income in central cities nationwide. (See Table XXXIII)

- While the differential between central city and suburban median income is 19 percent nationwide, it is 27 percent in New England.

Because New Englanders living in cities make up a large proportion of the Region's population, especially in the three southern states, economic development strategies that target cities will have a significant impact on the Region.

- 25 percent of New Englanders live in central cities. 13 percent of the Region's city dwellers live in poverty areas and 12 percent have incomes below the poverty level. (See Table XXXIV)

- 26 percent of Massachusetts residents, 32 percent of Connecticut residents, and 34 percent of Rhode Island residents live in cities. In Rhode Island, 21 percent (over 1/5) of city dwellers reside in poverty areas.

- In suburban areas of New England, only 5 percent of residents are below the poverty level and only one percent live in poverty areas.

Characteristics Of The Central City Population

Minorities represent a disproportionate number of poor, central city New Englanders. Blacks make up only 4 percent of New England's population. However, they comprise 11 percent of the Region's center city population, 38 percent of New Englanders in central city poverty areas, and 29 percent of all central city New Englanders who live below the poverty level. The Region's minorities are concentrated in the central cities. Seventy-nine percent of all Blacks and 60 percent of all Hispanics in the Region live in central cities. Central city minorities in New England tend to be worse off than central city minorities nationwide. Nationwide, 27 percent of central city Blacks and 26 percent of central city Hispanics are below poverty level. In New England, 29 percent of central city Blacks and 37 percent of central city Hispanics are below poverty level.

They are poor because of under- and unemployment that results from poor quality education and long-term racial discrimination, which have barred them from decent paying jobs with advancement potential. Unemployment rates for minorities are available for only two New England states. In 1978, while 5.9 percent of Whites in Massachusetts were unemployed, 9.8 percent of minorities were jobless. In Connecticut, the disparity was even greater. 4.8 percent of Whites and 11.2 percent of minorities were unemployed.

Those who are employed tend to have lower paying jobs. For example, 53 percent of White working males in New England had an annual income of $10,000 or more in 1975. Only 39 percent of all working Black males had incomes this high. The disparity in white-collar occupations is even larger. Sixty-eight percent of White male, white-collar workers made $10,000 or more in 1978. Only 47 percent of Black male, white-collar workers made $10,000 or more.

Female-headed families represent a disproportionate number of central city families. While 27 percent of all U.S. families live in central cities, 42 percent of families headed by women live in central cities. In New England, female-headed families have a median income equal to half the median income of all families. The situation for Black female-headed families is even worse. Their median income is one-third of the median income of all New England families. While 8 percent of all New Englanders live below poverty level, 31 percent of all persons in female-headed families are below poverty level. For minorities, the situation is even worse. Fifty percent of persons in Black female-headed families, and 81 percent of persons in Hispanic female-headed families are below poverty level.

This poverty is a result of under- and unemployment. The median income of full-time working women is 59 percent of the median income of full-time working men in New England. Unem-

Table XXXIV

Central City and Suburban* Population Below the Poverty Level (1976)

New England and the U.S. Average

	Percent of Central City Population Below Poverty Level	Percent of Suburban Population Below Poverty Level	Percent Difference Between Central City and Suburban Populations Below Poverty Level
United States	14	7	7
New England	12	5	7
Connecticut	12	3	9
Maine	12	3	10
Massachusetts	12	5	7
New Hampshire	7	3	4
Rhode Island	12	6	6
Vermont**	NA	NA	NA

Source: U.S. Census, Series P-60, No. 110

* "Suburbs" refers to localities in SMSAs, but excludes the central city
** Vermont has no SMSAs   NA - not available

Table XXXV

Firms by Sector, All Firms, Black-Owned Firms

	Firms by Sector as a Percent of All Firms: 1976*	Black-Owned Firms by Sector as a Percent of Total Black-Owned Firms: 1977**	
	U.S.	U.S.	N.E.
Construction	10	9.0	8.0
Manufacturing	4	2.0	2.0
Transportation & Public Utilities	4	10.0	6.0
Wholesale Trade	5	1.0	2.0
Retail Trade	19	24.0	20.0
Finance, Insurance, Real Estate	13	4.0	4.0
Services	30	44.0	52.0
Other	15	6.0	6.0
Total:	100	100.0	100.0

Sources: * U.S. Census, Statistical Abstract of the U.S., Table No. 914
** U.S. Census, Survey of Minority-Owned Business Enterprises, MB 77-1

ployment is more severe for women. For example, the unemployment rate for Black women in 1978 was 15 percent in Connecticut, nearly one-sixth of the Black female labor force.

Unemployment is also a critical problem for urban youth. In 1978, youth unemployment among all races was 16 percent in New England. For Black youths, it was 21 percent in Massachusetts, and 43 percent in Connecticut.

Human Capital — Issues Of Under- And Unemployment

The most critical issue in distressed center city neighborhoods is unemployment. Since such unemployment exists for a variety of reasons, any efforts to combat it must be comprehensive: involving basic educational skills and specialized training for the unemployed; local capacity building; minority small business development; and corporate responsibility in hiring.

Education and Skills Training

The conclusions on the need for basic education discussed in the labor chapter are even more important in addressing the special needs of the urban poor. In order to take advantage of employment opportunities becoming available in cities, the urban unemployed require better job skills. They need basic educational skills and a better knowledge about how the working world operates.

In some instances, specialized skills training to match up worker skills with those skills required by employers is also necessary. But, the importance of specific skills training is often overplayed since most jobs are easy to learn, even if they are in high technology industries.

CETA programs often do not address the issues of basic knowledge about the workplace and productivity. Rather, they tend to teach specific skills over a limited time period. This is one

reason why CETA training is often unsuccessful for the hard-core unemployed despite the level of public investment.

Local Capacity Building

The local economies of distressed neighborhoods, characterized by deteriorated and abandoned commercial and industrial structures, could provide opportunities to local residents. Where commercial and industrial space is used productively, it can act as an incubator to develop employment and management skills and capacity for directing financial capital to community needs. Community-based economic development is an important vehicle for providing employment opportunities in distressed urban areas.

Such efforts are commonly carried out through organizations such as community development corporations (CDC) whose purposes are to (1) create new or better jobs for area residents; (2) provide opportunities for residents to learn technical, managerial, and entrepreneurial skills; (3) rehabilitate under-utilized or blighted real property to attract new businesses; (4) support businesses owned by local residents; and (5) provide accessible goods and services at competitive prices. CDCs channel capital into businesses whose profit-making potential is sufficient to meet the employment and income needs of the community. CDC-owned firms or firms owned by local residents or workers who receive management or financial assistance from a CDC provide a source of employment and income generating opportunities for local residents.

CDCs and other community-based organizations also work with the private and public sectors to develop innovative uses of employment training resources, and act as "chambers of commerce" to attract new business investment from outside the community. In order to build capacity and employment opportunity among residents in distressed neighborhoods, community based organizations require adequate funding as well as management and financial assistance. Financial assistance must be in the form of high-risk capital that can be used for existing projects and firms or for start-ups in which traditional investors are unwilling to become involved.

Entrepreneurship Among Minorities

Small business ownership provides an important source of employment and income growth opportunity for minorities. Jobs in firms owned by minorities provide an opportunity for minorities to gain employment experience and skills that will enable them to bypass racial discrimination in entry-level jobs and obtain better positions in overall job markets.

However, both potential minority entrepreneurs and existing firms owned by members of minority groups are constrained from contributing fully to New England's economy. Racial and ethnic minorities, and women in general, face discrimination in capital markets. Because most minority businesspeople are first generation entrepreneurs and are beginning to own businesses outside of the retail and service sectors, in which they have traditionally been concentrated, they are inexperienced in their new sectors and new product markets.

Minority entrepreneurship is disproportionately low relative to the size of the minority population. While Blacks make up 11 percent of the U.S. population, they own 2 percent of all firms. Minority-owned firms have lower gross receipts than all firms. Table XXXV shows that the distribution among sectors of Black-owned firms is different from the distribution of all firms. Most notably, firms owned by Blacks are

much more concentrated in the service sector, and much less concentrated in finance, insurance, and real estate.

Physical Capital

While unemployment is the most critical problem of distressed neighborhoods, the condition of a city's physical capital is also a major issue. Good capital stock is essential for employment growth. Cities should look upon their physical stock as an asset and attempt to maximize the return on it. It can be a city's primary tool to attract industry. Housing stock is also an important determinant of economic viability and quality of life.

Influencing Location Decisions of Firms

Physical amenities and public infrastructure are necessary for economic activity and opportunities. In those parts of New England's cities characterized by low income and high unemployment, commercial centers and industrial areas are often blighted, and sewer, water, and road systems tend to be old and inadequately maintained.

Cities, because they are population centers, are a natural location for New England's growth industries. High grade services and high technology manufacturing are major employers in many of New England's cities. However, they infrequently locate in distressed parts of these cities, and thus infrequently employ residents of low-income communities. A balanced mix of new construction and rehabilitation of old buildings to meet the needs of the growth industries is essential to the economic development of distressed urban communities. New construction in a physically deteriorated community can be a catalyst to major investment in nearby older structures. Firms that "spin off" from high tech manufacturing taking place in

Table XXXVI

Population Change in Twelve Selected New England Cities: 1970-1975, 1975-1980

	Annual Average Percent Change: 1970—1975	Annual Average Percent Change: 1975-1980
Bridgeport, CT	-2.0	+0.8
Hartford, CT	-2.8	+0.2
New Haven, CT	-1.8	+0.4
Portland, ME	-1.8	+0.8
Boston, MA	-0.2	+0.2
Brockton, MA	+1.4	+1.2
Springfield, MA	+0.8	+0.4
Worcester, MA	-0.6	-0.2
Manchester, NH	-1.0	+3.0
Pawtucket, RI	-1.4	-0.8
Providence, RI	-1.4	-2.0
Burlington, VT	-0.8	+1.0

1. Based on 1975 and 1979 population estimates rather than 1975 and 1980

Sources: U.S. Census, Connecticut Office of Policy and Management, Maine State Planning Office, Metropolitan Area Planning Council (Boston), Old Colony Planning Council (Brockton), Lower Pioneer Valley Regional Planning Commission (Springfield), Central Massachusetts Regional Planning Commission (Worcester), New Hampshire Office of State Planning, Vermont Office of State Planning

Table XXXVII

Indicators of Economic Distress In Ten Selected Rural Counties in New England

	Percent of Population Below Poverty Level	Unemployment Rate July 1977 to June 1979 (average percent)
Dukes, MA	8.6	7.9
Aroostock, ME	19.5	10.2
Somerset, ME	15.9	9.7
Waldo, ME	17.0	10.1
Coos, NH	12.6	6.3
Grafton, NH	10.7	3.9
Sullivan, NH	10.3	3.4
Essex, VT	18.5	9.9
Lamoille, VT	14.8	7.7
Bennington, VT	13.3	6.6

Source: Economic Development Administration, U.S. Census, 1970 Census of Population

new facilities may locate in neighboring older buildings.

Public and private participation are essential for improving physical capital to serve the needs of industry. Carefully placed public investment can orchestrate the placement of private investment. For example, public rehabilitation of a sewer system, parcel assembly and site clearance, construction of a highway access ramp, or provision of police services would reduce the private risks of investment in a physically deteriorated community.

Housing the Urban Population

A housing shortage and strong competition within a tight market exist in New England's cities. The size of the average household has declined from 2.9 persons in 1970 to 2.3 persons today. Despite population losses during the early 1970's, the Region's cities are currently experiencing population growth or a marked slowdown in population decline. As can be seen in Table XXXVI, between 1970 and 1975 ten out of twelve selected New England cities lost population. Between 1975 and 1980, nine of those twelve cities gained population.

Current residents in the city, with high unemployment and low income, will be unable to compete in urban housing markets as revitalization continues. If the disadvantaged cannot retain city housing, they will be unable to share in the benefits of that revitalization. The problem of "displacement" will arise when a population that has higher incomes than the current population enters a housing market. The most useful way of preventing such displacement is support of home ownership among low-income persons and non-profit corporations set up to serve the housing needs of such persons.

B / Distressed Rural Areas

Introduction

The common perception of New England is as a densely-populated northern extension of the Atlantic Megalopolis. Although this description fits much of southern New England, the bulk of the Region is a sparsely-populated area, consisting of relatively remote small towns and cities in an area dominated by forests. 23.7 percent of the population of New England lives in areas classified as rural by the Census. These areas have often been overlooked for both public and private investment, a situation that has begun to change only in the past several years. As a result of disinvestment and remoteness, these areas have chronically suffered a disproportionate share of poverty.

The chronic poverty that exists in much of rural New England is largely a result of a uniformity of the economic base. Rural areas have long been reliant on a few traditional industries and a few employers. When one or more of these industries enters a period of decline, the economy of the area suffers disproportionately. Underemployment is more of a problem than unemployment. Employment is often seasonal or low paying. Because adequately-paying full-time jobs are scarce, many members of the labor force try to supplement their income with part-time or counterseasonal employment, or by engaging in cottage industry.

The economies of most rural regions of the United States are based on agriculture or mineral extraction. In this regard, rural New England is unusual. While agriculture forms a basis of the economy of some select areas, the economy of rural New England is, for the most part, based on rural manufacturing and service centers. As a result of this small center-based economy, many rural residents travel long distances to employment in town centers. Rural New England has been characterized as a region of "rural commuters".

In discussing the economic development of rural New England, a fundamental issue must be resolved. A major attraction of living in a rural area is the quality of life: the natural scenic beauty and small town living. The challenge is maintaining this quality of life while promoting economic development. Some communities are more willing to accept and encourage development while other communities are unwilling to accept any growth at all. Each community must work for the type and scale of development that is most appropriate to its needs and objectives.

Most of the rapidly-growing sectors of New England's economy, specifically, high technology manufacturing and high grade services, are expanding in the cities and suburban areas of New England. The rural areas, for the most part, are bypassed by these industries.

However, there are some promising opportunities for the economic growth of rural New England. Several important resources have the potential to contribute to rural economic development. The harvesting and processing of (adding value to) these resources, notably the forests, fisheries, and agriculture, have been growing rapidly in recent years and have attracted much new investment. The tourism industry is important to the economies of certain rural areas and generally has been growing.

The principal focus of an economic development strategy for distressed rural New England is to enlarge and diversify the economic base to provide employment opportunities for residents. This can be done by capitalizing on the assets of rural areas — natural resources and labor. Development should be of a scale and magnitude that is compatible with the rural environment so that it does not impose social costs and fiscal burdens on rural communities.

Targeting Rural Distress In New England
Although there are several ways to classify the Region into rural versus non-rural, all definitions of rural indicate lower incomes and higher unemployment for rural New England than for the Region's non-rural areas. The United States Census Bureau breaks down the population as metropolitan versus non-metropolitan.

- The median income of New Englanders living in metropolitan areas was 12 percent higher than that of New Englanders in non-metropolitan areas in 1976. However, this disparity was smaller than the 26 percent disparity for the Nation as a whole.

- A greater proportion of non-metropolitan New Englanders' incomes than of metropolitan incomes in the Region are below poverty level. Again, this disparity was   r smaller than that of the Nation.

For the purpose of discussion, 36 counties in New England have been classified as rural. These counties are identified as having a population density of 200 persons per square mile or less and not encompassing any section of an SMSA. However, there are also rural areas in New England that are not included in the 36 counties identified. The county data are intended to provide a broad indication of the economic characteristics of the rural sections of New England.

- 27 out of 36 counties had unemployment rates greater than the average unemployment rates for New England during the base period (July 1977 - June 1979).

- Four counties in New England, all of them rural, had unemployment rates of 10 percent or greater.

Characteristics Of The Economy Of Rural New England
Ten distressed counties of the 36 rural counties have been identified as representative of rural New England. These counties are *Dukes*, Massachusetts; *Aroostook, Somerset*, and *Waldo*, Maine; *Coos, Grafton*, and *Sullivan*, New Hampshire; and *Essex, Lamoille*, and *Bennington*, Vermont.

The data from these 10 counties show the diversity of the economy in rural New England. Six out of these ten counties were more dependent on manufacturing employment than the regional average, while several of the counties had large employment shares in services. One common characteristic to rural New England is a strong orientation towards natural resource based industries including tourism, resource harvesting and natural resource value-added manufacturing. All ten counties had larger employment shares in the primary sector than did the Region. The resource that appears to have the greatest significance to the ecocomy of distressed rural New England is the forests, with eight out of the ten counties having significant employment shares in lumber and wood products.

Agriculture, forestry, and fishing were important in several of the counties, particularly Aroostook, reflecting the importance of farming there. The large share of employment in food processing emphasizes the role of agriculture-related manufacturing.

The importance of forest products to the economy of rural New England is illustrated by the large shares of employment in lumber and

Table XXXVIII

Shares of Employment by Industry For Ten Selected Distressed Rural Counties in New England 1978

(Percent of County Total)

Industry	Dukes, MA	Aroostook, ME	Somerset, ME	Waldo, ME	Coos, NH	Grafton, NH	Sullivan, NH	Essex, VT	Lamoille, VT	Burlington, VT
Ag. Serv., For., Fish, etc.*	2.5	14.7	6.0	(D)	2.7e	2.3	3.2e	6.4e	6.9	2.4
Goods Producing	9.7e	19.6	33.6	29.0e	33.2	21.2	39.7e		15.8	34.4
Mining	—	(L)	0	—	+0	0.1	+0	—	0.1	0
Construction	7.2	2.5	3.8	3.0	3.0	3.4	3.3	(D)	5.5	4.6
Manufacturing	2.4	17.0	29.9	26.0	30.2	17.7	36.3	47.9	10.2	29.8
non-durables	1.5	10.6	18.7	20.7	26.2	7.0	16.1	(D)	3.8	8.2
durables	1.0	6.5	11.1	5.3	4.1	10.7	20.2	(D)	6.5	21.5
Service Producing	72.8	58.0e	49.8		55.4	68.9	47.8		65.8	54.1
Transp.,Comm.,Pub.Ut.	3.3	(D)	1.8	4.4	3.3	2.7	2.1	3.5	3.3	2.1
Trade	22.4	14.5	12.6	11.8	15.1	16.2	17.2	3.7e	17.5	17.1
wholesale	2.5	3.8	2.2	2.3	2.1	1.8	2.9	(L)	1.0	1.2
retail	19.9	10.8	10.4	9.5	13.1	14.4	14.3	3.5	16.4	15.9
Fire	5.3	2.3	1.5	(D)	1.7	2.3	3.5	0.6	2.5	2.3
Services	25.3	(D)	13.6	15.9	19.4	34.4	12.6	(D)	26.0	21.6
Government	16.5	26.4	20.3	15.3	15.8	13.3	12.4	24.2	16.4	11.1
federal civ.	0.5	4.0	0.9	1.5	0.9	1.7	0.8	2.2	0.9	0.7
federal mil.	0.6	9.0	1.5	1.7	1.1	0.9	1.4	2.3	1.8	1.6
state & local	15.4	13.4	18.0	12.0	13.8	10.7	10.2	19.8	13.7	8.8
Total Excl. Non-farm Prop.	85.0	92.3	89.5	87.5	91.4	92.4	90.7	90.9	88.4	90.9
Non-Farm Prop.	15.0	7.7	10.5	12.5	8.6	7.6	9.3	9.1	11.6	9.1
Total Employment (persons)	4680	41373	17011	9191	15577	34441	13070	2297	6768	16056

(L) Fewer than 10 employees
(D) No figures available because of disclosure rules
(e) Estimate
 * Includes farm workers and farm proprietors
Computations may not sum to totals due to rounding

Source: Bureau of Economic Analysis

wood products in six of the counties (Aroostook, Somerset, Coos, Sullivan, Essex, and Lamoille) and the large share of paper in Sullivan County. Interestingly enough, only Bennington County had significant employment in furniture manufacturing, which implies that there might be a potential for this industry in other wood processing areas.

Tourism is an important industry in certain areas of rural New England. High employment shares in retail trade and services in Dukes and Lamoille Counties indicate their dependence on tourism.

Manufacturing industries, both traditional and non-traditional, are important in many of the counties. Leather and leather products comprise a very large share of employment in Somerset County and a smaller one in Grafton County. Fabricated metal products and non-electrical machinery provide large shares of Sullivan County's employment, while a large share of Bennington County's workforce is employed in the manufacture of electrical equipment.

Issues

The most critical economic issue for distressed rural areas is the lack of employment opportunities. This manifests itself through both high unemployment and under-employment. Many rural residents of New England have only seasonal or part-time employment. In 1978, the rates of people working part-time who wished to work full-time were significantly higher in Maine and Vermont, the two most rural states, than in the other four states.

The insufficiency of employment opportunities suggests the need to expand the economic base of rural areas through fostering a diversification of industries.

Utilizing Natural Resources For Economic Development

Although New England is a region with limited natural resources, it does have resources with economic potential. These resources, primarily forests, fish, and agriculture, have traditionally been important to rural New England but have suffered a long period of decline and disinvestment. However, in recent years this trend has been reversed. These industries are showing signs of future growth, with many of the economic benefits of the growth going to rural New England.

The fishing industry in New England has been expanding, largely as a result of the Fisheries Conservation and Management Act of 1976 which extended United States jurisdiction over the fishery resources out to 200 miles offshore. This extension has reduced overfishing by foreign fleets and has stimulated investment in the industry.

The dramatic increase in transportation costs over the last decade has made the transport of high-bulk items such as lumber more nearly prohibitive. This encourages production closer to markets. Since rural New England is closer to the major eastern markets of the Nation, the utilization of its resources can be expected to increase.

The cost of transportation also encourages value-added and refinement of resources near their source. High cost encourages the shipment of a resource in its lowest-bulk, highest-value form. It is far less expensive to ship furniture parts from the hardwood forests of Maine to a furniture plant in North Carolina than it is to ship the rough-cut lumber there.

There are other factors which tend to encourage the processing of a resource near the source. Fish is a highly perishable item which loses quality rapidly. It is therefore most efficient to process it as quickly as possible. The situation is similar for most agricultural commodities such as dairy products.

Natural-resource-based industries are growing in New England, as witnessed by the large investments in paper and wood products facilities that have been made in recent years. However there are certain impediments that must be overcome in order for there to be substantial future investment in value-added industries.

- Forest product industries are reluctant to locate in an area unless they are assured of a supply of certain species. Currently, there are very poor data on the local level as to the supply of a given species. There must be better data on a local level so that potential investors will know what is available.

- Unlike the West, New England's forests are largely owned by small non-commercial land-owners, for whom woodcutting is not a primary objective. The resources owned by the small landowners are currently grossly under-utilized.

- The fishing industry of New England suffers from severe fragmentation. Processors are unwilling to invest unless they are assured a constant supply of fish, which is difficult because of the fragmentation. In addition, the marketing mechanisms tend to draw fresh fish away from the ports to Boston or New York.

- As with fishing, agriculture in New England lacks an effective marketing mechanism that benefits the farmer. As in the case of forestry and fishing, processors are reluctant to invest unless assured a constant supply of the produce.

Appropriate Scale Development

Each rural community, in pursuing economic development, must strike a balance between providing sufficient and adequate employment for its residents and preserving its character and quality of life. Development that is too large disturbs the scale and balance of the community and creates a fiscal burden from the forced rapid expansion of services and facilities, such as water and sewer capacity, police, fire, schools, etc.

Traditional economic development efforts have been oriented toward locating a new plant in a community. However, studies have shown that only a small percentage of new jobs in the economy are created this way. Most jobs are created through the expansion of existing industry. This suggests that rural communities should devote a significant portion of their efforts and resources to meeting the needs of the existing local industry. Such efforts include training programs for the workforce, assistance in obtaining financing and cooperation with the firm's expansion planning efforts. Every effort should be made to ensure that a firm in the process of expansion does not find it advantageous to relocate out of the community.

Firms that employ fewer than 20 people, "microbusinesses," are an important component of the rural economy. These firms often provide necessary services to local residents and keep funds within the community. Other microbusinesses produce goods or services for export from the community, contributing to the local economic base. In addition to providing employment and income for many rural residents micro-businesses are the major generators of new jobs. There is the possibility that micro-businesses can grow and expand into major employers in the community.

Microbusinesses have special needs and problems that are often overlooked in economic development efforts. A major problem has been accessing capital. The capital requirements of these firms are small, usually only several thousand dollars. However, transactions costs make it very difficult to secure small loans through conventional financial mechanisms.

Lack of expertise in business practices is also a major problem of microbusinesses. Often the entrepreneur is knowledgeable in the skill or craft required to produce his good or service but inexperienced in operating a business. Technical expertise to small entrepreneurs is essential.

Physical Capital

As has been mentioned previously in this document, adequate physical capital is essential for economic growth. Disinvestment in rural New England has resulted in a public infrastructure that is often antiquated or otherwise inadequate to serve modern economic development needs.

Another important feature of rural New England's physical capital is that it is generally concentrated in town centers. The adequacy of this infrastructure varies, largely corresponding to the size and scale of the center. The larger centers tend to offer a greater range of existing infrastructure, sewers, more housing, a greater amount of available industrial space, public or private transportation services, better highway and rail access and even an airport. They also offer a wider range of services, both public and private, such as health, education, retail, and professional services. Therefore these larger centers are better able to support larger scale economic development. Development in smaller centers, which lack a range of services and facilities, should be of a smaller scale so as not to overburden existing facilities.

Government has traditionally been the provider of much of this physical capital. However, many government infrastructure programs were designed for cities. Trying to use them for rural areas does not serve the rural community in an effective way. Two examples of this are mass transportation and housing.

Federal mass transit programs have generally been geared toward rapid transit rail systems and fixed route bus systems. Lower population bases make these systems unsuited for rural areas. The Section 18 Program is a response to this problem. It provides money to make up the deficit of existing providers. This acts as a disincentive to cost effective operations. Mass transportation programs that more effectively utilize existing services and are not as capital intensive as the typical system would be much better suited to the needs of rural New England.

Similarly, federal housing programs and formulas are more appropriate to urban areas because of guidelines, regulations, and cost structure.

In rural New England there already exists an abundance of centers containing a full range of "infrastructure packages". New investments in public physical capital should be aimed at strengthening and upgrading these centers rather than creating new ones or dramatically altering the scale of existing centers. Such an approach involves an emphasis on upgrading the existing infrastructure and building new infrastructure of an appropriate scale in town centers.

Expansion Of Local Capacity Through Regionalization Of Economic Development Activities

Economic development is a regional multicommunity activity, with costs and benefits that transcend municipal boundaries. Presently,

only the community in which development facilities are located achieves the tax benefits, while neighboring communities are often burdened with part of the costs, such as the cost of providing police and fire protection to the workers. This situation leads to competition between adjacent municipalities for the location of the development facilities, since each jurisdiction wants the tax revenue.

At the same time, most individual communities lack the capacity to perform economic development planning. They usually lack professional staff and the fiscal capacity to hire staff. This suggests that the most appropriate mechanism for rural economic development is at the regional level. At that level a professional staff could serve the needs of several communities. Substate regional planning agencies and economic development districts are the ideal vehicles since they are composed of communities related by common problems and issues. The staff of such an agency is typically in a position to link the economic development needs of a community with other community issues.

Targeting Strategies For Distressed Populations

The role of government in economic development is to address the special needs of communities and population groups which are less likely to share in the benefits of growth while promoting the overall climate for economic activity. Each New England state and the Federal government currently practice policies that target programs and public investments to communities in need. Connecticut has enacted an Urban Action Grants Program to package and target state aid to distressed cities and towns. New Hampshire attempts to direct private investment toward slower growth rural counties in the North Country. The need for special public intervention takes two forms: (1) to encourage private industrial location and (2) to help the affected population through training, business self-help and community rebuilding assistance so that they can better participate in the overall growth of the Region.

Basic Targeting Strategies

1 / The encouragement of economic activity within access of distressed populations should be given high priority. State policy should direct both public infrastructure investments and financial incentives, (IRBs etc.) to facilitate job creation for unemployed and low income groups.

2 / Human capital is the most underutilized resource in distressed parts of the Region. Public and private investment in the labor force, through basic education and specialized skills training is the cornerstone of a strategy to extend economic opportunity to distressed populations.

3 / Barriers to employment of women and minorities and other groups have resulted in high unemployment and low income. Affirmative action by both the public and private sector will prevent the continued underutilization of an important resource.

4 / Unemployed workers in high unemployment areas tend to require unskilled and semi-skilled blue-collar job opportunities. Many such opportunities have and continue to be provided by manufacturing. Manufacturing industries identified as "traditional;" or "less competitive" — machinery, leather, food processing, toys, jewelry, etc. — are important employers. Every effort should be made to sustain this employment base through identifying and assisting viable enterprises to remain and grow.

5 / Distressed populations and poor communities tend to lack the business and managerial skills to fully benefit from the opportunities of regional growth. Special policies and programs such as the Northern Community Investment Corporation in New Hampshire and Vermont and Massachusetts' Community Development Finance Corporation should be expanded and replicated throughout the Region. These mechanisms are important in the development of entrepreneurial and employment opportunities.

6 / Both rural towns and inner-city communities often lack the capability to manage government services necessary for community improvement. Their effectiveness in working with state and federal programs must be enhanced.

7 / Viable neighborhood commercial districts and adequate housing are necessary to provide for economic opportunity and improved quality of life in distressed areas. State targeting policies should address these issues.

8 / The federal government should be responsive to state targeting strategies and give priority to areas of economic distress. Federal agencies should work together to coordinate flexible responses to the special economic needs of target population groups.

Targeting Public Policy Recommendations

1 / States should build local capacity in low-income communities by offering technical and financial assistance to local residents or organizations involved in business ownership and development and by offering incentives to attract business investment from outside the community.

2 / State and federal programs should continue to provide rent subsidies (such as HUD Section 8, and Section 707 in Massachusetts) and scattered site public housing to ensure that a diversity of housing types is available to people in various geographic areas and income groups.

3 / State and federal agencies should continue to provide funding (such as CDBGs) to revitalize and ensure the continued viability of distressed neighborhood commercial areas and downtowns.

4 / States should develop urban and rural targeting priorities which provide for a wide array of state agencies (including the departments of transportation, housing, human resources, and economic development) to offer coordinated assistance and/or funding to specific projects in state-designated target areas.

5 / NERCOM should work through FRC to encourage Federal and Regional officials (i.e. EDA, FmHA, and UMTA) to respond to state targeting strategies by packaging assistance to special community needs.

6 / New England should capitalize on its potential for entrepreneurship among women and minorities. The Region's economy can benefit from public sector procurement and contract procedures that require participation of such firms. States should assist these firms in obtaining information about public sector procurement.

Special Urban Targeting Public Policy Recommendations

1 / CETA training should be channeled into programs that, in addition to teaching specific job skills, provide trainees with an understanding of the economic system and the work environment.

2 / U.S. Department of Labor should provide research and demonstration grants to organizations and firms that gear their training to the long-term urban unemployed to do research on the educational, skill, and basic knowledge needs of the disadvantaged and to develop demonstration programs to meet those needs.

3 / States should offer technical assistance to potential and existing minority entrepreneurs, helping with business planning and loan packaging and providing information about, and linkages to, appropriate state, federal and private sources of financing targeted to minority-owned enterprises.

4 / Public investment programs such as Industrial Revenue Bonds and Industrial Park Loan Programs should require recipient firms to develop strategies to hire unemployed or under-employed persons where possible.

5 / Unemployment among residents of distressed urban neighborhoods is of such a magnitude that skills training programs and community-based development efforts cannot address the problem without concerted private-sector participation. A primary thrust of public policy should be toward encouraging major corporations and large employers in ensuring that affirmative action is practiced in all job levels and in training and tuition reimbursement programs, and that contracts with government agencies have covenants requiring firms to train and hire the unemployed.

Special Rural Targeting: Public Policy Recommendations

1 / Since rural economic development is multi-community activity, with costs and benefits that transcend municipal boundaries, economic development planning should be done on a sub-regional basis. Regional planning agencies and economic development districts (EDDs) should take a major role in providing technical assistance to promote economic development to constituent communities. The states should permit and encourage "coinvestment" among communities in facilities to encourage economic development in conjunction with the sharing of tax revenues to finance such facilities.

2 / Rural economic development efforts must recognize the desire of most small communities to remain rural in character. Development should be scaled to the needs and desires of the community so as to avoid undesired urbanization.

3 / Existing employment and service centers should be the focus of economic development efforts. Investments in infrastructure should be targeted to growth centers.

4 / Rural economic development efforts should include emphasis on existing businesses which have been able to sustain their viability despite such problems as small markets, high energy costs and inadequate transportation. This emphasis should include fostering the growth and development of microbusinesses. Communities should establish business technical assistance centers to aid them. Community capital pools should be established by both the local financial institutions and public financing programs to provide capital in the small amounts needed by these businesses.

5 / A major emphasis should be placed on the management and utilization of the Region's natural resources, such as forest, fish, and agriculture to promote economic development. NERCOM should work with the states and private interests to identify investment opportunities that would increase the value added to these resources. The Federal government should support these efforts by providing better inventories of resources and more emphasis on resource management programs.

6 / Federal economic development programs should be more sensitive to the special needs of rural communities. Programs should reinforce and help implement local and state plans and policies. The Governors' Rural Advisory Committees, consisting of federal and state officials, are an appropriate vehicle. In addition, the Federal Regional Council should assist state and local officials in packaging various programs for an economic development project.

7 / Many federal economic development programs are modifications or adjustments of programs designed to aid urban areas and therefore are not totally appropriate to rural scale development. These programs should be altered to better reflect rural needs.

8 /   The Rural Growth Policy Act of 1980
       allowed for the extension of Farmers Home
       Section III planning grants, which are ex-
       tremely useful in strengthening the capa-
       city of both regional and state rural econo-
       mic development organizations. Such
       capacity enables the regional planning
       agencies to provide technical expertise to
       local communities and the states to coor-
       dinate federal and local activities. This
       program should be funded at its fully au-
       thorized level.

9 /   Public policy should support and encour-
       age a range of economic development or-
       ganizations that are appropriate to the
       needs of local communities including com-
       munity development corporations and pro-
       ducer cooperatives.

Agenda For Action: Strategies and Policies for Regional Cooperation

12

Recognizing both the new development potential of the Region and the constraints to growth, a series of strategies and policy recommendations have been developed to enhance New England's overall economic development prospects and to direct development to those population groups and geographic locations that lag behind the Region in overall prosperity. These strategies capitalize on the Region's comparative advantages and mitigate weaknesses through state actions, regional self-help initiatives, and by impacting decision making at the Federal level.

The New England states comprise the oldest and one of the most homogeneous regions of the country, sharing both the traditions and some of the problems that reflect their age. While significant differences among the economies of the states and sub-regions do exist, the planning process has identified an agenda of common prospects and problems that merit region-wide attention. New England is in many ways significantly different from the rest of the Nation and there is a clear need for interstate cooperation to address these common issues.

The New England Regional Commission should play a significant role in reinforcing interstate cooperation. The Commission should play an expanded role as information gatherer for the six states and as a monitor of the potential impact of federal policy and the national economy on the Region. The Commission is in

The interconnected electronics of a computer's printed circuit board suggests the interdependence of the many population groups and geographic areas that define the New England region—an interrelationship which establishes the principle of mutual cooperation as the only effective way to successful economic development for New England as a whole.

many ways the ideal convener of regional leaders, public and private, to forge consensus on strategies to address regional concerns. Issues that have emerged from this planning process include: building a consensus on energy needs and improving the regional dialogue on capital availability. The Commission should also continue to be used as a catalyst, both in developing programs to promote the economy of the Region and by investing in specific development projects.

Federal Coordination — New England is very different from the rest of the Nation in scale, problems and needs. Federal sensitivity to these differences is important in maximizing the effectiveness of very necessary program dollars and in preventing the development of policies and programs detrimental to the competitive position of the Region. For New England, federal programs often need to stress retrofitting and maintenance of existing facilities over new construction. Investment needs are sometimes smaller-scale: rural problems are significantly different than in the rest of the Nation. The Commission should work more closely with regional federal officials through the vehicle of the Federal Regional Council (FRC) to tailor and package federal programs to regional needs and priorities.

Pending Regional Commission legislation calls for enhanced federal responsiveness to regional priorities, both through the Secretary of Commerce and through an inter-agency coordinating mechanism representing all federal agencies. The Region and the Commission should use these mechanisms as well as links to the New England Congressional delegation to communicate regulatory and legislative issues which impact on the health of the Region.

State Government — It is important to recognize that state and local governments are the principal public sector initiators of economic development policies and projects. The six New England states all utilize a range of tax incentives, financing and investment policies to promote economic growth. The specific recommendations which emerge from the Plan are intended to supplement current state activities.

Public-Private Sector Cooperation — Most of the specific recommendations which emerge from the planning process call for governmental initiatives. However, implicit in these recommendations is the recognition that it is private industry and private investment capital which are the prime vehicles for economic growth. These strategies and policy recommendations suggest improved mechanisms for government to work with the private sector, to facilitate an investment climate and to encourage private sector decisions which would benefit the Region.

But there is also a need for direct private-sector action in several key areas: upgrading the labor force and improving training and labor market information mechanisms requires business initiatives; better utilization of financing mechanisms and finance packaging must involve private financial institutions; transportation carriers from all modes need to work together with the public sector to coordinate transportation planning.

The Regional Plan calls for these combined forces to work together on a New England agenda which includes the following major issues:

The Labor Market
To more effectively meet labor supply and demand needs, as reflected in skills shortages simultaneous with significant unemployment, all sectors must work together to improve regional education and training and labor market forecasting. The maintenance of an educated and skilled labor force is primarily the responsibility of local government, with state and federal support through CETA and vocational education. The Regional Commission can help with improved labor demand/supply forecasting and by working with the U.S. Manpower Administration to design new programs tailored to the educational needs of disadvantaged members of the labor force and the skills requirements of emerging occupations.

Capital Availability
The continued growth of the regional economy depends on the availability of investment capital. New England's rapid-growth industries are difficult to lend to, and reinvestment in new technology for traditional industries is perceived as high risk. New England has evolved an innovative mix of public and private financing mechanisms to meet special lending requirements. Yet the need for capital persists and the public sector and private sector must work more closely together to: (1) identify tax and regulatory priorities to stimulate investment in the Region, (2) better utilize in-place development financing mechanisms including federal programs to meet special needs,and (3) convene the parties at interest to further identify unmet capital needs and the mechanisms that should be developed to meet them.

Capital is also an important component of a targeting strategy. The states should continue to use public dollars to supplement private investment in geographic areas of distress through revolving loan funds and other appropriate development mechanisms.

Research and Development
Research and development and investment in new technology are very important to the New

England economy. Regional leaders should promote increased federal attention and investment in technology development as a national priority which improves productivity and as a regional benefit which creates jobs and promotes business expansion.

Small Business

The climate for incubating and expanding small business is critical to the growth of new jobs in New England. Recognizing that regional economic growth is dependent, in large part, on a dynamic process involving the birth and growth of home-grown industries, the states should review tax and regulatory policies in terms of their impact on entrepreneurship and business development.

To increase the ability of small and young firms to access capital, regional leaders should advocate Congressional action to: (1) amend the Securities and Exchange Act of 1933 to raise the exemption level of "small issues" in the issuance of revenue bonds and (2) change tax legislation to liberalize depreciation allowances to encourage financing from retained earnings.

Energy

The Commission, state energy offices and utility companies must work together to build a consensus on the real long-term energy options and needs of New England. Improvements in energy forecasting and the planning of a realistic fuel mix, consistent with the best interests of the Region, are critical to the development of that consensus.

To insure reliability of energy supply for a region disproportionately dependent on foreign oil, the Commission should take a lead in contingency planning and in demanding a strategic petroleum reserve to serve the Region. The

Federal government should also move more forcefully toward the solution of the nuclear waste disposal issue. New England is more dependent on nuclear power than the Nation and the lack of adequate disposal solutions jeopardizes current and projected facility operations.

The deregulation of oil prices will increase income from depletion taxes in energy producing states, exacerbating the differences between energy producing and energy consuming regions by impacting on state and local taxes. The New England states not only pay more for energy, but also pay more in taxes which affects the competitive location of industrial expansion. The Federal government must address this discrepancy to prevent a serious imbalance in economic growth among regions.

A regional energy strategy must include concerted efforts at promoting conservation and alternative energy development. The outmigration of capital to other regions and the concern over supply interruptions can be mitigated through better use of resources within New England.

Transportation

Although the deregulation of the transportation industry has achieved many benefits on the national level, the impact on in-region transportation may be negative, as already demonstrated in the decline in small community air service. Deregulation plus increases in fuel costs will augment the Region's locational disadvantages unless the Commission, the states and the transportation carriers work together to maintain and improve service. The Commission should continue to monitor impacts of air deregulation and the potential impact of rail and truck deregulation. Transportation is of particular concern to target rural communities where both passenger and goods movement are dis-

proportionately impacted by increasing fuel costs and decline in service. State government should be in the forefront in designing innovative approaches to rural transportation needs.

Infrastructure

New England must invest in the upgrading and retrofitting of its capital stock and federal infrastructure programs must be redesigned to reflect this need. The reuse of abandoned mill buildings, the upgrading of deteriorated sewer lines and the replacement of old bridges should receive equal attention with new investments.

Regional targeting strategies should be reflected in state and federal infrastructure investments. In the decision making process regarding the expenditure of scarce public resources, special attention should be given to job creation projects in areas of distress.

Hazardous Waste

In the development of a region-wide network for the safe, efficient treatment of industrial waste to comply with the Resource Conservation and Recovery Act, the Commission should continue its collaboration among government, industry and the general public to promote environmentally sound hazardous waste management.

Export Promotion

Because of its leadership in high technology and specialized products and services, New England has a special advantage in generating jobs and income through selling abroad. Dependent on imported fuel from abroad and on food-stuffs from outside the Region, New England needs to realize more fully its potential in exporting to foreign markets. The Commission and the States need to increase attention to export development through export information services, promoting trade shows and working with regional trade associations on trade shows and other international marketing efforts.

Ports and Airport Development

Currently the preponderance of New England exports are shipped through other regions. To take better advantage of the jobs and income potential from exports, the Region's leaders should act collaboratively to insure the adequacy of international port and airport facility development.

Targeting

Special attention should be directed to populations of geographic areas that do not share naturally in the benefits of the Region's development. Ensuring that this attention is forthcoming is one of the most important responsibilities of those charged with making and implementing public policy.

The preceding strategies represent a summary of the priority issues which have emerged from the planning process and suggest the appropriate actors for the implementation of these strategies. These issues should become the framework for interstate cooperation over the next five years. These issues and the planning process have also generated a series of specific federal policy and legislative issues. The following is an identification of Regional priorities for Federal action in 1981.

Regional Priorities For Federal Action
Labor

- The Comprehensive Employment and Training Act should be reauthorized in 1982 with the following changes:

-Expansion of private sector involvement in skills training activities.

-Targeting of funding to on-the-job and skills training to meet the needs of growing occupations.

-Expansion of the 112 Discretionary Program to allow for the introduction of experimental programs that better fit labor market needs and coordinate with occupational education programs.

Capital and Small Business
- Specific changes in federal tax legislation are needed in order to make capital available for economic expansion with special attention to small firms, start-ups and growing high technology ventures.

-The Securities and Exchange Act of 1933 should be amended so as to raise the exemption level on bond issues.

-Depreciation allowances should be liberalized, corporate income tax schedules should be lowered, and capital gains roll-over provisions should be enacted to encourage investment from retained earnings.

-Legislation like the Public Works and Economic Development Act amended to include a development financing program should be passed and implemented in such a way as to facilitate growth of target industries and distressed communities in the New England Region.

-Proposed modifications of federal tax legislation should not eliminate tax exempt industrial revenue bonds.

Innovation and Technology
- Congress should legislate increased federal

expenditures for research and development, directed to both public and private research.

- Congress should appropriate funding equal to the full level authorized in the Stevenson-Wydler Act to establish centers for industrial technology affiliated with universities and other non-profit organizations.

Export Trade
- Upcoming changes in federal legislation, agreements and rulings in the area of export trade should take a form that benefits the industrial and geographic configuration of the New England Region. Specifically:

-Export Promotion-The Stevenson Export Trading Company legislation should be passed and implemented on a regional basis.

-Multinational Trade Negotiation Agreements should be sensitive to both the Region's growth and declining industries.

-Civil Aeronautics Board Rulings should promote expansion of international service to New England airports.

Infrastructure
- New legislative initiatives should provide for federal financial assistance for rehabilitating and maintaining older systems comparable to that provided for constructing new systems.

- Federal tax depreciation allowances on the cost of improvements should be liberalized to encourage renovation and re-use of existing structures.

- Federal legislation on tax exempt bond issues for housing should allow for state targeting to reasonable housing market needs.

Appendixes

Bibliography

Bibliography

APTER I

eau of the Census, U. S. Department of Commerce. (Source of data on
0 and preliminary 1980 population and on median incomes).

eau of Economic Analysis, Regional Economic Measurement Division,
S. Department of Commerce. (Source of aggregate and industry-specific
a on employment, income and population for the U. S., New England,
individual states).

eau of Labor Statistics, U. S. Department of Labor. (Source of
mployment rates and data on women and minority populations).

obs, Jane, The Economy of Cities, Random House, New York, 1969.

zies, Ian, interpreting Robert A. Leone, The Boston Globe, Globe
spaper Co., Boston, MA, March 19, 1979.

ional Development Plan 1976, New England Regional Commission.

PTER II

eau of the Census, Demographic Division, U. S. Department of Commerce.
urce of data on 1970 and preliminary 1980 population and on median
omes).

eau of the Census, Economic Division, U. S. Department of Commerce.
urce of Census of Agriculture data).

eau of Economic Analysis, Regional Economic Measurement Division,
S. Department of Commerce. (Source of aggregate and industry-specific
a on employment, income and population for the U. S., New England and
ividual states).

eau of Labor Statistics, U. S. Department of Labor. (Source of unem-
yment rates and data on women and minority populations).

eral Reserve Bank of Boston. (Source of data on gross state product
gross regional product by industry).

S. National Marine Fisheries Service Bureau

S. Travel Data Center. (Source of information on the importance of
rism to New England).

ner, Ralph R., "Revising Our Development Strategies: A Challenge for
80's", CUED Commentary, January 1980.

PTER III

eau of the Census, Demographic Division, U. S. Department of Commerce.
urce of data used to calculate population density by county).

eau of the Census, Economic Division, U. S. Department of Commerce.
74, 1978 Census of Agriculture).

eau of Economic Analysis, Regional Economic Measurement Division,
S. Department of Commerce. (Source of county data on employment).

hing and Petroleum Interactions on Georges Bank, Volume II, Parts A and
prepared for the New England Regional Commission by the Capital Resources
ter, Graduate School of Oceanography, University of Rhode Island, 1976.

ional Marine Fisheries Bureau.

The Nation's Water Resources 1975 - 2000, Volume 4, New England Region,
U. S. Water Resources Council, 1975.

Pierce, Neil, The New England States, W. W. Norton & Company, Inc., New
York, NY, 1976.

Reidel, Carl, The Yankee Forest: A Prospectus, Yale School of Forestry
and Environment Studies Fifth Forest Project, 1975.

U. S. Forest Service, U. S. Department of Agriculture.

CHAPTER IV

An Assessment of CETA, Third Annual Report, National Commission for
Manpower Policy, May 1978.

Annual Plan for Vocational-Technical Education in New Hampshire, State
Department of Education, Volcational-Technical Division, 1981.

Annual Planning Information Fiscal Year 1981, Connecticut Labor Department,
Employment Security Division.

Bureau of the Census, U. S. Department of Commerce. (Source of educational
attainment data from 1976 Population Estimates, Series P25).

Bureau of Labor Statistics, U. S. Department of Labor. (Source of wage
data).

Directory of National Unions and Employee Associations, Bureau of Labor
Statistics, U. S. Department of Labor, September, 1980.

Employment and Training Report of the President 1980, Manpower Administration,
U. S. Department of Labor.

Employment and Unemployment During 1979: An Analysis, Bureau of Labor
Statistics, U. S. Department of Labor.

Geographic Profile of Employment: States, 1979, Bureau of Labor Statistics,
U. S. Department of Labor.

Massachusetts Annual Program Plan for Vocational Education, State Department
of Education, June 1, 1979.

Neglected Resource - The Use of Employment and Training Programs in Economic
Development Strategies, Northeast-Midwest Institute, September, 1979.

Osterman, Paul, The Politics and Economics of CETA Youth Programs, Department of Economics, Boston University, January, 1980.

Report of the Task Force on Capital and Labor Markets, New England Regional
Commission, November, 1975.

Schumacher, E. F., Small is Beautiful: Economics as if People Mattered,
Harper Torchbooks, Harper & Row, New York, 1973.

State of Maine Annual Plan for Vocational Education 1981, Maine Department
of Educational and cultural services.

The Unfulfilled Promise of Postsecondary Vocational Education: Graduates
and Dropouts in the Labor Market, Willford W. Wilms Graduate School of
Education, University of California and Stephen Hansell Center for Social
Organization of Schools, Johns Hopkins University, October 28, 1980.

Work Stoppages, Bureau of Labor Statistics, U. S. Department of Labor.

CHAPTER V

Adams, Russell B. Jr., The Boston Money Tree, Thomas Y. Crowell Company,
New York, 1977.

American Council of Life Insurance.

Bureau of Economic Analysis, Regional Economic Measurement Division, U. S.
Department of Commerce.

Federal Deposit Insurance Corporation Annual Reports.

Hovey, Harold A., Development Financing for Distressed Areas, Northeast-
Midwest Institute, 1979.

Katzman, Martin T. And Daniels, Belden H., Development Incentives to Induce
Efficiencies in Capital Markets, prepared for the New England Regional
Commission and the International Center of New England, Inc., 1976.

Kelley, Paul and Erlichman, Howard, Capital: the Real Problem of Small
Business, Massachusetts Technology Development Council, 1979.

Seymour, Craig and Wetzel, William E., Jr., An Economic Strategy for New
England - the Role of Informal Equity Capital, University of New Hampshire,
1979.

Verification of Capital Gaps in New England 1976, prepared by T. A.
Associates for the New England Regional Commission.

Von Hausen, Michael and Plofker, Steven D., Sources of Capital for Community
Economic Development in Rural Massachusetts, Harvard University, 1980.

Wetzel, William E., Jr., The Cost and Availability of Credit and Risk
Capital in New England, University of New Hampshire, 1979.

Wetzel, William E., Jr., Risk Capital Research, University of New Hampshire,
1980.

CHAPTER VI

Birch, David, The Job Generation Process, Massachusetts Institute of Technology, Cambridge, MA.

Birch, David, The Role of Small Business in New England, MIT Program on
Neighborgood Regional Change, 1979.

Bureau of Economic Analysis, Regional Economic Measurement Division,
U. S. Department of Commerce.

Dun Bradstreet data, Dun's Marketing Service, 1980.

Geographic Distribution of Federal Funds (Each New England State), Fiscal
1979, compiled for the Executive Office of the President by the Community
Services Administration, published by NTIS.

Hekman, John S., "The Future of High Technology Industry in New England:
A Case Study of Computers", New England Economic Review, Federal Reserve
Bank of Boston, January/February, 1980.

National Science Foundation

Reports on the White House Conference on Small Business, Executive Office
of the President, 1979.

Schmenner, Roger W., The Manufacturing Location Decision: Evidence from Cincinnati and New England, Economic Development Research Report, Harvard Business School and the Harvard-MIT Joint Center for Urban Studies, March, 1978.

Small Business and Innovation, Report of the Small Business Administrative Office of Advocacy Task Force, 1979.

U. S. Department of Defense.

Wetzel, William E., Jr., Risk Capital Research, University of New Hampshire, 1980.

CHAPTER VII

Arthur D. Little Company, Cambridge, MA.

Boyan, Douglas R. (editor), Foreign Students in Institutions of Higher Education, Open Doors Report 1978-79, Institute of International Education, New York.

Compendium of Hearings Concerning the Small Business Export Expansion Act of 1979, compiled by the Select Small Business Committee, U. S. Senate, March, 1980.

Fisheries in the U. S. 1979, National Oceanic and Atmospheric Administration, U. S. Department of Commerce.

"Foreign Investment in the United States", Survey of Current Business, Bureau of Economic Analysis, U. S. Department of Commerce, September, 1980.

Highlights of U. S. Export and Import Trade, Bureau of the Census, U. S. Department of Commerce, 1976.

National Maritime Administration.

Origins of Exports of Manufacturing Establishments, Bureau of the Census, Annual Survey of Manufactures, 1976.

A Regional Analysis of International Travel to the United States, U. S. Travel Service, U. S. Department of Commerce, 1979.

State Export Series, States Reports, Office of International Economic Research, Industry and Trade Division, U. S. Department of Commerce, 1976.

CHAPTER VIII

Analysis of Energy Use in the Manufacturing Sector of New England, New England Regional Commission, Energy Program Report 79-1, March, 1979.

A Blueprint for Energy Action, Final Report of the New England Energy Congress, May, 1979.

"New England Energy Situation at a Glance", fact sheet prepared by the New England Regional Commission Energy Program, November 29, 1979.

State Energy Data Report, U. S. Department of Energy, Energy Information Administration, Report No. DOE/EIA-0214 (78).

Stobaugh, Robert and Yergin, Daniel, editors, Energy Future, Report of the Energy Project at the Harvard Business School, Random House, New York, 1979.

Why Wood? An Introduction to the Industrial Use of Wood Fuel, New England Regional Commission, Energy Program Report 79-8, November, 1979.

CHAPTER IX

Civil Aeronautics Board data obtained through NEMTRIC data system of the New England Regional Commission.

Dodge, Marshall, "Which Way to Vassalboro?", Bert and I and Other Stories from Down East.

Maio, Dominic J., Freight Transportation Petroleum Conservation Opportunities - Viability Evaluation, U. S. Department of Transportation Research and Special Programs Administration, Transportation Systems Center, March, 1979.

National Energy Transportation Study, A Preliminary Report to the President by the Secretary of Transportation and the Secretary of Energy, July, 1980.

The New England Rail Study, U. S. Railway Association and New England Regional Commission, March, 1980.

U. S. Army Corps of Engineers.

U. S. Maritime Administration.

CHAPTER X

Additional Federal Aid for Urban Water Distribution Systems Shoud Wait Until Needs Are Clearly Established, U. S. General Accounting Office, Comptroller General Report to The Congress, CED-81-17, November 24, 1980.

America's Urban Capital Stock, prepared by the Urban Institute for the U. S. Department of Housing and Urban Development. Final Report expected June, 1981.

Bureau of the Census, Demographic Division, U. S. Department of Commerce. (Source of preliminary 1980 population data).

Bureau of Labor Statistics, U. S. Department of Labor. (Source of consumer price index).

Connecticut Department of Health, Environmental Health Services Division, Hartford, CT September, 1976.

The Economic Impact Analysis on the Hazardous Waste Management Regulation published May 19, 1980. U. S. Environmental Protection Agency.

An Economic Impact of Hazardous Waste Regulations on New England, June 6, 1978. New England Regional Commission.

Environmental Quality: The Tenth Annual Report of the Council on Environmental Quality, December, 1979. U. S. Government Printing Office #041-011-00047-5.

Franklin County Water Quality Management Plan, Mass. Department of Environmental Quality Engineering, 208 Program, 1980.

Inventory of Federal Assistance Programs for Urban Water Supply Systems, U. S. Water Resources Council, Washington, D. C. January 15, 1980.

Jacobs, Jane, The Death and Life of Great American Cities, Random House, Inc., New York, 1961.

National Interim Primary Drinking Water Regulations, U. S. Environmental Protection Agency Office of Water Supply, EPA 570-9-76-003 Fed. Reg. (6-24-77, 7-9-76, 11-29-79, 3-11-80, 8-27-80)

National Rural Community Facilities Assessment Study: Pilot Phase Final Report, undertaken by Abt. Associates for the U. S. Farmers Home Administration, March 1, 1980.

The Nation's Water Outlook to the Year 2000, Congressional Research Services, Library of Congress, Report No. 78-26 ENR, January, 1978.

1978 Needs Survey Costs Estimate for Construction of Publicly Owned Wastewater Treatment Facilities. U. S. Environmental Protection Agency Office of Water Program Operations, Washington, D. C., Publication #FRD-1, February 10, 1979.

The Northeast Water Resources Project (V. I, II, III) Prepared by the Nova Institute for the Consortium of Northeast Organizations, September, 1979.

Parallel Goals: Clean Air and Economic Development -- Exploring New Strategies for Urban Areas, prepared by the National League of Cities and the National Association of Counties for the U. S. Environmental Protection Agency, March, 1980.

Peterson, George E., The Urban Institute, Washington, D. C.

A Plan for the Development of Hazardous Waste Management Facilities in the New England Region, (Volumes I and II) Prepared for the New England Regional Commission by Arthur D. Little, Inc. September, 1979.

Public Water Supply Inventory, Environmental Protection Agency, Region I, Water Supply Branch, Boston, 1980.

Regional Administrator's Annual Report - Environmental Quality in New England, U. S. Environmental Protection Agency -- Region I, December, 1979.

Report of the Special Commission Relative to Determining the Adequacy of Water Supply in the Commonwealth, The Commonwealth of Massachusetts, House Bill No. 5596, January, 1979.

Safe Drinking Water for Connecticut: Report on Economic Impact Analys and Possible Forms of Financial Assistance, by the Office of Policy an Management Comprehensive Planning Division, Hartford, Connecticut, Mar 1979.

A Study of Public Works Investment in the United States, prepared by Consad Research Corporation for the U. S. Department of Commerce, Apri 1980.

Urban Water Systems: Problems and Alternative Approaches to Solutions The President's Intergovernmental Water Policy Task Force Subcommittee Urban Water Supply, June, 1980.

Water Purification Plants Needed - Surface Supplies, Memo from George Coogan, former Director, Water Supply Division, Mass. Department of E mental Quality Engineering, to Hon. Thomas W. McGee. Background to Ho Bill No. 5073, April 18, 1978.

Water Resources Planning, Management, and Development: What Are the Nation's Water Supply Problems and Issues, U. S. General Accounting Office, Community and Economic Development Division, Washington, D. C. GED-77-100, July 28, 1977.

CHAPTER XI

Bureau of Economic Analysis, Regional Measurement Division, U. S. Depa of Commerce.

Bureau of the Census, Demographic Division, U. S. Department of Commer (Source of data on poverty, minorities and women).

Bureau of Labor Statistics, U. S. Department of Labor. (Source of dat on unemployment and wages).

Business Perspectives on Urban Issues, Connecticut Business and Indust Association, 1980.

Central Massachusetts Regional Planning Commission (Worcester).

Connecticut Office of Planning and Management.

Dearborn, Philip M., The Financial Health of Major U. S. Cities in 19 The Urban Institute, Washington, D. C.

Economic Development Administration, U. S. Department of Commerce.

Economic Development in New England - Targeting for Distressed Urban Areas, Conference Report for the New England Regional Commission, Har MIT Joint Center for Urban Studies, 1980.

Hamnock, John C. and Dodd, Gerard, Microbusiness and Employment in Ce Maine: A Summary, Accion International, Cambridge, MA 1979.

Kennedy, John F., Speech, February 2, 1961.

Lower Pioneer Valley Regional Planning Commission (Springfield, MA).

Maine State Planning Office.

Metropolitan Area Planning Council (Boston, MA).

Microbusiness and Local Development, presented to the Office of Techr Assessment, U. S. Congress by Accion International, Cambridge, MA, 19

New Hampshire Office of State Planning.

Old Colony Planning Council (Brockton, MA).

A Regional Development Strategy for New England: Special Concerns o Rural Communities, workshop sponsored by the New England Regional Com at the New England Municipal Center, July, 1980.

State Departments of Employment Security (Individual New England sta

Vaughn, Roger J., A Local Economic Development Strategy, Citibank, N. New York, 1980.

Vermont Office of State Planning.

Appendixes

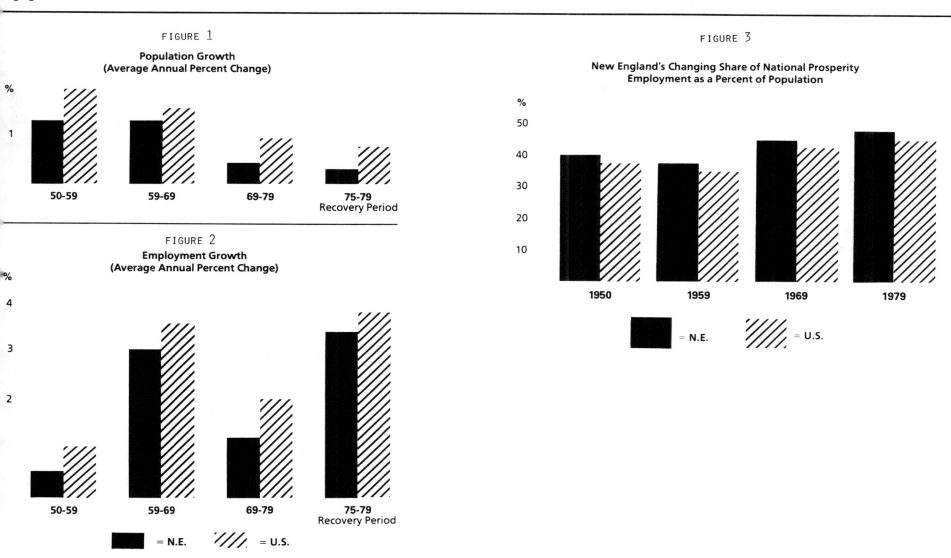

FIGURE 1

Population Growth
(Average Annual Percent Change)

%

1

50-59   59-69   69-79   75-79
Recovery Period

FIGURE 2

Employment Growth
(Average Annual Percent Change)

%

4

3

2

50-59   59-69   69-79   75-79
Recovery Period

■ = N.E.   ///// = U.S.

FIGURE 3

New England's Changing Share of National Prosperity
Employment as a Percent of Population

%

50

40

30

20

10

1950   1959   1969   1979

■ = N.E.   ///// = U.S.

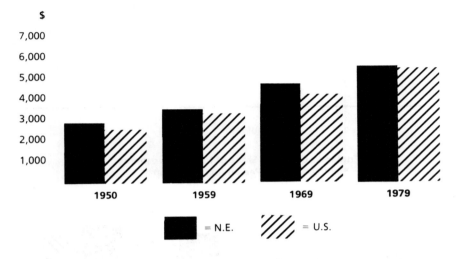

FIGURE 4

Real per Capita Income (1972 Dollars)

$

7,000

6,000

5,000

4,000

3,000

2,000

1,000

1950   1959   1969   1979

■ = N.E.   ▨ = U.S.

FIGURE 5

**Unemployment Rates: New England and the United States
1970-1979 Annual Averages
(Percent)**

10
9
8
7
6
5
4
3
2
1

1970 1971 1972 1973 1974 1975 1976 1977 1978 1979

1980
Seasonally Adjusted

Jan Feb Mar Apr May June

——— New England   - - - U.S.

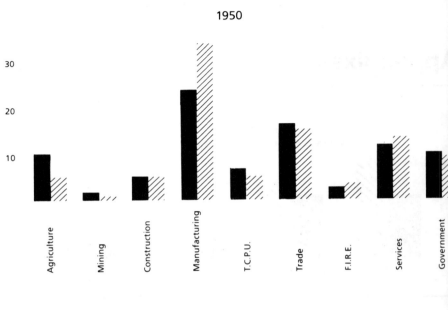

FIGURE 6

The Changing Industrial Structure of the N.E. Region and the Nation

Shares of Area Totals 1950 and 1979 (% of area totals)

1950

30

20

10

Agriculture Mining Construction Manufacturing T.C.P.U. Trade F.I.R.E. Services Government

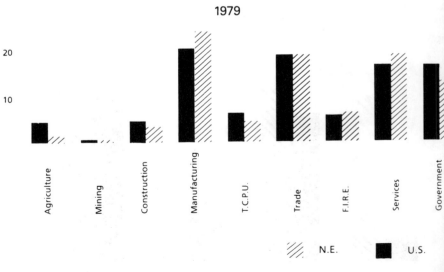

1979

20

10

Agriculture Mining Construction Manufacturing T.C.P.U. Trade F.I.R.E. Services Government

▨ N.E.   ■ U.S.

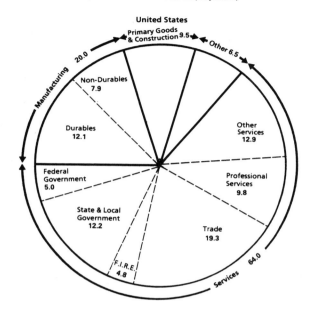

FIGURE 7

1979
Industrial Mix
New England and the United States
(Percent of Total Area Employment)

United States

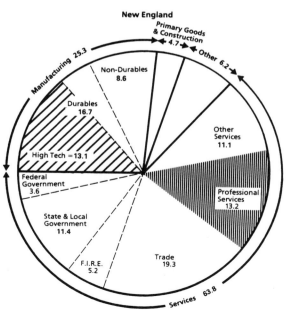

New England

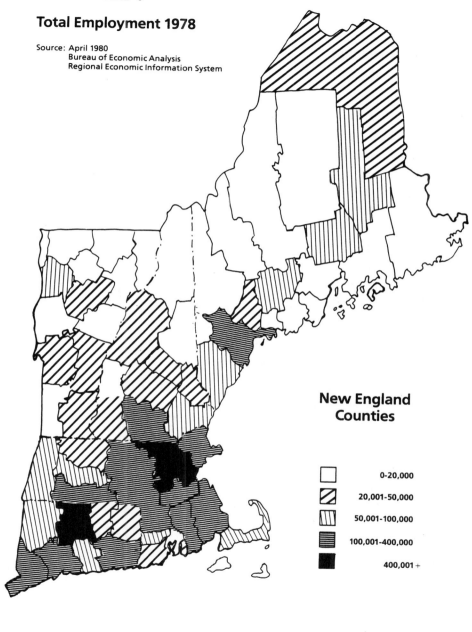

FIGURE 8

Total Employment 1978

Source: April 1980
    Bureau of Economic Analysis
    Regional Economic Information System

New England Counties

☐	0-20,000
▨	20,001-50,000
▥	50,001-100,000
▤	100,001-400,000
■	400,001 +

FIGURE 9

U.S. WATER RESOURCES COUNCIL

NEW ENGLAND REGION

- ⬤ Urban
- Cropland
- Forest/Cropland
- Forest

N

SCALE 1:3,900,000

0   50   100 MILES

75°   70°

45°   45°

101

MAINE

Houlton

Plattsburgh

106

Johnsbury

Littleton

Barre

Montpelier

VERMONT

Bangor

Augusta

Brunswick

Portland

Lebanon

Glens Falls

Springfield

Franklin

Concord

102

Portsmouth

Saratoga Springs

Manchester

NEW HAMPSHIRE

Brattleboro

Albany

105

Lawrence

ATLANTIC OCEAN

MASS

Worcester

Boston

Springfield

103

Hartford

104

Taunton

Providence

New Bedford

100

R I

CONN

New London

Newport

New Haven

Stamford

Hudson River

Yonkers

NEW YORK

70°

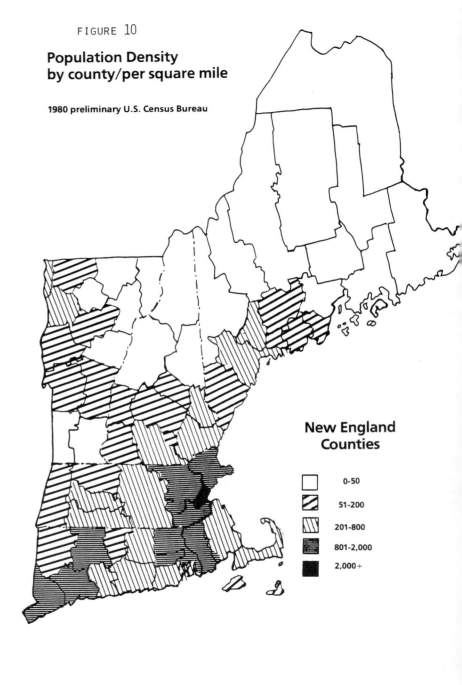

FIGURE 10

Population Density
by county/per square mile

1980 preliminary U.S. Census Bureau

New England
Counties

- ☐ 0-50
- ▨ 51-200
- ▨ 201-800
- ▦ 801-2,000
- ■ 2,000+

110

FIGURE 11

State Public Works Investments by Region
(Per Capita Percent of U.S. Average Constant 1972 Dollars)

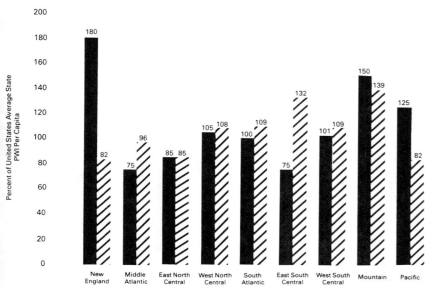

1957 1977

Source: *"A STUDY OF PUBLIC WORKS INVESTMENT IN THE UNITED STATES,"*
U.S. DEPARTMENT OF COMMERCE/CONSAD RESEARCH CORP., APRIL 1980

FIGURE 12

Management of Hazardous Waste In New England

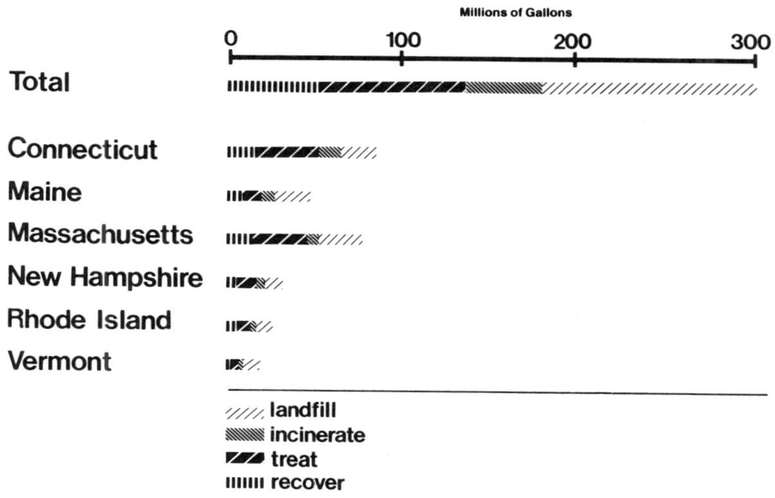

Millions of Gallons

	0	100	200	300

Total

Connecticut

Maine

Massachusetts

New Hampshire

Rhode Island

Vermont

///// landfill
incinerate
treat
recover

111

FIGURE 13

1978
Total Energy Consumption By Source
United States and New England — % of Total

United States

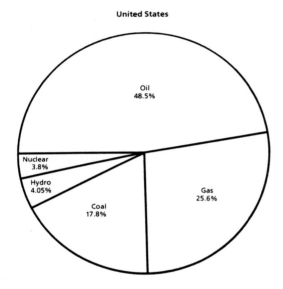

Oil
48.5%

Nuclear
3.8%

Hydro
4.05%

Coal
17.8%

Gas
25.6%

New England

Oil
79%

Gas — 8.3%

Hydro — 2.51%

Nuclear — 9.4%

Coal — 0.7%

FIGURE 14

1978
Total Energy Consumption for Residential Sector by Source
United States and New England —%of Total

United States

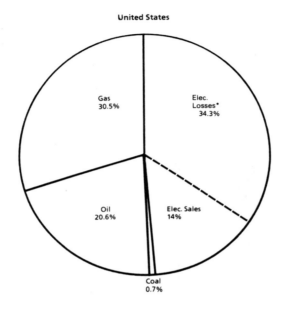

Gas
30.5%

Elec.
Losses*
34.3%

Oil
20.6%

Elec. Sales
14%

Coal
0.7%

New England

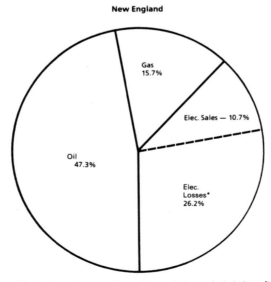

Gas
15.7%

Elec. Sales — 10.7%

Oil
47.3%

Elec.
Losses*
26.2%

*Energy losses in generation and transmission are included to reflec
total energy consumed for electric generation.

FIGURE 15

1978
Total Energy Consumption for Industries by Source
United States and New England —%of Total

United States

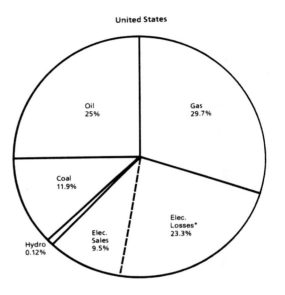

Oil
25%

Gas
29.7%

Coal
11.9%

Hydro
0.12%

Elec.
Sales
9.5%

Elec.
Losses*
23.3%

New England

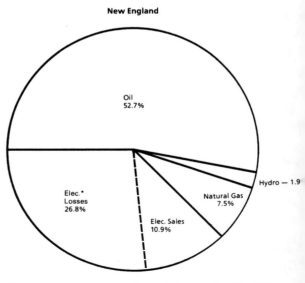

Oil
52.7%

Hydro — 1.9

Elec.*
Losses
26.8%

Natural Gas
7.5%

Elec. Sales
10.9%

*Energy losses in generation and transmission are included to reflect
total energy consumed for electric generation.

112

FIGURE 16

1978
Total Energy Consumption for Commercial Sector by Source
United States and New England — % of Total

United States

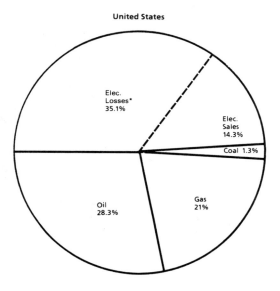

New England

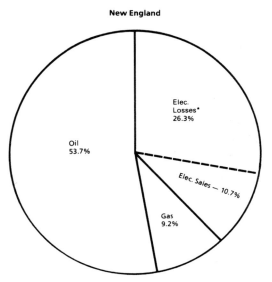

*Energy losses in generation and transmission are included to reflect total energy consumed for electric generation.

FIGURE 17

1978
Fuel Sources for Electric Power
United States and New England — % of Total

United States

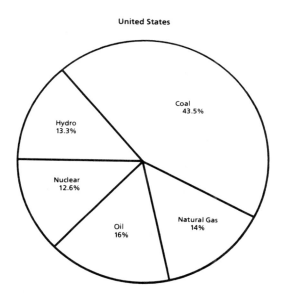

New England

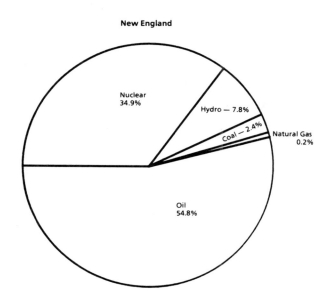

113

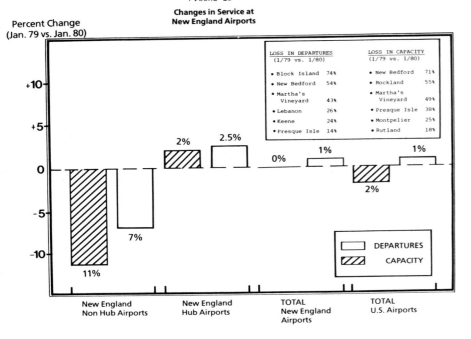

FIGURE 18

Changes in Service at New England Airports

Percent Change (Jan. 79 vs. Jan. 80)

LOSS IN DEPARTURES (1/79 vs. 1/80)		LOSS IN CAPACITY (1/79 vs. 1/80)	
• Block Island	74%	• New Bedford	71%
• New Bedford	54%	• Rockland	55%
• Martha's Vineyard	43%	• Martha's Vineyard	49%
• Lebanon	26%	• Presque Isle	38%
• Keene	24%	• Montpelier	25%
• Presque Isle	14%	• Rutland	18%

□ DEPARTURES
▨ CAPACITY

New England Non Hub Airports · New England Hub Airports · TOTAL New England Airports · TOTAL U.S. Airports

FIGURE 19

Major New England Ports

	Main Channel Depth (in feet)	Dry and Liquid Bulk Terminals	General Cargo Terminals	Number of Petroleum Storage Tanks	Capacity of Petroleum Storage in 1,000's of lbbls. Petroleum	Percentage of Total Cargo Tonnage*	Major Non-Petroleum Cargoes Handled**
SEARSPORT	35	3	1	14	1,454	83	salt, potatoes, chemical products, newsprint
PORTLAND	40	10	1	136	8,898	99	fish and shellfish, woodpulp, fresh and frozen vegetables
PORTSMOUTH	35	11	1	37	1,683	88	salt, limestone, scrap metal, steel cable
BOSTON	40	33	3	387	17,534	73	general cargo, sugar, salt, limestone, lumber, motor vehicles, liquefied natural gas
NEW BEDFORD	30	2	1	14	1,450	63	fresh fish, lumber
FALL RIVER	35	10	1	112	6,054	98	crude rubber/allied gums, coal
NARRAGANSETT BAY, RI	40	15	2	467	11,931	83	cement, scrap metal, lumber, liquefied natural gas
NEW LONDON	36	13	1	38	1,640	88	molasses, woodpulp, sulphuric acid, chemicals
NEW HAVEN	35	19	1	914	10,045	91	chemicals, cement, scrap metal, steel products, seafood
BRIDGEPORT	35	12	1	54	2,599	82	steel products, scrap metal, paper products

Sources: U.S. Army Corps of Engineers Port Series No. 1 (Rev. 1976) Port Series No. 4 (Rev. 1976) Port Series No. 3 (Rev. 1979) Waterborne Commerce of the United States, 1977

* Does not include liquefied gases
** Relative to each port

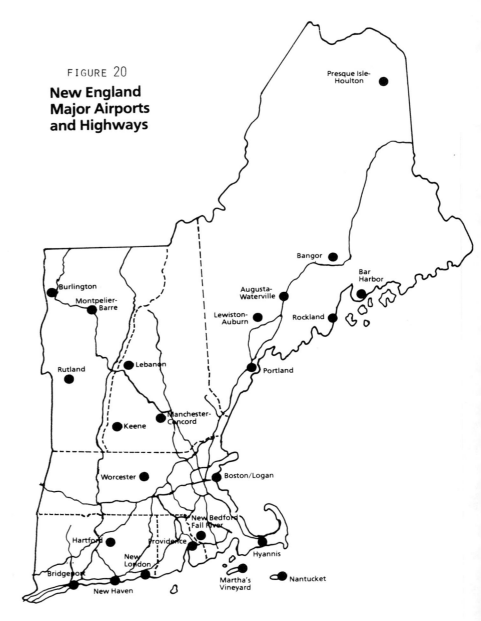

FIGURE 20

New England Major Airports and Highways

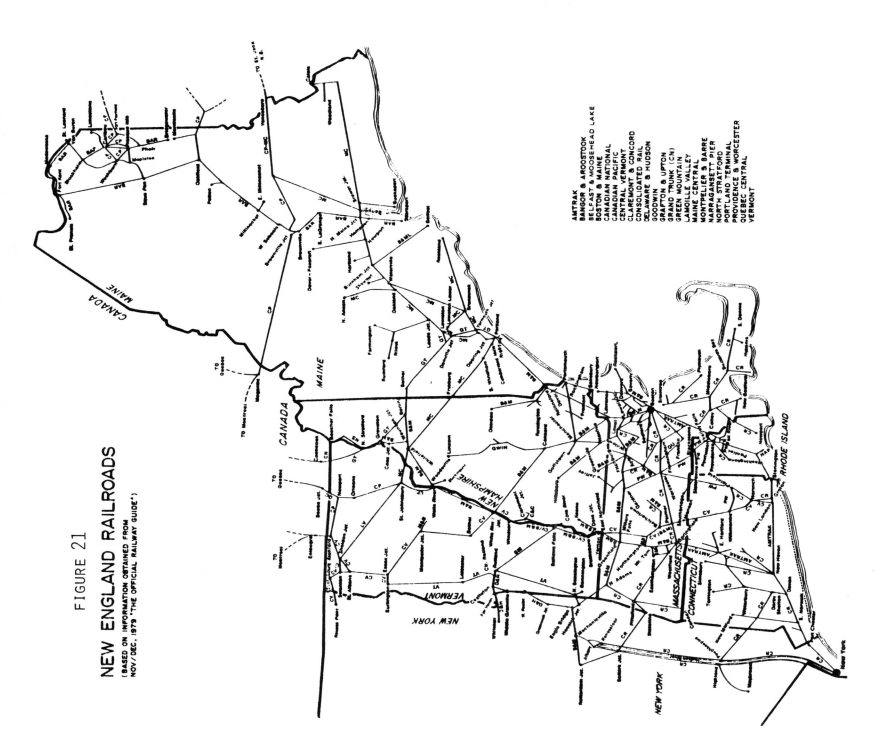

FIGURE 21

NEW ENGLAND RAILROADS

(BASED ON INFORMATION OBTAINED FROM
NOV./DEC. 1979 "THE OFFICIAL RAILWAY GUIDE".)

AMTRAK
BANGOR & AROOSTOOK
BELFAST & MOOSEHEAD LAKE
BOSTON & MAINE
CANADIAN NATIONAL
CANADIAN PACIFIC
CENTRAL VERMONT
CLAREMONT & CONCORD
CONSOLIDATED RAIL
DELAWARE & HUDSON
GOODWIN
GRAFTON & UPTON
GRAND TRUNK (CN)
GREEN MOUNTAIN
LAMOILLE VALLEY
MAINE CENTRAL
MONTPELIER & BARRE
NARRAGANSETT PIER
NORTH STRATFORD
PORTLAND TERMINAL
PROVIDENCE & WORCESTER
QUEBEC CENTRAL
VERMONT

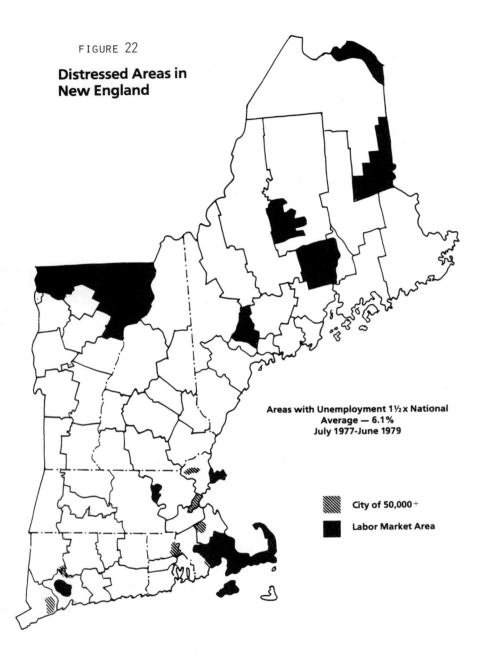

FIGURE 22

Distressed Areas in New England

Areas with Unemployment 1½ x National
Average — 6.1%
July 1977-June 1979

░░ City of 50,000+

■ Labor Market Area

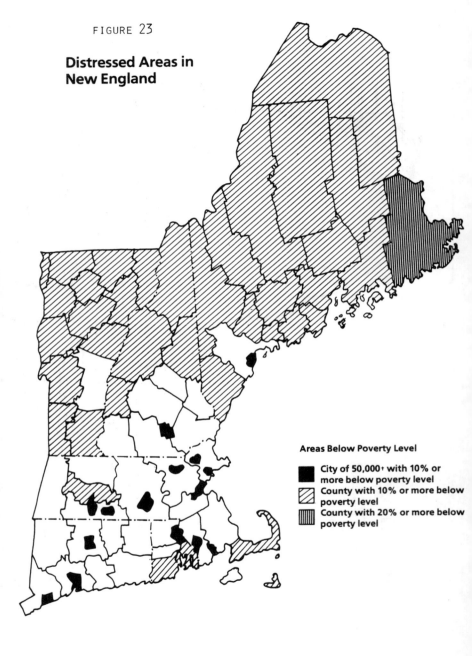

FIGURE 23

Distressed Areas in New England

Areas Below Poverty Level

■ City of 50,000+ with 10% or
more below poverty level

▨ County with 10% or more below
poverty level

▦ County with 20% or more below
poverty level

TABLE 1

POPULATION IN NEW ENGLAND
1970 AND 1980
(NUMBER OF PERSONS)

	1970	1980*	AVERAGE ANNUAL PERCENT CHANGE 1970-1980
MASSACHUSETTS	5,689,170	5,725,985	0.1%
CONNECTICUT	3,032,217	3,096,951	0.2
MAINE	993,722	1,123,560	1.3
RHODE ISLAND	949,723	945,761	-.04
NEW HAMPSHIRE	737,681	918,959	2.5
VERMONT	444,732	510,711	1.5
NEW ENGLAND	11,847,245	12,321,927	0.4

SOURCE: U.S. DEPARTMENT OF COMMERCE, DEPARTMENT OF THE CENSUS

*April 1, 1980 PRELIMINARY DATA

TABLE 2

THE NEW ENGLAND ECONOMY IN NATIONAL PERSPECTIVE
ECONOMIC EXPANSION 1950-1979
(average annual percent changes)

	New England	United States	difference (percentage points)
Employment Growth			
1950-1959	0.5	1.1	-0.6
1959-1969	3.0	3.5	-0.5
1969-1979	1.5	2.1	-0.6
1975-1979	3.2	3.4	-0.2
Population Growth			
1950-1959	1.3	1.9	-0.6
1959-1969	1.2	1.4	-0.2
1969-1979	0.5	0.9	-0.4
1975-1979	0.2	0.8	-0.6
Personal Income Growth			
1950-1959	7.2	7.6	-0.4
1959-1969	9.1	9.4	-0.3
1969-1979	13.4	16.2	-2.8
1975-1979	12.3	13.7	-1.4
Per Capita Real Personal Income Growth			
1950-1959	1.9	1.6	0.3
1959-1969	3.3	3.5	-0.2
1969-1979	1.7	2.4	-0.7
1975-1979	3.4	3.7	-0.3

TABLE 4

NEW ENGLAND'S CHANGING SHARE OF NATIONAL PROSPERITY
A PERSISTENT REGIONAL EDGE ON A PER CAPITA BASIS

	Employment as a Percent of Population			Per Capita Personal Income (dollars)		
	New England	U.S.	(percentage points)	New England	U.S.	ratio (N.E./U.S.)
1950	41.4%	38.7%	2.7	$1,598	$1,496	1.07
1959	38.8	36.2	2.6	2,346	2,145	1.09
1962	38.8	35.6	3.2	2,608	2,353	1.11
1967	43.9	42.0	1.9	3,440	3,142	1.09
1969	44.7	43.2	1.5	3,994	3,667	1.09
1970	44.0	42.6	1.4	4,245	3,893	1.09
1973	44.6	44.0	0.6	5,167	4,981	1.04
1974	45.0	44.4	0.6	5,635	5,428	1.04
1975	43.4	43.3	0.1	6,026	5,861	1.03
1976	44.3	44.1	0.2	6,559	6,401	1.02
1977	45.7	45.4	0.3	7,163	7,043	1.02
1978	47.5	46.9	0.6	7,956	7,854	1.01
1979	49.0	47.9	1.1	8,910	8,733	1.02

TABLE 3

UNEMPLOYMENT RATES
NEW ENGLAND AND THE UNITED STATES: 1970-1979
Annual Averages
(percent)

	U.S.	NEW ENGLAND	MASSACHUSETTS	CONNECTICUT	MAINE	RHODE ISLAND	NEW HAMPSHIRE	VERMONT
1970	4.9	4.9	4.6	5.7	5.5	4.1	3.8	4.5
1971	5.9	6.9	6.6	8.4	7.4	5.4	5.1	6.3
1972	5.6	6.8	6.4	8.6	6.8	5.1	4.8	6.0
1973	4.9	6.1	6.7	6.3	5.8	4.8	4.4	5.3
1974	5.6	6.6	7.2	6.1	6.5	5.5	5.5	6.4
1975	8.5	10.4	11.2	9.1	10.3	11.2	9.0	9.4
1976	7.7	9.1	9.5	9.5	8.9	8.1	6.4	8.7
1977	7.0	7.7	8.1	7.0	8.4	8.6	5.9	7.0
1978	6.0	5.7	6.1	5.2	6.1	6.6	3.8	5.7
1979	5.8	5.4	5.5	5.1	7.2	6.6	3.1	5.1

TABLE 5

THE NEW ENGLAND REGION'S CHANGING INDUSTRIAL STRUCTURE

1950-1979

Industry Employment Shares of New England Totals
(percent)

Industry	1950	1959	1969	1975	1979
Agriculture, Forestry, Fishery*	4.6	2.5	1.7E	1.4	1.4
Goods Producing	44.0	41.8	33.5E	28.0	28.6
Mining	0.2	0.1	0.1E	0.1	0.1
Construction	5.5	5.4	4.1	3.3	3.2
Manufacturing	38.3	36.3	29.3	24.6	25.3
Nondurables	19.8	16.3	11.6	9.1	8.6
Durables	18.5	19.9	17.7	15.5	16.7
Service Producing	51.4	55.7	58.9	64.4	63.8
Transportation, Communication, Public Utilities	5.4	4.9	4.2	4.1	3.9
Trade	18.1	17.5	17.7	19.0	19.3
Finance, Insurance, Real Estate	3.9	4.7	4.6	5.2	5.2
Services	13.4	15.5	16.9	19.4	0.4
Government	10.5	13.2	15.6	16.7	15.0
Total Excluding Non-farm Proprietors			94.1	93.8	93.8
Non-farm Proprietors			6.9	6.2	6.2
Total			100.0	100.0	100.0

E = Estimate

* Includes farm workers and proprietors

TABLE 6

THE NATION'S CHANGING INDUSTRIAL STRUCTURE

1950-1979

Industry Employment Shares of United States Totals
(percent)

Industry	1950	1959	1969	1975	1979
Agriculture, Forestry, Fishery*	11.6	7.6	5.5	4.9	4.3
Goods Producing	34.3	33.4	28.2	24.5	25.2
Mining	1.7	1.2	0.7	0.8	0.9
Construction	5.8	5.7	4.2	3.9	4.3
Manufacturing	26.8	26.5	23.3	19.8	20.0
Nondurables	12.5	11.6	9.6	8.2	7.9
Durables	14.3	14.9	13.7	11.6	12.1
Service Producing	54.1	59.0	60.0	64.2	64.0
Transportation, Communication, Public Utilities	7.1	6.2	5.1	4.9	4.9
Trade	18.4	18.8	17.2	18.6	19.3
Finance, Insurance, Real Estate	3.5	4.2	4.1	4.6	4.8
Services	13.6	15.3	15.3	17.0	17.9
Government	11.5	14.5	18.3	19.1	17.2
Total Excluding Non-farm Proprietors			93.7	93.6	93.5
Non-farm Proprietors			6.3	6.4	6.5
Total			100.0	100.0	100.0

* Includes farm workers and proprietors

TABLE 7

THE NEW ENGLAND REGION'S CHANGING INDUSTRIAL STRUCTURE

PATTERNS OF EMPLOYMENT GROWTH

(average annual percent changes)

Industry	1950-59	1959-69	1969-79	1975-79	1950-79
Agriculture, Forestry, Fishery	-4.8	-1.0e	-0.7e	2.7	-1.8
Goods Producing					
Mining	-5.3	-1.8e	0.6e	6.7	-1.5
Construction	0.2	-0.0	-1.1	2.6	-0.3
Manufacturing	-0.1	0.5	-0.1	4.3	0.1
Service Producing					
Transportation, Communication, Public Utilities	-0.6	1.0	0.8	2.1	0.5
Trade	0.1	3.1	2.5	3.8	2.2
Finance, Insurance, Real Estate	2.6	2.8	3.1	3.5	3.7
Services	2.3	4.1	3.9	4.9	4.7
Government	3.4	5.4	1.1	0.6	4.2

TABLE 8

THE NATION'S CHANGING INDUSTRIAL STRUCTURE

PATTERNS OF EMPLOYMENT GROWTH

(average annual percent changes)

INDUSTRY	1950-59	1959-69	1969-79	1975-79	1950-79
Agriculture, Forestry, Fishery	-3.2	-0.2	-0.5	-0.0	-1.1
Goods Producing					
Mining	-2.4	-1.8	5.3	7.0	-0.0
Construction	0.8	-0.0	2.6	6.8	1.2
Manufacturing	1.0	1.9	0.4	3.8	1.2
Service Producing					
Transportation, Communication, Public Utilities	-0.3	1.1	1.5	3.3	0.8
Trade	1.3	2.4	3.6	4.6	3.0
Finance, Insurance, Real Estate	3.7	3.4	4.0	4.5	5.1
Services	2.6	3.6	4.1	5.0	4.7
Government	4.2	7.0	1.4	0.7	5.9

TABLE 9

SHARES* OF REAL GROSS PRODUCT BY INDUSTRY
NEW ENGLAND AND THE UNITED STATES
1978
(% of area totals)

	U.S.	N.E.	MA	CT	ME	RI	NH	VT
Agriculture**	2.4	0.6	0.3	0.4	2.2	0.2	0.6	4.7
Goods Producing	30.4	31.9	29.6	33.5	32.8	36.2	36.4	33.3
Mining	1.5	0.1	0.0	0.2	0.0	0.1	0.2	0.5
Construction	4.3	3.4	3.0	3.3	4.8	3.4	5.4	5.1
Manufacturing	24.6	28.4	26.6	30.0	28.0	32.7	30.8	27.7
Nondurable	9.9	9.8	9.5	7.8	18.4	10.6	12.2	7.3
Durable	14.7	18.6	17.0	22.2	9.7	22.1	18.6	20.5
Service Producing	66.7	67.5	70.1	66.1	64.5	63.6	63.1	62.0
Transportation, Communication, Public Utilities	9.8	8.4	9.2	7.4	8.9	6.5	8.1	9.2
Trade	17.2	17.1	17.4	16.1	18.8	17.0	18.6	16.5
Wholesale	7.2	6.8	7.0	6.8	6.5	6.5	6.2	5.2
Retail	10.0	10.3	10.4	9.2	12.3	10.4	12.4	11.3
Finance, Insurance, Real Estate	15.5	18.1	17.6	22.4	11.8	15.3	14.3	12.0
Services	12.2	14.6	16.3	12.7	12.8	13.7	13.0	14.5
Government	12.0	9.3	9.6	7.5	12.6	11.1	9.1	9.8
Federal	4.1	2.4	2.2	1.7	5.1	2.9	2.4	2.1
State & Local	7.9	7.0	7.4	5.8	7.4	8.1	6.7	7.7
Total	100.0	100.0	100.0	100.0	100.0	100.0	100.0	100.0

*Components may not add to totals due to rounding error.
**Includes Farm, Agricultural Services, Forestry, Fishery

SOURCE: Data from Federal Reserve Bank of Boston and Bureau of Economic ANalysis

TABLE 10A

1978 SERVICE-PRODUCING INDUSTRIES' SHARE
OF AREA REAL GROSS PRODUCT
(%)

	U.S.	N.E.	MA	CT	ME	RI	NH	VT
Transportation, Communications, Public Utilities	9.8	8.4	9.2	7.4	8.9	6.5	8.1	9.2
Transportation	3.9	2.7	2.9	2.3	3.3	2.1	2.1	3.0
Communications	3.4	3.5	3.9	3.0	3.4	2.4	3.7	3.6
Public Utilities	2.3	2.3	2.4	2.1	2.2	2.1	2.4	2.7
Trade	17.2	17.1	17.4	16.1	18.8	17.0	18.6	16.5
Wholesale	7.2	6.8	7.0	6.8	6.5	6.5	6.2	5.2
Retail	10.0	10.3	10.4	9.2	12.3	10.4	12.4	11.3
Finance, Insurance, Real Estate (FIRE)	15.5	18.1	17.6	22.4	11.8	15.3	14.3	12.0
Banking	1.7	1.9	2.0	1.7	1.9	2.2	1.7	2.0
Other FIRE	13.8	16.2	15.6	20.7	9.9	13.1	12.6	10.0
Services	12.2	14.6	16.3	12.7	12.8	13.7	13.0	14.5
Business and Repair Services	2.1	3.0	3.5	3.1	1.6	2.5	2.2	1.5
Professional, Social & Related Services	6.0	9.5	10.8	7.8	8.6	9.3	7.9	9.0
Other Services	4.1	2.1	2.0	1.9	2.7	1.9	2.9	4.0
Government	12.0	9.3	9.6	7.5	12.6	11.1	9.1	9.8
Federal	4.1	2.4	2.2	1.7	5.1	2.9	2.4	2.1
Civilian		1.8	1.8	1.2	3.6	2.1	1.6	1.8
Military		0.6	0.4	0.5	1.5	0.8	0.8	0.3
State and Local	7.9	7.0	7.4	5.8	7.4	8.1	6.7	7.7
Total Service-Producing	66.7	67.5	70.1	66.1	64.5	63.6	63.1	62.0

TABLE 10B

1978 MANUFACTURING INDUSTRIES' SHARE
OF AREA REAL GROSS PRODUCT
(%)

	U.S.	N.E.	MA	CT	ME	RI	NH	VT		U.S.	N.E.	MA	CT	ME	RI	NH	VT
Nondurables	9.9	9.8	9.5	7.8	18.4	10.6	12.2	7.3	Durables	14.7	18.6	17.1	22.2	9.7	22.1	18.6	20.5
Food	2.3	1.4	1.4	1.1	3.0	1.2	1.3	1.6	Lumber	0.8	0.5	0.2	0.2	3.6	0.1	1.3	1.9
Tobacco	0.4	0.1	0.0	0.2	0.0	0.0	0.0	0.0	Furniture	0.4	0.3	0.3	0.3	0.2	0.2	0.4	1.0
Textiles	0.7	1.0	1.0	0.6	1.9	2.9	1.3	0.3	Stone, Clay and Glass	0.8	0.7	0.6	0.7	0.4	0.9	0.8	1.5
Apparel	0.9	0.8	1.1	0.5	0.8	0.7	0.6	0.5	Primary Metals	1.4	0.9	0.6	1.4	0.1	1.7	0.8	0.2
Paper	0.9	1.6	1.4	0.8	6.9	0.8	2.2	1.6	Fabricated Metals	1.7	2.6	2.0	4.3	0.9	2.2	1.8	0.6
Printing and Publishing	1.2	1.5	1.6	1.5	0.8	1.5	1.5	1.9	Nonelectrical Machinery	2.7	3.9	3.8	4.5	1.0	2.7	6.0	3.7
Chemicals	1.8	1.2	1.1	1.9	0.5	1.2	0.3	0.5	Electrical Machinery	2.3	4.1	4.5	3.5	1.6	3.1	4.9	9.3
Petroleum	0.7	0.2	0.2	0.2	0.1	0.0	0.0	0.0	Transportation Equipment	3.4	2.5	1.6	5.0	1.5	1.6	1.3	1.0
Rubber and Plastics	0.8	1.3	1.2	1.0	0.9	1.8	2.9	0.8	Instruments	0.7	1.9	2.4	1.6	0.2	1.2	1.8	0.8
Leather	0.2	0.7	0.6	0.1	3.4	0.5	2.0	0.2	Miscellaneous	0.5	1.4	1.0	0.9	0.2	8.4	0.5	0.6
									Total Manufacturing	24.6	28.4	26.6	30.1	28.0	32.7	30.8	27.7

1978 AGRICULTURE, MINING AND CONSTRUCTION INDUSTRIES' SHARE
OF AREA GROSS PRODUCT
(%)

	U.S.	N.E.	MA	CT	ME	RI	NH	VT
Farm	2.5	0.6	0.3	0.4	2.2	0.2	0.6	4.7
Mining	1.5	0.1	0.0	0.2	0.0	0.1	0.2	0.5
Construction	4.3	3.4	3.0	3.3	4.8	3.4	5.4	5.1

TABLE 11A

1979 SERVICE PRODUCING INDUSTRIES' SHARE
OF TOTAL AREA EMPLOYMENT
(%)

	U.S.	N.E.	MA	CT	ME	RI	NH	VT
Transportation, Communications, Public Utilities	4.9	3.9	4.3	3.9	3.6	3.0	3.1	3.8
Trade	19.3	19.3	20.0	19.0	17.7	17.8	19.5	17.3
Wholesale Trade	5.0	4.3	4.5	4.7	3.8	3.9	3.5	3.3
Retail Trade	14.3	14.9	15.5	14.3	13.9	13.9	16.0	13.9
Finance, Insurance and Real Estate	4.8	5.2	5.3	6.5	3.3	4.7	4.4	3.4
Banking	1.4	1.5	1.6	1.6	1.3	1.6	1.3	1.5
Other FIRE	3.3	3.7	3.7	4.9	2.0	3.1	3.1	1.9
Credit Agencies Other Than Banks	0.5	0.3	0.3	0.4	0.2	0.3	0.3	0.2
Security Commodity Brokers and Services	0.2	0.2	0.3	0.2	0.1	0.1	0.0	0.1
Insurance Carriers	1.2	2.0	1.8	3.2	0.9	1.7	1.6	0.8
Insurance Agents, brokers, Services	0.4	0.5	0.5	0.4	0.4	0.4	0.5	0.4
Real Estate	0.9	0.6	0.6	0.6	0.3	0.5	0.6	0.4
Holding and Other Investment Companies	0.1	0.1	0.1	0.1	0.0	0.1	0.1	0.0
Other	0.0	0.0	0.0	0.0	0.1	0.0	0.0	0.0
Services	17.9	20.4	22.5	18.8	17.1	19.6	17.1	20.1
Hotels and Other Lodging	1.0	0.8	0.8	0.4	1.1	0.5	1.5	3.0
Personal Services	0.9	0.9	0.9	0.9	0.6	0.8	0.8	0.7
Private Households	1.7	1.1	0.9	1.1	1.9	0.9	1.2	2.2
Business and Repair Services	3.6	3.6	4.2	3.9	1.6	3.2	2.3	1.5
Miscellaneous Business Services	2.8	2.9	3.4	3.2	1.0	2.4	1.7	1.1
Auto Repairs, Services, Garages	0.6	0.5	0.6	0.5	0.5	0.5	0.5	0.3
Miscellaneous Repair Serv.	0.3	0.2	0.3	0.2	0.2	0.2	0.2	0.1
Amusement	0.9	0.7	0.7	0.8	0.5	0.8	1.0	0.6
Professional, Social Services	9.8	13.2	15.0	11.6	11.3	13.5	10.3	12.2
Medical	4.7	6.4	6.9	5.8	6.4	6.8	4.8	5.8
Private Educational	1.2	2.6	3.3	2.1	1.1	2.4	2.1	2.2
Other	3.9	4.1	4.8	3.6	3.9	4.3	3.5	4.1
Government	17.2	15.0	15.1	13.1	19.1	16.0	15.3	16.2
Federal	5.0	3.6	3.3	3.0	6.6	4.4	3.5	3.6
Civilian	2.8	2.0	2.0	1.4	3.5	2.0	1.7	1.8
Military	2.2	1.6	1.3	1.6	3.1	2.3	1.8	1.8
State and Local	12.2	11.4	11.8	10.1	12.6	11.6	11.9	12.5
Total Service Producing	64.0	63.8	67.2	61.3	60.9	61.1	59.4	60.7

TABLE 11B

1979 MANUFACTURING INDUSTRIES SHARE
OF TOTAL AREA EMPLOYMENT
(%)

	U.S.	N.E.	MA	CT	ME	RI	NH	VT
Nondurables	7.9	8.6	8.5	6.5	14.2	9.2	10.5	6.0
Food	1.6	1.0	1.0	0.8	2.1	0.7	0.7	1.1
Tobacco	0.1	0.0	(L)	0.0	0	0	0	0
Textiles	0.8	1.0	0.9	0.6	1.8	2.8	1.2	0.3
Apparel	1.2	1.1	1.4	0.7	0.9	0.8	0.6	0.7
Paper	0.7	1.1	1.0	0.6	3.6	0.7	1.5	1.1
Printing and Publishing	1.2	1.4	1.5	1.5	0.7	1.2	1.4	1.7
Chemicals	1.1	0.7	0.6	1.1	0.3	0.7	0.2	0.3
Petroleum	0.2	0.0	0.1	0.0	0.0	0.0	0.0	0.0
Rubber and Plastics	0.7	1.2	1.1	0.9	0.8	1.6	2.5	0.7
Leather	0.2	1.0	0.8	0.1	4.1	0.8	2.4	0.1
Durables	12.1	16.7	15.1	21.6	8.4	20.1	16.4	15.6
Lumber	0.7	0.5	0.2	0.1	2.9	0.2	1.2	1.8
Furniture	0.5	0.3	0.3	0.3	0.2	0.3	0.4	1.2
Stone, Clay and Glass	0.7	0.5	0.5	0.6	0.2	0.7	0.7	1.0
Primary Metals	1.2	0.8	0.6	1.4	0.1	1.8	0.7	0.2
Fabricated Metals	1.6	2.4	1.9	4.3	0.8	2.2	1.7	0.6
Nonelectrical Machinery	2.4	3.4	3.6	3.9	0.9	2.1	4.9	3.0
Electrical Machinery	2.0	3.4	3.7	3.2	1.5	2.6	4.3	5.5
Transportation Equipment	2.0	2.3	1.3	5.4	1.3	1.4	0.2	0.9
Instruments	0.7	1.6	2.0	1.6	0.2	1.2	1.8	0.8
Miscellaneous	0.4	1.3	1.0	0.8	0.2	7.7	0.5	0.6
Total Manufacturing	20.0	25.3	23.6	28.0	22.6	29.3	26.9	21.6

1979 AGRICULTURE, MINING, CONSTRUCTION INDUSTRIES'
NONFARM PROPRIETORS' SHARES* OF TOTAL AREA EMPLOYMENT
(%)

	U.S.	N.E.	MA	CT	ME	RI	NH	VT
Agriculture, Forestry, Fisheries**	4.3	1.4	0.9	1.2	3.9	0.7	1.5	4.9
Farm Workers and Farm Proprietors	3.8	1.1	0.6	0.9	3.5	0.4	1.2	4.5
Agricultural Services, Forestry & Fisheries	0.5	0.3	0.4	0.3	0.4	0.3	0.3	0.4
Agricultural Services	0.4	0.3	(D)	(D)	0.3	0.2	0.2	0.4
Forestry, Fisheries & Other	0.0	0.1	(D)	(D)	0.1	0.1	0.0	0.0
Forestry	0.0	0.0	(D)	(D)	0.1	0.0	(D)	(D)
Fisheries	0.0	0.1	0.1	0.0	0.1	0.1	(D)	(D)
Other	0.0	0	0	0	0	0	0	0
Mining	0.9	0.1	0.0	0.1	0.0	0.1	0.1	0.3
Coal Mining	0.2	(D)	(L)	(D)	(D)	0	0	0
Anthracite	0.0	0	0	0	0	0	0	0
Bituminous & Lignite	0.2	(D)	(L)	(D)	(D)	0	0	0
Oil & Gas Extraction	0.4	0.0	(D)	(D)	(D)	0.0	0.0	(D)
Metal Mining	0.1	(D)	(D)	0.0	0.0	0	0	(D)
Non Metallic Except Fuels	0.1	0.1	0.0	0.0	0.0	0.0	0.1	0.3
Construction	4.3	3.2	2.7	3.3	3.8	3.1	4.9	4.3
General Building Contractors	1.2	1.0	0.8	0.9	1.4	1.0	1.6	1.8
Heavy Construction Contractors	0.9	0.5	0.3	0.5	0.7	0.3	1.2	0.6
Special Trade Contractors	2.2	1.8	1.6	1.9	1.8	1.8	2.1	1.9
Non-Farm Proprietors	6.5	6.2	5.6	6.1	8.7	5.7	7.2	8.1

Components may not sum to totals due to rounding error.

Includes Farm Workers and Farm Proprietors

Not shown to avoid disclosure of confidential information

Less than 10 wage and salary jobs

SOURCE: Bureau of Economic Analysis Data

TABLE 12

EXPORT-RELATED SERVICE INDUSTRIES (1979)

	N.E. % Employment	U.S. % Employment
Finance, Insurance, Real Estate	5.2	4.8
Insurance Carriers	2.0	1.2
Professional Services	13.2	9.8
Medical	6.4	4.7
Education	2.6	1.2

TABLE 13

SELECTED NON-DURABLE GOODS EMPLOYMENT (1979)
AS PERCENT OF TOTAL EMPLOYMENT

	N.E. Share of Total Employment	Average Annual Rate of Growth 1975-9	U.S. Share of Total Employment	Average Annual Rate of Growth 1975-9
All Non-Durables	8.6 %		7.9 %	
Printing	1.4 %	2.8 %	1.2 %	3.7%
Paper	1.1	2.2	.7	2.5
Food	1.0	0.6	1.6	1.1
Apparel	1.1	0.5	1.2	1.2
Textiles	1.0	1.3	.8	0.7
Leather	1.0	2.0	.2	0.2

TABLE 15

THE CHANGING INDUSTRIAL STRUCTURE OF MANUFACTURING
IN NEW ENGLAND
Industry Employment Shares of New England Manufacturing Total
(percent)

	TOTAL GOODS MANUFACTURED	
	1950	1979
Nondurables	51.8	33.9
Food & Tobacco	6.1	4.0
Textiles	17.2	4.2
Apparel	6.3	4.3
Paper	4.7	4.5
Printing & Publishing	4.1	5.7
Chemicals	1.7	2.7
Petroleum	0.2	0.2
Rubber & Plastics	3.8	4.6
Leather	7.8	3.9
Durables	48.2	66.1
Lumber	3.2	2.2
Furniture	1.5	1.3
Stone, Clay & Glass	1.6	2.1
Primary Metals	5.3	3.3
Fabricated Metals		9.5
Nonelectrical Machinery	9.7	13.5
Electrical Machinery	7.2	13.5
Transportation Equipment	3.3	9.0
Instruments & Miscellaneous	8.1	11.6
Ordnance, Fabricated Metals & Transportation	11.5	18.5

TABLE 14

SELECTED DURABLE GOODS MANUFACTURING EMPLOYMENT (1979)
AS PERCENT OF TOTAL EMPLOYMENT

	N.E. Share	Average Annual Rate of Growth 1975 - 1979	U.S. Share	Average Annual Rate of Growth 1975 - 1979
All Durables	16.7 %		12.1 %	
Electrical	3.4 %	7.2 %	2.0 %	6.2 %
Machinery	3.4	7.3	2.4	5.2
Fabricated Metals	2.4	3.3	1.6	4.3
Transportation Equip.	2.3	5.1	2.0	5.7
Instruments	1.6	7.7	.7	6.7
Miscellaneous Mfg.	1.3	3.6	.4	2.4
Lumber	.5	6.8	.7	6.2
Furniture	.3	1.0	.5	4.9

Industries in New England which are candidates for growth in the 1980's, based on recent positive trends, comprise 38% of employment in the Region.

Rapid-Growth Industries in the Service-Producing Sector

Within the service-producing sector the following rapid-growth industries emerge as especially good candidates for rapid growth in the medium-term future on the basis of their growth performance in recent years, both in New England and nationally:

	1978 share of total New England employment
Miscellaneous Business Services	2.7%
Holding and other Investment Companies	0.1%
Credit Agencies	0.3%
Professional and Social Services (including Medical and Educational)	13.2%
	16.3%

The following service-producing industries within the moderate growth range--or, like wholesale trade, in the rapid-growth group during the decade but in the moderate-growth group during the 1975-1978 expansion-- expanded rapidly enough to be considered additional candidates for further healthy expansion on this basis:

	1978 share of total New England employment
Wholesale Trade	4.3%
Insurance Agents, Brokers, Services	0.5%
Auto Repairs, Services, Garages	0.5%
	5.3%
	21.6%

The significance of strong recent national growth in these industries for our purposes is that, when concurrent with healthy expansion in New England, it suggests that the recent regional expansion in these industries is robust, partaking of growing broadly-based demand. Taken together, these industries comprised 21.6% of total New England employment in 1978.

Rapid-Growth Industries in the Manufacturing Sector

In the manufacturing sector the potential rapid-growth industries, based on recent rapid growth in New England and at least moderate recent growth in the nation, are:

	1978 share of total New England employment
Instruments and Related Products	1.6%
Lumber and Wood Products	0.6%
Electrical and Electronic Equipment	3.3%
Miscellaneous Manufacturing	1.4%
Stone, Clay and Glass Products	0.5%
Nonelectrical Machinery	3.2%
	10.6%

Of these, only Instruments performed well over the entire decade; the others were included in this group based on their performance during the recent expansion. The justification for drawing optimistic tentative conclusions based only on the recent expansion is that it is reasonable to assume a degree of structural evolution of the economy in the wake of the oil-related shocks of 1973-1974, particularly since the expansion has been an exceptionally long one. Additional candidates for rapid growth on this basis from among the manufacturing industries are:

	1978 share of total New England employment
Fabricated Metal Products	2.4%
Transportation Equipment	2.2%
	4.6%
	15.2%

These manufacturing industries, taken together, comprised 16.1% of total New England employment in 1978.

Rapid-Growth Industries in Construction and Primary Industries

In construction and the primary industries--agriculture, forestry, fishing and mining--the following industries grew rapidly in recent years, although their share of total employment was miniscule in 1978:

	1978 share of total New England employment
Bituminous and Lignite Mining	.01%
Oil and Gas Extraction	.01%
	.02%

The following industries in this sector are candidates for rapid expansion, based on recent rapid growth in some of the New England states and moderate growth in the region as a whole:

	1978 share of total New England employment
Fisheries	.08%
Forestry	.01%
Agricultural Services	.25%
General Building Contractors	.95%
	1.29%
	1.31%

Taken together, these tertiary industries comprised 1.31% of the total New England employment in 1978.

TABLE 16

MARKET VALUE OF AGRICULTURAL PRODUCTS SOLD IN NEW ENGLAND

1974 - 1978

(THOUSANDS OF DOLLARS)

	1974	1978	% Change
Massachusetts	$179,653	$215,943	+ 20.2%
Connecticut	186,921	228,749	+ 22.4%
Maine	359,612	399,723	+ 11.2%
Rhode Island	22,219	26,402	+ 18.8%
New Hampshire	72,192	89,209	+ 23.6%
Vermont	207,889	274,745	+ 32.2%
New England	$1,028,486	$ 1,234,771	+ 20.1

TABLE 17

USE OF FARMLAND IN NEW ENGLAND IN ACRES

1974 AND 1978

	TOTAL FARMLAND			HARVESTED FARMLAND		
	1974	1978	% Change	1974	1978	% Change
Mass.	601,734	680,513	+ 13.1	188,015	214,220	+ 13.9
Conn.	440,056	501,419	+ 13.9	159,157	178,476	+ 12.1
Maine	1,523,696	1,614,180	+ 5.9	449,601	488,043	+ 8.5
R.I.	61,068	75,791	+ 24.1	21,422	25,141	+ 17.4
N.H.	506,464	543,347	+ 7.3	118,186	136,925	+ 15.9
Vermont	1,667,561	1,756,062	+ 5.3	514,801	581,583	+ 13.0
New England	4,800,561	5,171,312	+ 7.7	1,451,182	1,624,388	+ 11.2

Source: 1974, 1978 Census of Agriculture

TABLE 18

VALUE OF AGRICULTURAL PRODUCTS SOLD IN NEW ENGLAND IN 1974
FARMS WITH SALES OF $2,500 OR MORE
(THOUSANDS OF DOLLARS)

	MA	CT	ME	RI	NH	VT	NE	% OF TOTAL NE VALUE
...PS	85,347	74,863	131,103	11,986	16,549	15,106	334,954	32.9
...ins	281	343	3,143	24	78	394	4,263	0.4
...acco	9,925	28,952	―	―	―	―	38,877	3.8
...ton & Cottonseed	―	―	―	―	―	―	―	0.0
...ld Seeds, Hay, Forage & Silage	4,136	5,096	4,714	331	2,410	7,544	24,231	2.4
...er Field Crops**	3,330	2,067	103,952	2,835	474	806	113,464	11.2
...etables, Sweet Corn & Melons	10,200	4,214	4,582	1,067	1,999	548	22,610	2.2
...its, Nuts & Berries	20,452	6,157	10,553	776	5,697	4,298	48,023	4.7
...sery & Greenhouse Products	36,933	28,033	4,158	6,955	5,891	1,515	83,485	8.2
...EST PRODUCTS	679	405	2,739	28	1,158	2,592	7,601	0.7
...ESTOCK & POULTRY PRODUCTS	91,086	109,766	223,149	9,972	52,561	188,272	674,806	66.3
...ltry & Poultry Products	23,977	49,274	158,226	3,275	17,722	8,753	261,227	25.7
...ry Products	50,396	50,551	54,662	5,278	29,337	160,265	350,489	34.5
...tle & Calves	7,405	8,034	9,428	911	4,494	18,589	48,861	4.8
...eep, Lambs & Wool	74	43	164	8	68	130	487	0.0
...gs & Pigs	3,346	484	257	391	434	172	5,084	5.0
...er Livestock & Livestock Prod.	5,888	1,379	412	110	506	364	8,659	0.9
...AL Agricultural Products	177,112	185,034	356,991	21,986	70,268	205,970	1,017,361	100.0

...he sum of the figures may not equal total due to rounding off.
...ncludes, Potatoes, Sweet Potatoes, Sugar Beets, Etc.

SOURCE: 1974 Census of Agriculture; Bureau of the Census.

TABLE 19

TEN LARGEST AGRICULTURAL COUNTIES IN NEW ENGLAND BY VALUE OF
PRODUCTS SOLD 1978

(Includes Farms with Sales of $2,500 or More)

	Value of Agric. Products Sold ($1,000)	Avg. Val. Per Farm	Acreage in Farms	Percent of Land In Farms
Androscoggin, ME	76,636	304,111	71,693	23.6
Aroostook, ME	71,004	59,071	420,247	9.6
Hartford, CT	53,989	93,730	79,490	16.8
Addison, VT	52,790	85,560	238,745	47.6
Kennebec, ME	48,706	111,967	120,217	21.5
Franklin, VT	48,172	71,366	226,205	53.6
Waldo, ME	47,174	130,676	94,514	20.0
New London, CT	46,470	121,332	80,378	18.8
Windham, CT	42,426	119,173	70,478	21.4
Middlesex, MA	40,657	93,038	41,866	7.9

SOURCE: 1978 Census of Agriculture

TABLE 20

NEW ENGLAND COMMERCIAL FISH LANDINGS

	VOLUME (thousand pounds)	VALUES ($000)
76	544,119	175,436
77	581,247	202,786
78	660,717	256,510
79	708,606	302,037

SOURCE: National Marine Fisheries Service

TABLE 21

VALUE AND OUTPUT IN NEW ENGLAND'S FISHING INDUSTRY
(1979)

	Millions of Dollars	Millions of Pounds
New England	302	709
Massachusetts	176	375
Maine	80	232
Rhode Island	26	22
Connecticut	7	7
New Hampshire	3	8

SOURCE: National Marine Fisheries Bureau

TABLE 22

COMMERCIAL TIMBERLAND OWNERSHIP
NEW ENGLAND AND THE UNITED STATES
1977
(1,000 ACRES)

	Total	Federally Owned or Mngd	State, County, Municipal	Private
Mass.	2,798	10	356	2,432
Conn.	1,806	2	144	1,659
Maine	16,894	73	238	16,583
N.H.	395	--	32	363
N.H.	4,692	472	108	4,112
Vermont	4,430	213	209	4,008
New England	31,015	770	1,088	29,158
United States	487,726	105,744	30,858	351,124

SOURCE: U.S. Forest Service

TABLE 23

POPULATION AGE DISTRIBUTION: 1979

NEW ENGLAND AND THE UNITED STATES
(percent)

	UNDER 5 YEARS	5-17 YEARS	18-64 YEARS	65 AND OVER
UNITED STATES	7.3	21.9	59.3	11.5
NEW ENGLAND	6.0	21.5	60.1	12.4
MASSACHUSETTS	5.8	21.3	60.3	12.7
CONNECTICUT	5.8	21.3	61.2	11.8
MAINE	7.2	22.6	57.5	12.7
RHODE ISLAND	5.9	21.4	59.1	13.6
NEW HAMPSHIRE	6.9	22.3	59.4	11.3
VERMONT	7.1	22.6	58.7	11.6

SOURCE: U.S. Census Bureau Population Division

TABLE 24

CIVILIAN NON-INSTITUTIONAL POPULATION (16 YRS. AND OVER)
BY SEX
NEW ENGLAND AND THE UNITED STATES
1979
(000)

	U.S.	N.E.	MA	CT	ME	RI	NH	VT
MALES	76,448	4,375	2,057	1,113	383	330	316	175
FEMALES	85,083	4,872	2,312	1,245	417	370	337	187
TOTAL	161,531	9,247	4,369	2,358	800	700	653	362
MALES AS A % OF TOTAL	47.3	47.3	47.1	47.2	47.9	47.1	48.4	48.3
FEMALES AS A % OF TOTAL	52.7	52.7	52.9	52.8	52.1	52.9	51.6	51.7

SOURCE: U.S. Department of Labor, Bureau of Labor Statistics

TABLE 25

MINORITY POPULATION (16 YRS. AND OVER) IN NEW ENGLAND
AND
THE UNITED STATES: 1979

	NON-WHITE CIVILIAN NON-INSTITUTION POPULATION (thousands)	% OF TOTAL CIVILIAN NON-INSTITUTION POPULATION
UNITED STATES	19,918	12.3
NEW ENGLAND	386	4.2
MASSACHUSETTS	199	4.6
CONNECTICUT	148	6.3
MAINE	2	.03
RHODE ISLAND	5	.1
NEW HAMPSHIRE	31	4.8
VERMONT	1	.03

SOURCE: U.S. Department of Labor Bureau of Labor Statistics
Report 571, September 1979.

TABLE 26

LABOR FORCE PARTICIPATION RATES: 1978 AND 1979
NEW ENGLAND AND THE UNITED STATES

(percent of civilian non-institutional population 16 & over)

1978

	U.S.	N.E.	MA	CT	ME	RI	NH	VT
All Races	63.2	64.8	65.5	65.1	60.0	61.9	67.4	66.7
Men	77.9	78.5	79.5	78.1	74.3	76.4	80.2	78.4
Women	50.0	52.6	53.1	53.3	47.7	49.3	55.4	55.7
White	63.4	64.7	65.4	64.9	60.1	62.2	67.5	66.6
Men	78.6	78.6	79.6	78.2	74.5	76.7	80.4	78.4
Women	49.5	52.2	52.7	52.6	46.9	49.6	55.4	55.2
Black & Other	61.8		69.3	68.5				
Men	72.1		77.3	78.0				
Women	53.4		63.1	61.9				

1979*

	U.S.	N.E.	MA	CT	ME	RI	NH	VT
All Races	63.7	65.9	66.1	67.1	61.0	64.3	68.2	66.3
Men	77.9	78.9	79.3	79.7	73.6	76.4	90.2	78.9
Women	51.0	54.3	54.5	55.7	49.6	53.5	54.9	54.6
White	64.0	65.8	66.0	66.8	61.0	64.0	68.2	66.4
Black & Other	61.8	69.4	68.3	70.2				

SOURCES: Statistical Abstract of the United States, 1979 Edition.

Employment & Unemployment During 1978: An Analysis, Bureau of Labor Statistics.

* Further Breakdown Not Available

TABLE 27

EDUCATIONAL ATTAINMENT OF PERSONS AGED 18 AND OVER

NEW ENGLAND AND THE UNITED STATES

PERCENT COMPLETING YEARS OF SCHOOL

	CUMULATIVE DISTRIBUTION						MEDIAN SCHOOL YEARS COMPLETED
	ELEMENTARY		HIGH SCHOOL		COLLEGE		
	0-4	5-8	1-3	4	1-3	4+	
MASSACHUSETTS	100.0	97.6	86.4	72.3	35.1	16.8	12.6
CONNECTICUT	100.0	97.9	84.7	70.3	35.3	18.3	12.6
MAINE	100.0	98.9	84.6	67.8	29.0	13.6	12.5
RHODE ISLAND	100.0	96.5	80.1	61.8	28.9	14.9	12.4
NEW HAMPSHIRE	100.0	98.7	85.2	70.3	34.0	15.3	12.6
VERMONT	100.0	98.4	82.8	69.4	33.1	15.6	12.5
NEW ENGLAND	100.0	97.8	85.2	70.4	34.0	16.6	12.6
UNITED STATES	100.0	96.6	82.5	66.6	30.6	13.9	12.5

SOURCE: U.S. Census, 1976 Population Estimates, Series P 25

TABLE 28

AVERAGE HOURLY EARNINGS IN MANUFACTURING
NEW ENGLAND AND THE UNITED STATES

Dollars/Hour

	1949	1959	1969	1970	1971	1972	1973	1974	1975	1976	1977	1978	1979
U.S.	1.38	2.24	2.29	3.46	3.70	3.98	4.24	4.68	5.03	5.46	5.92	6.47	6.69
MA	NA	2.03	3.04	3.23	3.42	3.65	3.89	4.16	4.48	4.79	5.13	5.54	6.05
CT	1.37	2.26	3.28	3.43	3.61	3.87	4.14	4.42	4.78	5.12	5.56	5.96	6.43
ME	1.15	1.70	2.55	2.71	2.86	3.03	3.23	3.51	3.81	4.16	4.52	4.91	5.42
RI	1.23	1.82	2.69	2.85	2.99	3.15	3.37	3.62	3.84	4.15	4.39	4.71	5.10
NH	1.18	1.71	2.61	2.81	3.03	3.20	3.39	3.65	3.97	4.26	4.56	4.93	5.39
VT	1.14	1.78	2.76	2.93	3.12	3.26	3.50	3.78	4.07	4.40	4.70	5.10	5.53

SOURCE: U.S. Department of Labor, Bureau of Labor Statistics

TABLE 29

1979 MANUFACTURING WAGES BY INDUSTRY
NEW ENGLAND AND THE UNITED STATES
(DOLLARS PER HOUR)

		US	MA	CT	ME	RI	NH	VT
20	Food	6.272	6.128	6.666	4.654	5.657	6.386	5.183
21	Tobacco	6.702	NA	NA	NA	NA	NA	NA
22	Textiles	4.658	4.984	4.975	4.401	4.648	4.489	NA
23	Apparel	4.240	4.632	4.213	4.152	4.293	4.171	4.014
24	Lumber & Wood Products	6.083	4.773	4.944[1]	5.482	5.627[1]	4.928	4.357
25	Furniture	5.061	4.972	4.944[1]	NA	5.627[1]	4.921	4.532
26	Paper	7.116	6.126	6.645	7.437	4.920	6.368	6.042
27	Printing & Publishing	6.904	6.809	6.507	NA	6.818	6.012	6.055
28	Chemicals	7.590	7.242	7.034	NA	6.895	5.483[4]	NA
29	Petroleum Refining	9.364	5.042[3]	NA	NA	NA	NA	NA
30	Rubber & Plastics	5.962	5.806	5.753	NA	NA	5.483[4]	4.700
31	Leather	4.225	4.428	NA	4.230	3.519	4.251	NA
32	Stone, Clay & Glass	6.841	7.070	NA	NA	5.760	5.689	5.871
33	Primary Metals	8.977	6.323	7.259	5.268[2]	5.840	5.482	NA
34	Fabricated Metals	6.817	6.367	6.005	NA	5.192	5.357	NA
35	Machinery, Except Electrical	7.327	6.366	7.056	NA	NA	5.744	6.482
36	Electrical Machinery	6.308	6.131	5.323	5.268[2]	4.983	5.436	6.073
37	Transportation Equipment	8.524	7.653	7.800	NA	6.372	5.763[5]	NA
38	Instruments	6.168	6.612	5.902	NA	5.238	5.763[5]	NA
39	Miscellaneous Manufacturing	5.034	5.042[3]	NA	NA	4.218[6]	NA	NA
	All Manufacturing	6.688	6.046	6.426	5.413	5.101	5.386	5.525

[1]Data for SIC 24 (Lumber & Wood Products) and SIC 25 (Furniture) combined

[2]Data for SIC 33 (Primary Metals) and SIC 36 (Electrical) combined

[3]Data for SIC 29 (Petroleum Refining) and SIC 39 (Miscellaneous Manufacturing) combined

[4]Data for SIC 28 (Chemicals) and SIC 30 (Rubber and Plastics) combined

[5]Data for SIC 37 (Transportation Equipment) and SIC 38 (Instruments) combined

[6]Includes only SIC 39 (Jewelry, Silverware and Platedware)

SOURCE: U.S. Department of Labor, Bureau of Labor Statistics

TABLE 30

UNIONIZATION
NEW ENGLAND AND THE UNITED STATES: 1978

	NUMBER OF MEMBERS (000)	PERCENT UNIONIZATION OF NON-AGRICULTURAL EMPLOYEES
NEW ENGLAND	1,371	26.2
UNITED STATES	23,306	26.8
MASSACHUSETTS	692	27.7
CONNECTICUT	356	26.4
MAINE	100	24.7
RHODE ISLAND	119	29.9
NEW HAMPSHIRE	61	16.8
VERMONT	43	22.7

SOURCE: U.S. Department of Labor, Bureau of Labor Statistics, "Directory of National Unions and Employee association", Sept. 1980.

TABLE 31

WORK STOPPAGES IN NEW ENGLAND AND THE UNITED STATES

1959-1978

1959	NUMBER OF WORK STOPPAGES	WORKERS INVOLVED
NEW ENGLAND	264	73,000
UNITED STATES	3,708	1,880,000
MASSACHUSETTS	134	43,000
CONNECTICUT	68	20,500
MAINE	19	1,280
RHODE ISLAND	20	5,430
NEW HAMPSHIRE	14	1,250
VERMONT	9	1,640
1969		
NEW ENGLAND	373	155,900
UNITED STATES	5,700	2,481,000
MASSACHUSETTS	172	85,400
CONNECTICUT	99	47,200
MAINE	18	2,100
RHODE ISLAND	52	15,700
NEW HAMPSHIRE	23	3,100
VERMONT	9	2,400
1978		
NEW ENGLAND	246	52,400
UNITED STATES	4,230	1,622,600
MASSACHUSETTS	117	25,200
CONNECTICUT	55	8,400
MAINE	24	7,600
RHODE ISLAND	36	7,200
NEW HAMPSHIRE	15	3,100
VERMONT	11	900

SOURCE: U.S. Department of Labor, Bureau of Labor Statistics, "Work Stoppages"

TABLE 32

LABOR FORCE STATUS BY OCCUPATION

1979 AVERAGE

(NUMBERS IN THOUSANDS)

	TOTAL	WHITE COLLAR WORKERS	BLUE COLLAR WORKERS	SERVICE WORKERS
UNITED STATES				
EMPLOYMENT	96,945	49,342	32,065	12,834
UNEMPLOYMENT RATE	5.8	3.3	6.9	7.1
NEW ENGLAND	5,765	3,083	1,856	781
UNEMPLOYMENT RATE	5.4	3.1*	6.7*	6.5*
MASSACHUSETTS				
EMPLOYMENT	2,731	1,502	830	388
UNEMPLOYMENT RATE	5.5	3.6	7.1	5.3
CONNECTICUT				
EMPLOYMENT	1,500	834	473	187
UNEMPLOYMENT RATE	5.1	2.8	5.7	6.7
MAINE				
EMPLOYMENT	453	202	178	64
UNEMPLOYMENT RATE	7.2	3.6	9.0	8.4
RHODE ISLAND				
EMPLOYMENT	420	212	149	59
UNEMPLOYMENT RATE	6.6	4.4	8.6	6.9
NEW HAMPSHIRE				
EMPLOYMENT	431	224	155	48
UNEMPLOYMENT RATE	3.1	2.1	3.7	5.5
VERMONT				
EMPLOYMENT	228	108	70	35
UNEMPLOYMENT RATE	5.1	3.0	6.9	7.3

SOURCE: Geographic Profile of Employment: States, 1979, U.S. Department of Labor, Bureau of Labor Statistics

* NERCOM Estimates

TABLE 33

DISTRIBUTION OF ASSETS OF U.S. LIFE INSURANCE COMPANIES
(000,000)

CORPORATE SECURITIES

YEAR	GOVERNMENT SECURITIES	%	BONDS	%	STOCKS	%	MORTGAGES	%	REAL ESTATE	%
1975	$15,177	5.2	$105,837	36.6	$28,605	9.7	$ 89,167	30.8	$ 9,621	3.3
1976	20,260	6.3	120,666	37.5	34,262	10.7	91,552	28.5	10,476	3.3
1977	23,555	6.7	137,889	39.2	33,763	9.6	96,848	27.5	11,060	3.2
1978	26,552	6.8	156,044	40.0	35,518	9.1	105,790	27.1	11,764	3.0

YEAR	POLICY LOANS	%	MISCELLANEOUS ASSETS	%	TOTAL	%
1975	$24,467	8.5	$16,974	5.9	$289,304	100
1976	25,834	8.0	18,502	5.7	321,552	100
1977	27,556	7.8	21,051	6.0	351,722	100
1978	30,146	7.8	24,110	6.2	389,924	100

TABLE 34

NON-INSURED PRIVATE PENSION FUNDS

(In Millions)

	1976	1977	1978
Total Assets	160,414	181,509	202,237
Cash & Deposits	2,199	3,721	8,110
US Govt. Securities	14,713	20,138	19,695
Corporate Bonds	39,070	45,580	53,824
Pfd. & Common Stocks	94,600	98,152	101,698
Mortgages	2,369	2,497	2,789
Other Investments	7,463	11,421	16,121
		% SHARES	
Total Assets	100	100	100
Cash & Deposits	1.4	2.1	4.0
US Govt. Securities	9.2	11.1	9.7
Corporate Bonds	24.4	25.1	26.6
Pfd. & Common Stocks	59.0	54.1	50.3
Mortgages	1.5	1.4	1.4
Other Investments	4.7	6.2	8.0

TABLE 35A

ASSETS AND LIABILITIES OF COMMERCIAL AND SAVINGS BANKS
In Dollars (000)

UNITED STATES

	COMMERCIAL BANKS			SAVINGS BANKS		
	June 30 1976	June 30 1977	June 30 1978	June 30 1976	June 30 1977	June 30 1978
Real Estate	143,699,265	163,007,362	194,466,559	69,751,108	75,010,824	81,926,715
-Construction and Land Development	17,236,423	19,002,395	24,091,877	813,117	924,861	1,300,404
Loans to Farmers	22,185,324	25,776,934	27,063,534	990	1,350	1,318
Commercial and Industrial	176,597,620	194,653,208	223,934,656	472,519	622,428	410,855
Loans to Individuals	111,269,691	128,729,693	154,829,544	2,184,137	2,604,060	3,216,884
Other Loans	67,717,462	71,255,914	79,498,723	129,395	199,427	152,645
TOTAL GROSS LOANS	521,469,362	583,423,111	679,793,016	72,538,149	78,438,089	85,708,417
TOTAL DEPOSITS	782,424,554	853,581,778	952,781,113			
C+I/Total Deposit	22.6%	22.8%	23.5%			

Source: Federal Deposit Insurance Corporation Annual Reports

TABLE 35B

ASSETS AND LIABILITIES OF COMMERCIAL AND SAVINGS BANKS
In Dollars (000)

NEW ENGLAND

	COMMERCIAL BANKS			SAVINGS BANKS		
	June 30 1976	June 30 1977	June 30 1978	June 30 1976	June 30 1977	June 30 1978
Real Estate	6,622,620	7,377,892	6,242,810	13,789,214	15,673,877	17,501,645
-Construction and Land Development	376,167	389,579	497,593	277,264	325,796	410,571
Loans to Farmers	46,603	55,406	69,448	897	1,249	1,220
Commercial and Industrial	7,602,165	8,126,615	9,026,833	66,780	117,891	163,992
Loans to Individuals	4,637,692	5,104,270	5,758,568	815,804	968,634	1,183,507
Other Loans	1,574,122	1,528,275	1,477,038	32,510	61,919	60,817
TOTAL GROSS LOANS	20,483,202	22,183,458	25,067,354	14,705,203	16,823,570	18,917,481
TOTAL DEPOSITS	29,862,514	32,322,199	34,193,985			
C+I/Total Deposit	25.5%	25.1%	26.4%			

Source: Federal Deposit Insurance Corporation Annual Reports

TABLE 35C

ASSETS AND LIABILITIES OF COMMERCIAL AND SAVINGS BANKS
In Dollars (000)

MASSACHUSETTS

	COMMERCIAL BANKS			SAVINGS BANKS		
	June 30 1976	June 30 1977	June 30 1978	June 30 1976	June 30 1977	June 30 1978
Real Estate	2,040,769	2,226,082	2,597,338	2,927,803	3,530,823	3,765,496
-Construction and Land Development	220,898	187,285	199,131	23,833	25,645	51,998
Loans to Farmers	7,767	11,008	23,590	0	0	0
Commercial and Industrial	4,405,608	4,558,000	4,967,141	1,474	15,735	18,934
Loans to Individuals	2,003,495	2,139,063	2,364,069	112,043	139,600	165,537
Other Loans	1,086,865	974,078	1,051,979	2,234	30,325	29,948
TOTAL GROSS LOANS	9,544,504	9,908,231	11,004,117	3,043,574	3,716,483	3,979,915
TOTAL DEPOSITS	14,249,514	15,195,248	16,358,425			
C+I/Total Deposit	30.9%	30.0%	30.4%			

Source: Federal Deposit Insurance Corporation Annual Reports

TABLE 35D

ASSETS AND LIABILITIES OF COMMERCIAL AND SAVINGS BANKS
In Dollars (000)

CONNECTICUT

	COMMERCIAL BANKS			SAVINGS BANKS		
	June 30 1976	June 30 1977	June 30 1978	June 30 1976	June 30 1977	June 30 1978
Real Estate	1,674,176	1,829,175	2,211,885	6,977,578	7,879,628	8,928,954
-Construction and Land Development	95,837	112,653	154,655	180,173	210,326	235,003
Loans to Farmers	7,130	8,901	9,679	1	4	4
Commercial and Industrial	1,541,592	1,666,479	1,866,186	30,178	58,286	107,170
Loans to Individuals	1,254,324	1,430,912	1,664,140	434,917	505,626	615,673
Other Loans	250,012	309,951	196,772	19,176	17,746	15,753
TOTAL GROSS LOANS	4,727,234	5,245,418	6,103,317	7,461,850	8,461,290	9,667,854
TOTAL DEPOSITS	7,235,074	7,810,224	8,763,193			
C+I/Total Deposit	21.3%	21.3%	21.3%			

Source: Federal Deposit Insurance Corporation Annual Reports

TABLE 35E

ASSETS AND LIABILITIES OF COMMERCIAL AND SAVINGS BANKS
In Dollars (000)

MAINE

	COMMERCIAL BANKS			SAVINGS BANKS		
	June 30 1976	June 30 1977	June 30 1978	June 30 1976	June 30 1977	June 30 1978
Real Estate	524,894	603,387	699,416	1,197,126	1,368,004	1,572,102
-Construction and Land Development	17,603	23,267	34,983	21,639	25,008	27,105
Loans to Farmers	12,087	13,154	13,210	9	23	5
Commercial and Industrial	421,479	503,784	561,710	5,125	6,426	9,714
Loans to Individuals	427,652	479,207	526,220	79,357	101,918	135,350
Other Loans	32,101	27,643	24,563	2,600	2,883	3,094
TOTAL GROSS LOANS	1,418,213	1,627,175	1,825,121	1,284,214	1,479,254	1,720,265
TOTAL DEPOSITS	2,059,218	2,280,870	1,179,096			
C+I/Total Deposit	20.5%	22.1%	47.6%			

Source: Federal Deposit Insurance Corporation Annual Reports

TABLE 35F

ASSETS AND LIABILITIES OF COMMERCIAL AND SAVINGS BANKS
In Dollars (000)

RHODE ISLAND

	COMMERCIAL BANKS			SAVINGS BANKS		
	June 30 1976	June 30 1977	June 30 1978	June 30 1976	June 30 1977	June 30 1978
Real Estate	1,271,076	1,396,198	1,514,426	966,359	1,025,988	1,108,492
-Construction and Land Development	22,319	30,103	59,416	18,615	20,878	25,978
Loans to Farmers	47	105	38	0	0	0
Commercial and Industrial	712,496	790,655	955,660	10,605	19,817	9,748
Loans to Individuals	391,037	385,479	437,975	55,901	63,367	71,542
Other Loans	169,213	186,606	171,129	5,403	7,068	5,449
TOTAL GROSS LOANS	2,543,869	2,759,043	3,079,228	1,038,268	1,116,240	1,195,231
TOTAL DEPOSITS	3,235,795	3,502,980	3,880,287			
C+I/Total Deposit	22.0%	22.6%	24.6%			

Source: Federal Deposit Insurance Corporation Annual Reports

ASSETS AND LIABILITIES OF COMMERCIAL AND SAVINGS BANKS
In Dollars (000)

NEW HAMPSHIRE	COMMERCIAL BANKS			SAVINGS BANKS		
	June 30 1976	June 30 1977	June 30 1978	June 30 1976	June 30 1977	June 30 1978
Real Estate	547,467	680,815	811,696	1,266,991	1,369,064	1,546,790
-Construction and Land Development	10,451	18,809	31,103	22,415	31,893	50,191
Loans to Farmers	3,154	2,658	2,985	246	202	209
Commercial and Industrial	317,041	378,221	411,593	16,748	14,918	15,821
Loans to Individuals	331,976	403,721	472,571	116,670	138,960	169,522
Other Loans	16,100	16,125	16,843	778	1,683	914
TOTAL GROSS LOANS	1,215,738	1,481,540	1,715,688	1,401,433	1,524,827	1,733,256
TOTAL DEPOSITS	1,716,603	2,013,307	2,295,679			
C+I/Total Deposit	18.5%	18.8%	17.9%			

Source: Federal Deposit Insurance Corporation Annual Reports

ASSETS AND LIABILITIES OF COMMERCIAL AND SAVINGS BANKS
In Dollars (000)

VERMONT	COMMERCIAL BANKS			SAVINGS BANKS		
	June 30 1976	June 30 1977	June 30 1978	June 30 1976	June 30 1977	June 30 1978
Real Estate	564,238	642,235	746,049	453,357	500,370	579,811
-Construction and Land Development	9,059	17,462	18,305	10,589	12,046	20,296
Loans to Farmers	16,418	19,580	19,946	622	1,020	1,002
Commercial and Industrial	203,949	229,476	264,543	2,650	2,709	2,605
Loans to Individuals	229,208	256,888	293,593	16,916	19,163	25,883
Other Loans	19,831	13,872	15,752	2,319	2,214	5,659
TOTAL GROSS LOANS	1,033,644	1,162,051	1,339,883	475,864	525,476	614,960
TOTAL DEPOSITS	1,366,310	1,519,570	1,717,305			
C+I/Total Deposit	14.9%	15.1%	15.4%			

Source: Federal Deposit Insurance Corporation Annual Reports

TABLE 36

EDA BUSINESS LOANS AND GUARANTEES

	FY 1977	FY 1978	FY 1979	TOTAL
Connecticut	$ 6,750,000.	$ 8,570,000.	$ 1,280,000.	$16,600,000.
Maine	$ 2,000,000.	$ 8,471,200.	$ 8,900,000.	$19,371,200.
Massachusetts	$ 750,000.	$ 8,203,000.	$ 2,230,000.	$11,183,000.
New Hampshire		$ 2,250,000.	$ 2,000,000.	$ 4,250,000.
Rhode Island	$ 4,900,000.	$ 600,000.	$ 1,400,000.	$ 6,900,000.
Vermont			$ 483,400.	$ 483,000.
New England	$14,400,000.	$28,094,200.	$16,293,400.	$58,787,600.
United States	$57,300,000.	$120,100,000.	$155,600,000.	$333,000,000.
New England as % of U.S.	25.1%	23.4%	10.5%	17.7%

TABLE 37
HUD URBAN DEVELOPMENT ACTION GRANTS (UDAG)

	NUMBER OF UDAGs	TOTAL AMOUNT OF UDAGs	TOTAL PRIVATE INVESTMENT	TOTAL OTHER PUBLIC INVESTMENT	AMOUNT OF UDAG USED FOR DIRECT FINANCING TO A FIRM/DEVELOPER
1978					
Connecticut	4	$ 9,486,070.	?	?	?
Maine	3	4,336,000.	$ 5,562,637.	$ 2,580,938.	?
Massachusetts	12	41,910,000.	232,104,000.	25,748,000.	?
New Hampshire	1	650,000.	?	187,500.	0
Rhode Island	1	5,900,000.	42,000,000.	425,000.	0
Vermont	1	2,957,000.	18,000,000.	0	0
TOTAL		65,239,070.			
1979					
Connecticut	5	$ 6,200,000.	?	?	?
Maine	5	4,615,000.	$ 18,304,785.	$ 3,387,800.	?
Massachusetts	10	33,832,125.	130,566,460.	913,200.	$ 7,186,200.
New Hampshire	1	1,200,000.	5,865,000.	453,000.	0
Rhode Island	0	0	0	0	0
Vermont	2	2,342,000.	7,282,385.	0	2,342,000.
TOTAL		48,189,125.			

TABLE 38

SMALL BUSINESS ADMINISTRATION

DIRECT LOANS AND GUARANTEES

TOTAL LOANS AND GUARANTEES

(in millions)

	FY 1978	%NE	%US	FY 1979	%NE	%US	%Δ
U.S.	$2,400		100	$ 2,500		100	4
Conn.	40	16	1.7	45	18	1.8	13
ME	40	16	1.7	35	14	1.4	-12
MA	65	27	2.7	72	29	2.9	11
N.H.	42	17	1.8	44	17	1.8	5
R.I.	38	16	1.6	35	14	1.4	-8
Vt.	20	08	0.8	21	08	0.8	5
N. Eng.	245	100	10.2	252	100	10.1	3

Notes

1. Approximately 97 percent of the amounts shown are guarantees of loans.

2. Approximately 60 percent of the loans and guarantees are used to purchase equipment or to construct facilities.

3. Approximately 40 percent of the loans and guarantees are used to finance working capital.

4. Less than 2 percent of the loans and guarantees are used to finance equipment required by OSHA or EPA.

5. Approximately 8 percent of the loans and guarantees are used to assist minority businesspeople.

TABLE 39

301(d)SBIC FINANCING TOTALS BY STATE DURING 1979
* *

New England	# of Financings Made in State by 301(d) SBIC's	$ Amount	East South Central	# of Financings Made in State by 301(d) SBIC's	$ Amount
Maine	0	0	Kentucky	7	311,204
New Hampshire	0	0	Tennessee	5	599,000
Vermont	0	0	Alabama	2	475,000
Massachusetts	5	198,500	Mississippi	3	190,649
Rhode Island	0	0			
Connecticut	11	1,030,500	Total	17	$1,575,853
Total	16	$1,229,000			

Middle Atlantic			West South Central		
New York	95	6,430,634	Arkansas	0	0
New Jersey	8	601,209	Louisiana	44	6,549,900
Pennsylvania	15	1,640,000	Oklahoma	2	150,009
			Texas	27	1,595,095
Total	118	$8,671,843	Total	73	$8,295,004

East North Central			Mountain Region		
Ohio	14	477,099	Montana	0	0
Indiana	1	150,000	Idaho	0	0
Illinois	10	1,055,153	Wyoming	0	0
Michigan	59	3,523,113	Colorado	6	820,016
Wisconsin	0	0	New Mexico	0	0
			Arizona	0	0
Total	84	$5,205,365	Utah	0	0
			Nevada	0	0
			Total	6	$820,016

West North Central			Pacific Region		
Minnesota	9	740,064			
Iowa	1	100,000	Washington	3	183,937
Missouri	2	120,000	Oregon	0	0
North Dakota	0	0	California	46	2,668,424
South Dakota	0	0	Alaska	1	24,505
Nebraska	1	10,000	Hawaii	4	214,333
Kansas	0	0	Total	54	$3,091,199
Total	13	$970,064			

South Atlantic			Territories		
Delaware	0	0	Puerto Rico	0	0
Maryland	1	15,395	Virgin Islands	0	0
Dist. of Col.	15	1,571,499	Total	0	$ 0
Virginia	8	831,195			
West Virginia	0	0			
North Carolina	5	550,000			
South Carolina	2	284,000			
Georgia	7	113,798	GRAND TOTAL	441	$35,103,231
Florida	22	1,879,000			
Total	60	$5,244,887			

<u>SUMMARY OF NEW ENGLAND INSTITUTIONS DESIGNED TO INFLUENCE THE FLOW OF CAPITAL</u>

Each state has public and private non-conventional sources of financing for firms which have difficulty accessing funds through conventional sources.

<u>PUBLIC SECTOR</u>

1. Industrial Development and Finance Authorities

   Connecticut:

   <u>CDA</u> <u>Connecticut Development Authority</u>

   Issues industrial revenue bonds and guarantees industrial loans.

   Maine:

   <u>MGA</u> <u>Maine Guarantee Authority</u>

   Issues industrial revenue bonds, guarantees industrial loans, and issues loans for industrial shell buildings and parks.

   Massachusetts:

   <u>MIFA</u> <u>Massachusetts Industrial Finance Agency</u>

   Issues industrial revenue bonds and guarantees industrial loans.

   New Hampshire:

   <u>IDA</u> <u>Industrial Development Authority</u>

   Issues industrial revenue bonds, makes direct industrial loans, and guarantees industrial loans.

   Rhode Island:

   <u>PAEDC</u> <u>Port Authority and Economic Development Corporation</u>

   Issues industrial revenue bonds.

   <u>IBA</u> <u>Industrial Building Authority</u>

   Guarantees industrial loans.

   <u>NIDC</u> <u>Narragansett Industrial Development Corporation</u>

   Makes direct industrial loans.

   Vermont:

   <u>VIDA</u> <u>Vermont Industrial Development Authority</u>

   Issues industrial revenue bonds, guarantees industrial loans, makes direct industrial loans, makes loans for industrial shell buildings and parks.

2. Revolving Loan Funds

Connecticut, Maine, Massachusetts, New Hampshire, and Vermont all have revolving loan funds (RLF) capitalized with grants from U.S. EDA. The revolving loan funds provide loan guarantees and direct financing through secured, subordinated junior mortgages for working capital, physical capital, and real estate. The financing can be used for start-ups and expansions. For every $1. that these funds lend out, they must leverage $4. from other sources (either public or private). Interest rates are below the prime.

The RLFs in Connecticut, Maine, New Hampshire and Vermont are geographically targeted to economically distressed parts of the state. The RLF in Massachusetts is targeted to technology-based firms and can be used anywhere in the state.

   Connecticut:

   <u>NVRLP</u> <u>Naugatuck Valley Revolving Loan Program</u>

Maine:

NMRPC   Northern Maine Regional Planning Council

    Revolving Loan Program (serving Aroostook County).

Massachusetts:

MTDC   Massachusetts Technology Development Corporation

New Hampshire:

BEDCO   Berlin Economic Development Corporation

Vermont:

The FUND, Inc.   Northern Vermont Economic Development Council

    Serving Essex, Orleans, and Caledonia Counties.

EDC Fund, Inc.   Southeastern Economic Development Council

    Serving Rutland and Bennington Counties.

3. Others

Connecticut:

CPDC   Connecticut Product Development Corporation

    CPDC, funded by the State of Connecticut, supplies money for risk capital specifically for the development of new products. It provides 60 percent of the cost of product development. In return, it receives royalties on the sales of the product if it is successfully developed and marketed. It does not finance start-up firms.

Massachusetts:

CDFC   Community Development Finance Corporation

    CDFC is a state authority financed by $10 million in General Obligation Bonds. The Corporation makes investments in the form of debt, equity, or some combination of the two, in conjunction with community development corporations (CDC) in economically depressed areas. Eligible businesses may be privately or CDC owned as long as the CDC has a major voice in business decisions of the company.

    CDFC will invest if the company is unable to obtain suitable financing from conventional sources. But, in every investment, the corporation uses its money to leverage outside funding; either public or private. In fact, CDFC cannot own more than 49 percent of the voting stock of any firm in which it invests. It has invested in worker-owned, and joint CDC-worker owned businesses.

PRIVATE SECTOR

Each state has private corporations, capitalized by banks, insurance companies, and other private conventional lenders. These corporations invest in riskier ventures than the lenders would individually finance. They provide necessary financing to businesses unable to obtain funds from conventional sources. They either take first mortgages themselves, or leverage conventional first mortgages by taking second mortgages. These corporations help to perfect the capital market by pooling and spreading risks, and by reducing information and transactions costs.

Connecticut:

CDCC   Connecticut Development Credit Corporation

    Comprised of banks and insurance companies.

Maine:

MCC   Maine Capital Corporation (an SBIC)

Massachusetts:

MCRC   Massachusetts Capital Resource Corporation

    Comprised of insurance companies.

MBDC   Massachusetts Business Development Corporation

    Comprised of banks and insurance companies.

New Hampshire:

BDC   New Hampshire Business Development Corporation

    Comprised of banks.

Rhode Island:

BDC   Rhode Island Business Development Corporation

    Comprised of banks and other financial institutions.

BOI   Business Opportunities, Inc.

    A subsidiary of BDC - finances firms owned by minorities.

Vermont:

VDCC   Vermont Development Credit Corporation

    Comprised of banks and insurance companies)

New Hampshire and Vermont:

NCIC   Northern Community Investment Corporation

    A non-profit capital corporation serving economically distressed areas: Carrol, Coos, and Grafton Counties in New Hampshire, and Caledonia, Essex, and Orleans Counties in Vermont.

TABLE 40

STATE INDUSTRIAL DEVELOPMENT AND FINANCE AUTHORITIES

STATE	INDUSTRIAL REVENUE BONDS	LOAN INSURANCE	DIRECT LOANS	LOANS FOR INDUSTRIAL BUILDINGS & PARKS
CONNECTICUT	CDA	CDA		
MAINE	MGA	MGA		MGA
MASSACHUSETTS	MIFA $352,936,190. (1979)	MIFA $2,317,000. (1979)		
NEW HAMPSHIRE	IDA $10,550,000. (1977) 14,210,000. (1978) 25,925,000. (1979)	IDA $ 850,000. (1977) 160,000. (1978) 150,000. (1979)	IDA $ 105,300. (1977) 108,300. (1978) 0 (1979)	
RHODE ISLAND	PAEDC	IBA	NIDC	
VERMONT	VIDA $ 9,062,000. (1977) 6,906,000. (1978) 19,019,000. (1979)	VIDA $ 647,500. (1977) 1,734,438. (1978) 1,144,063. (1979)	VIDA $1,308,000. (1977) 1,433,680. (1978) 1,120,000. (1979)	VIDA $3,023,700. (1977) 2,109,000. (1978) 1,182,422. (1979)

TABLE 41

REVOLVING LOAN FUNDS

STATE	CORPORATION'S PORTION	OTHER LENDERS' PORTION
CONNECTICUT	NVRLF - not yet investing	
MAINE	NMRPC - not yet investing	
MASSACHUSETTS	MTDC $950,000. (1979)	$3,150,000. (1979) all private
NEW HAMPSHIRE	BEDCO $685,000.(1/79-2/80)	$2,729,000. (1/79-2/80)
RHODE ISLAND		
VERMONT	The Fund, Inc.-not yet investing EDC Fund, Inc. $447,000.(9/78-2/80)	$3,092,000. (9/78-2/80)

TABLE 42

Private Credit and Development Corporations

	Corporation's Portion	Other Lenders' Portion
Connecticut	CDCC	
Maine	MCC - not yet operating	
Massachusetts	MCRC $20,700,000 (9/78-9/79) MBDC $2,146,000 (1977) $2,380,000 (1978) $2,610,000 (1979)	$494,000 (1977) 270,000 (1978) 300,000 (1979)
New Hampshire	NHBDC 0 (1977) $ 160,000 (1978) 1,118,000 (1979) NCIC 333,700 (1976-77) 421,100 (1977-78) 1,215,700 (1978-79)	0 (1977) 0 (1978) 5,000 (1979) 1,689,300 (1976-77) 194,300 (1977-78) 5,893,000 (1978-79)
Rhode Island	BDC 1 BDI	
Vermont	VOCC $208,000 (1977) 228,000 (1978) 1,366,000 (1979) NCIC *See under New Hampshire	

TABLE 43

EMPLOYMENT IN NEW ENGLAND-HEADQUARTERED FIRMS: SMALL-FIRM* EMPLOYMENT AS A PERCENT OF INDUSTRY

Industry	% of Employment in New England Headquartered Firms With 99 Employees or Fewer
Auto Repair, Services, and Garages	93.1
Fisheries	83.7
General Building Contractors	71.4
Insurance Agents and Brokers	70.2
Lumber and Wood Products	66.3
Wholesale Trade	57.8
Miscellaneous Business Services	45.1
Holding and other Investment Companies	30.4
Miscellaneous Manufacturing	30.2

SOURCE: Dun & Bradstreet data, July 1980.
*99 Employees or Fewer

TABLE 44

RESEARCH AND DEVELOPMENT EXPENDITURES IN FIVE MAJOR INDUSTRIES

Industry	% NE Manufacturing Employment (1978)	% Total R&D Dollars (1977) Nationwide
Electrical Equipment	13.0	19.9
Nonelectrical Machinery	12.5	13.3
Fabricated Metals	9.5	1.3
Transportation Equipment	8.5	11.4
Instruments	6.5	4.5

SOURCE: BEA Data, N.S.F.

TABLE 45

THE GEOGRAPHIC DISTRIBUTION IN NEW ENGLAND OF FEDERAL FUNDS:* FISCAL 1979

	TOTAL DIRECT		TOTAL INDIRECT		Population
	level ($ millions)	% of U.S.	level ($ millions)	% of U.S.	As % of U.S.
UNITED STATES	468,746	100.0	95,016	100.0	100.0
NEW ENGLAND	28,754	6.1	3,216	3.4	5.6
MASSACHUSETTS	13,711	2.9	1,208	1.3	2.6
CONNECTICUT	8,268	1.8	1,038	1.1	1.4
MAINE	2,263	0.5	371	0.4	0.5
RHODE ISLAND	1,927	0.4	205	0.2	0.4
NEW HAMPSHIRE	1,667	0.4	234	0.2	0.4
VERMONT	918	0.2	160	0.2	0.3

*Source: Geographic Distribution of Federal Funds in (Each New England State): Fiscal 1979, compiled for the Executive Office of the President by the Community Services Administration, published by NTIS.

TABLE 46

THE GEOGRAPHIC DISTRIBUTION IN NEW ENGLAND

OF

U.S. DEPARTMENT OF DEFENSE PRIME CONTRACT AWARDS
(1978)

	Level ($ millions)	% of Gross State or National Product	% Share of U.S.	% Change 1975-78
UNITED STATES	53,593	2.5	100.0	43.6
NEW ENGLAND	7,110	6.5	13.2	55.9
MASSACHUSETTS	2,787	5.3	5.2	57.5
CONNECTICUT	3,489	11.0	6.5	48.5
MAINE	341	4.6	0.6	608.9
RHODE ISLAND	156	2.1	0.3	210.8
NEW HAMPSHIRE	227	3.4	0.4	20.1
VERMONT	109	3.0	0.2	-11.4

Source: U.S. Department of Defense

TABLE 47

UNITED STATES DEPARTMENT OF DEFENSE

PRIME CONTRACTS FOR RESEARCH, DEVELOPMENT, TESTING, AND EVALUATION

	Level of Activity 1978 ($ millions)				% SHARE OF US TOTAL RDT&E	% CHANGE OF TOTAL RDT&E: 1975-1978
	TOTAL RDT&E	EDUCATIONAL INSTITUTIONS	OTHER NON PROFIT	BUSINESS FIRMS		
UNITED STATES	8,568	495	321	7,752	100.00	+37.7
NEW ENGLAND	1,077	132	146	798	12.57	+18.9
MASSACHUSETTS	881	128	146	606	10.28	+45.4
CONNECTICUT	135	2	0	132	11.57	+11.6
MAINE	2	0	0	2	0.02	-
RHODE ISLAND	4	2	0	2	0.04	-20.0
NEW HAMPSHIRE	55	0	0	55	0.64	+175.0
VERMONT	2	0	0	2	0.02	-90.0

Source: U.S. Department of Defense

TABLE 48

GEOGRAPHIC DISTRIBUTION OF FEDERAL EXPENDITURES FOR GENERAL SCIENCE, SPACE AND TECHNOLOGY: FISCAL 1979

	Level (Millions of $)	% of U.S. Total
United States	5,157.5	100.00
New England	206.2	4.00
Massachusetts	117.1	2.27
Connecticut	69.4	1.35
Maine	2.3	.05
Rhode Island	12.9	.25
New Hampshire	3.6	.07
Vermont	.9	.02

*Source: Geographic Distribution of Federal Funds

TABLE 49

EMPLOYMENT, PLANT AND EQUIPMENT OF U.S. AFFILIATES

OF FOREIGN OWNED COMPANIES: 1977

NEW ENGLAND AND THE U.S.

	Value of Plant and Equipment	Employment[1]
	$ Millions	
U.S. TOTAL	53,792	1,122,207
New England	1,629	70,097
Massachusetts	457	21,540
Connecticut	193	4,706
Maine	552	27,646
Rhode Island	160	8,318
New Hampshire	155	3,542
Vermont	111	4,345

[1]Average number of full-time and part-time employees during the year.

SOURCE: Bureau of Economic Analysis, U.S. Department of Commerce

TABLE 50

NEW ENGLAND'S LEADING EXPORT INDUSTRIES IN MANUFACTURING: 1976

RANKED BY VALUE OF EXPORTS

| Industry | Value of New England Export-Related Shipments (% millions) | | Value of Export-Related Shipments as % of Industry Shipments | | | | Value of Export-Related Shipments as % of Total Manufac. Exports In New England |
| | | | NEW ENGLAND | | UNITED STATES | | |
	Direct & Supporting	Direct	Direct & Supporting	Direct	Direct & Supporting	Direct	
1. Machinery	1542.6	1146.5	21.6	16.0	23.1	18.0	18.8
2. Transportation Equipment	1367.8	1143.6	25.2	21.1	14.5	11.7	16.7
3. Electrical Equipment	1017.3	729.7	19.6	14.1	17.8	12.4	12.4
4. Instruments	700.2	607.7	19.6	17.1	17.7	15.0	8.6
5. Chemicals	593.6	448.1	20.4	15.4	15.9	8.9	7.3
6. Fabricated Metals	555.8	306.6	11.0	6.1	11.3	4.8	6.9
7. Paper	493.0	248.8	11.5	5.8	10.6	4.7	6.0
8. Miscellaneous Manufactures	232.9	195.5	8.7	7.3	9.6	8.2	2.8
TOTAL: Leading Industries	6503.2	4826.5	17.9	13.3	15.9	11.0	79.5

Source: Bureau of Census, Annual Survey of Manufacturers, 1976, Origins of Manufacturing Establishments

TABLE 51

IMPORTANCE OF MANUFACTURING EXPORTS

NEW ENGLAND AND THE NATION

| | Value of Export-Related Shipments ($ millions) | | Value of Export-Related Shipments as % of Area Total | | Export-Related Manufacturing Employment (000) | | Export-Related Manufacturing Employment as % of Area Total Manufacturing Employment | |
	Direct & Supporting	Direct	Direct & Supporting	Direct	Direct & Supporting	Direct	Direct & Supporting	Direct
United States	137,729.9	83,098.0	11.6	7.0	2,125.4	1,173.2	11.3	6.3
New England	8,185.8	5,474.0	13.7	8.3	169.9	104.8	12.7	7.8
Massachusetts	3,662.7	2,502.4	13.6	9.3	77.1	48.2	13.0	8.2
Connecticut	2,820.9	1,957.6	15.5	10.7	57.7	36.6	14.2	9.0
Maine	433.5	254.9	9.8	5.8	7.9	4.2	8.0	4.2
New Hampshire	442.9	291.1	12.7	8.3	10.5	6.5	12.0	7.4
Rhode Island	515.2	268.5	11.4	5.9	11.1	5.8	9.6	5.0
Vermont	310.6	199.8	15.1	9.7	5.6	3.5	13.6	8.5

Source: Bureau of Census, Annual Survey of Manufacturers, 1976, Origins of Exports of Manufacturing Establishments

TABLE 52

NEW ENGLAND'S LEADING EXPORT INDUSTRIES IN MANUFACTURING: 1976
RANKED BY EMPLOYMENT

| | Export-Related Manufacturing Employment (persons) | | Export-Related Employment As Percent of Industry Employment | | | | Export-Related Employment as % of Total Export-Related Employment in New England Manufacturing |
| Industry | | | NEW ENGLAND | | UNITED STATES | | |
	Direct & Supporting	Direct	Direct & Supporting	Direct	Direct & Supporting	Direct	
1. Machinery	33,100	24,000	20.5	14.9	20.7	15.0	19.5
2. Electrical Equipment	27,200	19,000	20.5	14.3	18.6	12.4	16.0
3. Transportation Equipment	23,400	19,500	22.9	19.9	15.1	12.2	13.8
4. Instruments	15,000	12,900	19.3	16.6	18.6	15.5	8.8
5. Fabricated Metals	11,800	6,200	9.9	5.2	11.1	4.6	6.9
6. Miscellaneous Manufactures	6,600	5,600	9.2	7.8	7.5	6.1	5.4
7. Chemicals	5,800	4,100	19.1	13.5	15.3	8.8	3.4
8. Paper	7,200	3,400	11.3	5.3	9.5	3.4	4.2
TOTAL: Leading Industries	130,100	94,700	17.2	12.5	15.8	10.6	76.6

SOURCE: Bureau of the Census, Annual Survey of Manufacturers, 1976, Origins of Exports of Manufacturing Establishments

TABLE 54

PERCENTAGE CHANGE, POPULATION AND
DWELLING UNITS, 1970-1980, NEW ENGLAND AND STATES *

	% Change in Population	% Change in Dwelling Units
New England	4.0	20.0
Connecticut	2.1	18.0
Maine	13.1	26.1
Massachusetts	0.6	16.7
New Hampshire	24.6	37.5
Rhode Island	-0.4	16.6
Vermont	14.8	35.2

SOURCE: U.S. Census

*1980 figures are based on preliminary Census information and are subject to change.

A 93

TABLE 53

AVERAGE NUMBER OF PERSONS PER DWELLING UNIT
1970 AND 1980, STATES AND NEW ENGLAND *

	Average Persons Per Household in 1970	Average Persons Per Household in 1980
New England	2.94	2.54
Connecticut	3.10	2.67
Maine	2.50	2.24
Massachusetts	3.00	2.60
New Hampshire	2.63	2.38
Rhode Island	2.98	2.54
Vermont	2.69	2.30

SOURCE: U.S. Census

* 1980 figures are based on preliminary Census information and are subject to change.

TABLE 55

Variations in Housing Construction Costs Within Regions (October 1979)

Base = 1.00
(Average for Selected Areas)

Mid-Atlantic
Eastern Maryland	0.81
Vicinity of Reading, Pennsylvania	0.91
Southern New Jersey	1.01
Vicinity of District of Columbia	1.04

Midwest
Upper Penninsula, Michigan	0.93
Central Wisconsin	0.95
Vicinity of Milwaukee, Wisconsin	1.07
Vicinity of Detroit, Michigan	1.14

New England
Vicinity of Brattleboro, Vermont	0.87
Vicinity of Providence, Rhode Island	0.99
Vicinity of Boston, Massachusetts	1.03

Pacific West
Southeastern Washington	1.04
Vicinity of San Bernardino, California	1.12
Vicinity of Seattle, Washington	1.12
Vicinity of San Jose, California	1.22

Southeast
Vicinity of Greenville, South Carolina	0.75
Southeastern Alabama	0.83
Vicinity of Birmingham, Alabama	0.92
Vicinity of Memphis, Tennessee	0.95

Southwest
Central Texas	0.85
Central New Mexico	0.91
Vicinity of Houston, Texas	1.03
Vicinity of Phoenix, Arizona	1.05

West
Central Utah	0.91
Vicinity of Salt Lake City, Utah	0.96
Northeastern Colorado	1.01
Vicinity of Denver, Colorado	1.03

Source: E. H. Boeckn Co.

TABLE 56

MEDIAN INCOME OF PERSONS BY RACE AND SEX

NEW ENGLAND AND UNITED STATES: 1975 AND 1978
(dollars)

	ALL RACES		WHITE		BLACK		HISPANIC	
	MEN	WOMEN	MEN	WOMEN	MEN	WOMEN	MEN	WOMEN
NEW ENGLAND: 1975								
All	9,193	3,599	9,256	3,583	7,279	3,839	7,193	3,422
Full-Time Working	11,350	6,531	11,427	6,543	9,726	6,621	9,102	5,090
UNITED STATES: 1975								
All	8,974	3,462	9,450	3,482	5,710	3,273	6,753	3,210
Full-Time Working	11,412	6,285	11,827	6,349	8,172	5,866	8,315	5,007
NEW ENGLAND: 1978								
All	10,932	4,398	11,012	4,317	8,352	5,677	NA	NA
Full-Time Working	15,745	9,602	15,830	9,632	12,960	NA	NA	NA
UNITED STATES: 1978								
All	10,935	4,068	11,453	4,117	6,861	3,707	9,380	3,788
Full-Time Working	16,062	9,641	16,360	9,732	12,530	9,020	11,943	8,331

SOURCE: U.S. Census, Series P-60, No. 110, March 1978

TABLE 57

PERCENT PERSONS BELOW POVERTY LEVEL,* BY RACE (1975)

NEW ENGLAND AND THE UNITED STATES
(percent)

	ALL PERSONS	WHITES	BLACKS	HISPANICS
UNITED STATES	11.4	8.8	29.6	23.1
NEW ENGLAND	7.8	7.1	26.6	30.1
MASSACHUSETTS	7.1	6.4	24.6	31.5
CONNECTICUT	6.7	5.1	27.7	27.9
MAINE	12.0	12.0	-	-
RHODE ISLAND	8.7	8.0	34.3	34.3
NEW HAMPSHIRE	7.9	7.9	-	-
VERMONT	13.5	13.5	-	-

* Poverty level reflects an index of the Social Security Administration (SSA) that is adjusted for factors such as farm-non-farm residence, consumer price index, size of family, number of children in family, etc.

SOURCE: U.S. CENSUS, Series P60 No. 110, March 1978

TABLE 58

UNEMPLOYMENT RATES BY RACE AND SEX: 1978 AND 1979
NEW ENGLAND AND THE UNITED STATES
(percent)

1978

	U.S.	N.E.	MA	CT	ME	RI	NH	VT
All Races	6.0	5.7	6.1	5.2	6.1	6.6	3.8	5.7
Men	5.2	5.3	5.8	4.1	5.6	7.2	3.2	4.8
Women	7.2	6.4	6.5	6.7	6.8	5.9	4.6	7.1
Both Sexes, 16-19 years	16.3	15.6	15.9	16.0	16.3	18.2	12.2	9.1
White	5.2	5.5	5.9	4.8	6.1	6.2	3.9	5.8
Men	4.5	5.1	5.7	4.0	5.6	6.6	3.3	4.8
Women	6.2	6.1	6.3	6.0	6.8	5.7	4.7	7.1
Both Sexes, 16-19 yrs.	13.9	14.8	15.0	14.4	16.3	18.6	12.2	9.1
Black & Other	11.8		9.8	11.2				
Men	10.9		9.5	6.9				
Women	13.1		10.1	14.9				
Both Sexes, 16-19 yrs.	36.3		21.1	42.9				

1979 *

	U.S.	N.E.	MA	CT	ME	RI	NH	VT
All Races	5.8	5.4	5.5	5.1	7.2	6.6	3.1	5.1
Men	5.1	5.1	5.4	4.3	6.8	6.8	2.6	4.6
Women	6.8	5.9	5.7	6.1	7.7	6.5	3.9	5.7
White	5.1	5.2	5.5	4.5	7.1	6.5	3.1	5.1
Black & Other	11.3	10.3	7.0	14.3				

SOURCE: Employment and Unemployment During 1978: An Analysis, Bureau of Labor Statistics.

* Further Breakdown Not Available

TABLE 59

POVERTY IN FAMILIES

NEW ENGLAND AND THE UNITED STATES

1975 Median Income of Female-Headed Families (No Husband Present)
New England and the United States

	New England	United States
All Races	$ 7,523	$ 6,983
White	7,891	7,833
Black	4,918	5,279
Hispanic	-----	4,983

Percent of Households Headed by Women

	New England	United States
All Races	14%	13%
White	12%	11%
Black	46%	37%
Hispanic	36%	20%

Percent of Persons in Families Below the Poverty Level

	New England	United States
Male-headed (All races)	3%	6%
Female-headed " "	31%	35%
Male-headed (White)	3%	5%
Female-headed " "	28%	27%
Male-headed (Black)	6%	16%
Female-headed " "	50%	51%
Male-headed (Hispanic)	13%	16%
Female-headed " "	81%	54%

TABLE 60

DISTRESSED AREAS IN NEW ENGLAND AS IDENTIFIED BY POVERTY POPULATION

Cities and Counties with 10% or more of their population below poverty level.

MASSACHUSETTS		CONNECTICUT		MAINE	
CITIES	COUNTIES	CITIES	COUNTIES	CITIES	COUNTIES
Boston	Barnstable	Bridgeport	None	None	York
Cambridge	Hampshire	Hartford			Oxford
Fall River	Nantucket	New Haven			Androscoggin
Holyoke					Aroostook
Lawrence					Franklin
Lowell					Hancock
Lynn					Kennebec
New Bedford					Knox
Springfield					Lincoln
Worcester					Penobscot
					Pecataquin
					Saghadoc
					Somerset
					Waldo
					Washington

VERMONT			NEW HAMPSHIRE		RHODE ISLAND	
CITIES	COUNTIES		CITIES	COUNTIES	CITIES	COUNTIES
None	Addison	Franklin	Manchester	Carrol	Pawtucket	Newport
	Bennington	Grand Isle		Coos	Providence	Washington
	Caledonia	Lamoille		Grafton		
	Chittenden	Orange		Sullivan		
	Essex	Orleans				

SOURCE: 1970 Census of Population

TABLE 61

DISTRESSED AREAS IN NEW ENGLAND IDENTIFIED BY UNEMPLOYMENT RATES*

(AVERAGE UNEMPLOYMENT RATE JULY 1977-JUNE 1979)

	CITIES		LABOR MARKET AREAS	
MASSACHUSETTS	New Bedford	9.3%	Barnstable	8.7%
	Brockton	8.0	Clinton	8.8
	Lawrence	7.9	Gloucester	9.3
	Somerville	7.7	Newburyport	8.3
	Boston	7.6	Plymouth	9.5
			Taunton	7.7
			Dukes	7.9
CONNECTICUT	Bridgeport	7.7%	Ansonia	8.2%
	Waterbury	7.6		
MAINE			Southwest Penobscot	12.2%
			Madawaska-Van Buren	9.4
			Livermore Falls	8.5
			Houlton	8.5
			Greenville	8.3
RHODE ISLAND	Providence	8.0%		
	Pawtucket	7.6		
NEW HAMPSHIRE				
VERMONT			Newport	8.6%
			St. Johnsbury	7.7
			St. Albans	7.5

* Distressed cities and LMA's have unemployment rates of 7.5% or greater.

TABLE 62

UNEMPLOYMENT RATES IN SELECTED MEDIUM-SIZE CITIES AND NEW ENGLAND: 1979
(PERCENT)

New England	5.4
Torrington, CT	8.5
Norwich, CT	7.1
Willimantic, CT	5.8
Bangor, ME	7.6
Auburn, ME	7.2
Methuen, MA	7.1
North Adams, MA	8.9
Taunton, MA	7.2
Berlin, NH	8.2
East Providence, RI	7.5
Tiverton, RI	6.4
Woonsocket, RI	6.6

SOURCE: State Departments of Employment Security

TABLE 63

MEDIAN INCOME IN CENTRAL CITIES AND SUBURBS*(1976)
NEW ENGLAND AND U.S. AVERAGE

	MEDIAN INCOME OF CENTRAL CITY POPULATION	MEDIAN INCOME OF SUBURBAN POPULATION	PERCENT DIFFERENCE BETWEEN CENTRAL CITY AND SUBURBAN MEDIAN INCOMES
UNITED STATES	$13,280	$16,376	19
NEW ENGLAND	$12,564	$17,238	27
CONNECTICUT	$13,412	$18,124	26
MAINE	$11,881	$14,936	20
MASSACHUSETTS	$11,857	$17,336	32
NEW HAMPSHIRE	$15,838	$18,510	24
RHODE ISLAND	$13,814	$14,865	7
VERMONT**	NA	NA	NA

SOURCE: U.S. Census, Series P-60, No. 110

* "Suburbs" refers to localities in SMSAs, but excludes the central cities

** Vermont has no SMSAs

TABLE 64

CENTRAL CITY AND SUBURBAN* POPULATION BELOW THE POVERTY LEVEL (1976)
NEW ENGLAND AND THE U.S. AVERAGE

	PERCENT OF CENTRAL CITY POPULATION BELOW POVERTY LEVEL	PERCENT OF SUBURBAN POPULATION BELOW POVERTY LEVEL	PERCENT DIFFERENCE BETWEEN CENTRAL CITY AND SUBURBAN POPULATIONS BELOW THE POVERTY LEVEL
United States	14	7	7
New England	12	5	7
Connecticut	12	3	9
Maine	12	3	10
Massachusetts	12	5	7
New Hampshire	7	3	4
Rhode Island	12	6	6
Vermont**	NA	NA	NA

SOURCE: U.S. Census, Series P-60, No. 110

* "Suburbs" refers to localities in SMSAs, but excludes the central city

** Vermont has no SMSAs

TABLE 65

FIRMS BY SECTOR, ALL FIRMS, BLACK-OWNED FIRMS

	FIRMS BY SECTOR AS A PERCENT OF ALL FIRMS: 1976*	BLACK-OWNED FIRMS BY SECTOR AS A PERCENT OF TOTAL BLACK-OWNED FIRMS: 1977**	
	U.S.	U.S.	N.E.
CONSTRUCTION	10	9.0	8.0
MANUFACTURING	4	2.0	2.0
TRANSPORTATION & PUBLIC UTILITIES	4	10.0	6.0
WHOLESALE TRADE	5	1.0	2.0
RETAIL TRADE	19	24.0	20.0
FINANCE, INSURANCE, REAL ESTATE	13	4.0	4.0
SERVICES	30	44.0	52.0
OTHER	15	6.0	6.0
TOTAL:	100	100.0	100.0

SOURCES:
* U.S. Census, Statistical Abstract of the U.S., Table No.914
** U.S. Census, Survey of Minority-Owned Business Enterprises, MB 77-1

TABLE 66

POPULATION CHANGE IN TWELVE SELECTED NEW ENGLAND CITIES:

1970-1975, 1975-1980

	ANNUAL AVERAGE PERCENT CHANGE: 1970-1975	ANNUAL AVERAGE PERCENT CHANGE: 1975-1980
Bridgeport, CT	-2.0	+0.8
Hartford, CT	-2.8	+0.2
New Haven, CT	-1.8	+0.4
Portland, ME	-1.8	+0.8
Boston, MA	-0.2	+0.2
Brockton, MA	+1.4	+1.2
Springfield, MA	+0.8	+0.4
Worcester, MA	-0.6	-0.2
Manchester, NH	-1.0	+3.0
Pawtucket, RI	-1.4	-0.8
Providence, RI	-1.4	-2.0
Burlington, VT	-0.8	+1.0

1. Based on 1975 and 1979 population estimates rather than 1975 and 1980

SOURCES:
U.S. Census, Connecticut Office of Policy and Management, Maine State Planning Office, Metropolitan Area Planning Council (Boston), Old Colony Planning Council (Brockton), Lower Pioneer Valley Regional Planning Commission (Springfield), Central Massachusetts Regional Planning Commission (Worcester), New Hampshire Office of State Planning, Vermont Office of State Planning

TABLE 57

INDICATORS OF ECONOMIC DISTRESS IN TEN SELECTED RURAL COUNTIES IN NEW ENGLAND

	Percent of Population Below Poverty Level	Unemployment Rate July 1977 to June 1979 (average percent)
Dukes, MA	8.6	7.9
Aroostook, ME	19.5	10.2
Somerset, ME	15.9	9.7
Waldo, ME	17.0	10.1
Coos, NH	12.6	6.3
Grafton, NH	10.7	3.9
Sullivan, NH	10.3	3.4
Essex, VT	18.5	9.9
Lamoille, VT	14.8	7.7
Bennington, VT	13.3	6.6

Source: Economic Development Administration, U.S. Census, 1970 Census of Population

TABLE 68

SHARES OF EMPLOYMENT BY INDUSTRY FOR TEN SELECTED DISTRESSED RURAL COUNTIES IN NEW ENGLAND
1978
(Percent of County Total)

INDUSTRY	Dukes, MA	Aroostook, ME	Somerset, ME	Waldo, ME	Coos, NH	Grafton, NH	Sullivan, NH	Essex, VT	Lamoille, VT	Burlington, VT
Ag.Serv., For., Fish, etc.*	2.5	14.7	6.0	(D)	2.7e	2.3	3.2e	6.4e	6.9	2.4
Goods Producing	9.7e	19.6	33.6	29.0e	33.2	21.2	39.7e		15.8	34.4
Mining	-	(L)	0	-	+0	0.1	+0	-	0.1	0
Construction	7.2	2.5	3.8	3.0	3.0	3.4	3.3	(D)	5.5	4.6
Manufacturing	2.4	17.0	29.9	26.0	30.2	17.7	36.3	47.9	10.2	29.8
non-durables	1.5	10.6	18.7	20.7	26.2	7.0	16.1	(D)	3.8	8.2
durables	1.0	6.5	11.1	5.3	4.1	10.7	20.2	(D)	6.5	21.5
Service Producing	72.8	58.0e	49.8		55.4	68.9	47.8		65.8	54.1
Transp.,Comm.,Pub.Ut.	3.3	(D)	1.8	4.4	3.3	2.7	2.1	3.5	3.3	2.1
Trade	22.4	14.5	12.6	11.8	15.1	16.2	17.2	3.7e	17.5	17.1
wholesale	2.5	3.8	2.2	2.3	2.1	1.8	2.9	(L)	1.0	1.2
retail	19.9	10.8	10.4	9.5	13.1	14.4	14.3	3.5	16.4	15.9
Fire	5.3	2.3	1.5	(D)	1.7	2.3	3.5	0.6	2.5	2.3
Services	25.3	(D)	13.6	15.9	19.4	34.4	12.6	(D)	26.0	21.6
Government	16.5	26.4	20.3	15.3	15.8	13.3	12.4	24.2	16.4	11.1
federal civ.	0.5	4.0	0.9	1.5	0.9	1.7	0.8	2.2	0.9	0.7
federal mil.	0.6	9.0	1.5	1.7	1.1	0.9	1.4	2.3	1.8	1.6
state & local	15.4	13.4	18.0	12.0	13.8	10.7	10.2	19.8	13.7	8.8
Total Excl.Non-farm Prop.	85.0	92.3	89.5	87.5	91.4	92.4	90.7	90.9	88.4	90.9
Non-Farm Prop.	15.0	7.7	10.5	12.5	8.6	7.6	9.3	9.1	11.6	9.1
Total Employment (persons)	4680	41373	17011	9191	15577	34441	13070	2297	6768	16056

(L) Fewer than 10 employees

(D) No figures available because of disclosure rules

* Includes farm workers and farm proprietors

SOURCE: Bureau of Economic Analysis